D0520902

Advance Praise for *Exploiting On*

"Imagine trying to play defense in football
offense. You would not know when a run was coming, how to
defend pass patterns, nor when to blitz. In computer systems, as in
football, a defender must be able to think like an attacker. I say it in
my class every semester, you don't want to be the last person to
attack your own system—you should be the first.

"The world is quickly going online. While I caution against
online voting, it is clear that online gaming is taking the Internet by
storm. In our new age where virtual items carry real dollar value,
and fortunes are won and lost over items that do not really exist,
the new threats to the intrepid gamer are all too real. To protect
against these hazards, you must understand them, and this
groundbreaking book is the only comprehensive source of
information on how to exploit computer games. Every White Hat
should read it. It's their only hope of staying only one step behind
the bad guys."

—*Aviel D. Rubin, Ph.D.*
Professor, Computer Science
Technical Director, Information Security Institute
Johns Hopkins University

"Everyone's talking about virtual worlds. But no one's talking about
virtual-world security. Greg Hoglund and Gary McGraw are the
perfect pair to show just how vulnerable these online games
can be."

—*Cade Metz*
Senior Editor
PC Magazine

"If we're going to improve our security practices, frank discussions
like the ones in this book are the only way forward. Or as the
authors of this book might say, when you're facing off against
Heinous Demons of Insecurity, you need experienced companions,
not to mention a Vorpal Sword of Security Knowledge."

—*Edward W. Felten, Ph.D.*
Professor of Computer Science and Public Affairs
Director, Center for Information Technology Policy
Princeton University

"Historically, games have been used by warfighters to develop new capabilities and to hone existing skills—especially in the Air Force. The authors turn this simple concept on itself, making games themselves the subject and target of the 'hacking game,' and along the way creating a masterly publication that is as meaningful to the gamer as it is to the serious security system professional.

"Massively distributed systems will define the software field of play for at least the next quarter century. Understanding how they work is important, but understanding how they can be manipulated is essential for the security professional. This book provides the cornerstone for that knowledge."

—*Daniel McGarvey*
Chief, Information Protection Directorate
United States Air Force

"Like a lot of kids, Gary and I came to computing (and later to computer security) through games. At first, we were fascinated with playing games on our Apple][s, but then became bored with the few games we could afford. We tried copying each other's games, but ran up against copy-protection schemes. So we set out to understand those schemes and how they could be defeated. Pretty quickly, we realized that it was a lot more fun to disassemble and work around the protections in a game than it was to play it.

"With the thriving economies of today's online games, people not only have the classic hacker's motivation to understand and bypass the security of games, but also the criminal motivation of cold, hard cash. That's a combination that's hard to stop. The first step, taken by this book, is revealing the techniques that are being used today."

—*Greg Morrisett, Ph.D.*
Allen B. Cutting Professor of Computer Science
School of Engineering and Applied Sciences
Harvard University

"If you're playing online games today and you don't understand security, you're at a real disadvantage. If you're designing the massive distributed systems of tomorrow and you don't learn from games, you're just plain sunk."

— *Brian Chess, Ph.D.*
  Founder/Chief Scientist, Fortify Software
  Coauthor of Secure Programming with Static Analysis

"This book offers up a fascinating tour of the battle for software security on a whole new front: attacking an online game. Newcomers will find it incredibly eye opening and even veterans of the field will enjoy some of the same old programming mistakes given brilliant new light in a way that only massively-multiplayer-super-mega-blow-em-up games can deliver. w00t!"

— *Pravir Chandra*
  Principal Consultant, Cigital
  Coauthor of Network Security with OpenSSL

Exploiting
Online Games

Addison-Wesley Software Security Series

Gary McGraw, Consulting Editor

Titles in the Series

Exploiting Online Games: Cheating Massively Distributed Systems,
by Greg Hoglund and Gary McGraw
ISBN: 0-132-27191-5

Secure Programming with Static Analysis, by Brian Chess and Jacob West
ISBN: 0-321-42477-8

Software Security: Building Security In, by Gary McGraw
ISBN: 0-321-35670-5

Rootkits: Subverting the Windows Kernel, by Greg Hoglund and James Butler
ISBN: 0-321-29431-9

Exploiting Software: How to Break Code, by Greg Hoglund and Gary McGraw
ISBN: 0-201-78695-8

 For more information about these titles, and to read sample chapters, please visit
the series web site at www.awprofessional.com/softwaresecurityseries

Exploiting Online Games

Cheating Massively Distributed Systems

Greg Hoglund
Gary McGraw

✦Addison-Wesley

Upper Saddle River, NJ • Boston • Indianapolis • San Francisco
New York • Toronto • Montreal • London • Munich • Paris • Madrid
Capetown • Sydney • Tokyo • Singapore • Mexico City

The publisher offers excellent discounts on this book when ordered in quantity for bulk purchases or special sales, which may include electronic versions and/or custom covers and content particular to your business, training goals, marketing focus, and branding interests. For more information, please contact:

U.S. Corporate and Government Sales
(800) 382-3419
corpsales@pearsontechgroup.com

For sales outside the United States please contact:

International Sales
international@pearsoned.com

Visit us on the Web: www.awprofessional.com

Library of Congress Cataloging-in-Publication Data

Hoglund, Greg.
   Exploiting online games : cheating massively distributed systems / Greg Hoglund, Gary McGraw.
      p. cm.
   Includes index.
   ISBN 978-0-13-227191-2 (pbk. : alk. paper)
   1. Computer networks--Security measures. I. McGraw, Gary, 1966- II. Title.

TK5105.59.H64 2007
005.8--dc22   2007018716

ISBN 13: 978-0-13-227191-2
ISBN 10:   0-13-227191-5
Text printed in the United States on recycled paper at Courier in Stoughton, Massachusetts.
First printing, July 2007

For the gamers who stayed up
all night playing Wizardry
and Ultima I in 1981.

Contents

Foreword

It's wise to learn from your mistakes. It's wiser still to learn from the mistakes of others. Too often, we in the security community fail to learn from mistakes because we refuse to talk about them or we pretend they don't exist.

This book talks frankly about game companies' mistakes and their consequences. For game companies, this is an opportunity to learn from their own mistakes and those of their peers. For the rest of us, it's an opportunity to learn what can go wrong so we can do better.

The debate over full disclosure goes back a long way, so there is no need to repeat the ethical and legal arguments we have all heard before. For most of us in the security community, the issue is simple: Experts and the general public both benefit from learning about the technologies that they depend on.

In today's world, we are asked all the time to bet our money, our time, our private information, and sometimes our lives on the correct functioning of technologies. Making good choices is difficult; we need all the help we can get.

In some fields, such as aviation security, we can be confident that problems will be identified and addressed. Nobody would tolerate an aircraft vendor hiding the cause of a crash or impeding an investigation. Nor would we tolerate a company misleading the public about safety or claiming there were no problems when it knew otherwise. This atmosphere of disclosure, investigation, and remediation is what makes air travel so safe.

In game design, the stakes may not be as high, but the issues are similar. As with aviation, the vendors have a financial stake in the system's performance, but others have a lot at stake, too. A successful game—especially a virtual world like World of Warcraft—generates its own economy, in several senses. Objects in the game have real financial value, and a growing number of people make their living entirely or partially via in-game transactions. In-world currency trades against the dollar. Economists argue about the exact GDP of virtual worlds, but by any meaningful definition, virtual economies are just as "real" as the NASDAQ stock exchange.

Even nonplayers can have a lot at stake: the investor who bets his retirement account on a game company, the programmer who leaves a good job to work on a game, the family that owns the Indian restaurant across the street from the game company's headquarters. These people care deeply about whether the technology is sound. And would-be customers, before plunking down their hard-earned money for game software or a monthly subscription, want to know how well a game will stand up to attack.

If aviation shows us the benefits of openness, e-voting illustrates the harms caused by secrecy. We, the users of e-voting systems—citizens, that is—aren't allowed to know how the machines work. We know the machines are certified, but the certification process is itself shrouded in mystery. We're told that the details aren't really our concern. And the consequences are obvious: Designs are weak, problems go unfixed for years, and progress is slow. Even when things do go wrong in the field, it's very hard to get a vigorous investigation.

The virtue of this book is not only that it talks about real-world problems but also that it provides details. Some security problems exist only in theory but evaporate when real systems are built. Some problems look serious but turn out not to be a big deal in practice. And some problems are much worse than they look on paper. To tell the difference, we need to dig into the details. We need to see precisely how an attack would work and what barriers the attacker has to get over. This book, especially the later chapters, offers the necessary detail.

Because it touches on the popular, hot topic of massively multiplayer games, and because it offers both high-level and detailed views of game security, this book is also a great resource for students who want to learn how security really works. Theory is a valuable tool, but it does its best work when wielded by people with hands-on experience. I started out in this field as a practitioner, trying to learn how to get things done and how real systems behaved, before expanding my horizon to include formal computer science training. I suspect that many senior figures in the field would say the same. When I started out, books like this didn't exist (or if they did, I didn't know about them). Today's students are luckier.

Perhaps some vendors will be unhappy about this book. Perhaps they will try to blame the authors for the insecurity of their game software. Don't be fooled. If we're going to improve our security practices, frank discussions like the ones in this book are the only way forward. Or as the authors of this book might say, when you're facing off against Heinous Demons of Insecurity, you need experienced companions, not to mention a Vorpal Sword of Security Knowledge.

We all make mistakes. Let's learn from our mistakes and the mistakes of others. That's our best hope if we want to do better next time.

—*Professor Edward Felten*
Princeton, New Jersey
June, 2007

Preface

Online games, including World of Warcraft, EverQuest, Second Life, and online poker, have taken the computer world by storm. Gaming has always been (and remains) among the prime drivers of PC technology, with deep penetration into the consumer market. In the last ten years, computer games have grown just as quickly as the Internet and can now be found in tens of millions of homes.

The Internet is experiencing plenty of adolescent growing pains along with its phenomenal growth. These pains are experienced mostly in terms of problematic and pervasive computer security issues. Online games, especially massively multiplayer online role-playing games (or MMORPGs for short), suffer from these security problems directly.

MMORPGs are made of very sophisticated software built around a massively distributed client-server architecture. Because these games push the limits of software technology, especially when it comes to state and time (not to mention the real-time interaction of hundreds of thousands of users), they are particularly interesting as a case study in software security. In fact, MMORPGs are a harbinger of technical software security issues to come.

Modern software of all kinds (not just game software) is evolving to be massively distributed, with servers interacting with and providing services for thousands of users at once. The move to Web Services and Service Oriented Architectures built using technologies like AJAX and Ruby follows hard on the heels of online games. What we learn here today is bound to be widely applicable tomorrow in every kind of software.

Adding to the urgency of the security problem is the fact that online games are big business. The most popular MMORPG in the world, World of Warcraft by Blizzard Entertainment, has over 8 million users, each of whom pay $14 per month for the privilege of playing. Analysts estimate the gaming market will reach $12 billion by 2009.

Inside the virtual worlds created by MMORPGs, simple data structures come to have value, mostly a reflection of the time gamers spend playing the game. Players accumulate and trade virtual wealth (or play money). Many of these virtual economies have per capita GDPs greater than most small nations. Not surprisingly, direct connections between the virtual economies of games and the real economy exist all over the place. Until recently, it was possible to buy in-game play money with real dollars on eBay; now many other well-developed middle markets exist. And the reverse is possible, too. This has led to the emergence of a class of players more interested in wringing virtual wealth out of the game than playing the game itself.

Wherever money is at stake, criminals gather and linger. Cheating happens. In the case of MMORPGs, cheaters have real economic incentive to break the security of the game in order to accumulate virtual items and experience points for their characters. Many of these items and even the characters themselves are then sold off to the highest bidder.

Sophisticated hackers have been working the fertile fields of MMORPGs for years, some of them making a living directly from gaming (or cheating at gaming). This book describes explicitly and in a technical way the kinds of attacks and techniques used by hackers who target games.

Why Are We Doing This?

As you can imagine, game companies take a dim view of cheating in their games. If cheating becomes rampant in a game, unsatisfied noncheating players will simply move on to another. Game developers have taken a number of steps to improve security in their games, some of them controversial (monitoring game players' PCs behind the scenes), others legalistic (imposing strict software license agreements and terms of use), and some of them trivial to break (using symmetric cryptography but including the secret key in the game client code). Our hope is that by understanding the kinds of attacks and hacking techniques described in this book, game developers will do a better job with online game security.

We think our topic is important for several reasons: First, real money is at stake; second, many players are completely unaware of what is going on; and third, online game software security has many critical lessons that we can directly apply to other, more important software. Plus, it's fun and controversial.

For example, some game companies have been known to use stealthy techniques most often seen in rootkits to monitor gamers' PCs. They have also been known to resort to strong-arm tactics to suppress hackers, even those not attempting in any way to be malicious or to make money. Will manufacturers of other software or digital content adopt these techniques for themselves?

Not only are the technical issues captivating, the legal issues surrounding online games and their creative software license terms are also a harbinger of things to come. The legal battles between game companies, academics, and users are by no means over—in fact, they have just begun.

In the end, the topic of online game security poses a number of interesting questions, the most pressing one being this: How do you balance gamers' privacy rights against game developers' desires to prevent their games from being hacked?

Where Do We Draw the Line?

For the record, we do not condone cheating, malicious hacking, or any other game-related shenanigans. We are most interested in deeply understanding and discussing what's going on in online game security. As practical security experts, we believe that only by gaining direct technical understanding of what happens when games are exploited can we begin to build systems that can withstand real attacks. Because in this situation money is at stake, you can be sure that attacks and exploits today are both concerted and organized.

We think it is acceptable and necessary to understand both how games really work and how they fail. The only way to do this is to study them carefully. We pull no punches technically in this book, showing you how online game clients fail from a security perspective in living detail. We also explicitly describe techniques that can be used to exploit online games. We don't do this to create an army of online game hackers—that army is already brimming in numbers, and those already enlisted in it are unlikely to learn much from this book. We do this so that the good guys will know what they are really up against. Our main objective is to describe the kinds of weapons the existing active army of game attackers has.

In our research for this book, we have broken no laws. We expect our readers likewise not to break the law using the techniques we describe.

What's in the Book?

Like most books, this book starts out at a high level and becomes progressively more technical as it goes on.

Chapter 1, Why Games?, poses and answers some simple questions. How big are online games? How many people play? Why would anyone want to exploit them? What motivation is there to cheat in an online game? The answers to these questions will likely surprise you. Believe it or not, 10 million people play online games, billions of dollars are at stake, and some people even cheat for a living. We also provide a gentle introduction to game architecture in Chapter 1, describing the classic client-server model that most games use.

Things get more technical beginning in Chapter 2, Game Hacking 101, where we describe the very basics of game hacking. The chapter is organized around describing six basic techniques: (1) building a bot, (2) using the user interface, (3) operating a proxy, (4) manipulating memory, (5) drawing on a debugger, and (6) finding the future. We pay special attention to the topic of bots since most game exploits exist to create and operate them. Late in the chapter, we even show a very simple bot that we built so you can see exactly what bot software looks like. We then describe controversial moves taken by one game maker to thwart cheating—installing rootkit-like spyware on a gamer's PC to keep track of what's going on. We hold this approach in low opinion and have written a program to help you know what's going on with these monitoring programs on your own machine. We believe game makers would be better off spending their resources to build games that were less broken than to build monitoring technology.

The next two chapters take a break from technical material to cover money and the law. In particular, Chapter 3, Money, helps us understand why some players might want to cheat. The recent book *Play Money* by Julian Dibbell (Basic Books, 2006) describes one (pathetic) man's foray into professional game farming, something that a number of people actively pursue. There is enough money in play here that entire enterprises have grown up around providing middleman services for gamers, buying and selling virtual items in a marketplace. The biggest and most interesting company, Internet Gaming Entertainment, known as IGE to most people, deserves and gets a treatment of its own in this chapter.

Chapter 4, Enter the Lawyers, is about the law. Game companies (and indeed a whole host of other software makers) have created a licensing jungle in the form of end user license agreements (EULAs) and terms of use

(TOU) documents. Though we are not lawyers, and by no means should you rely on our advice, we provide a brief description of U.S. copyright law and the Digital Millennium Copyright Act (DMCA). Then we go through an entertaining (and somewhat scary) parade of EULAs gone bad—from Sony's rootkit debacle to viruses protected by EULAs. We end up with a discussion of your rights as a software user and gamer.

Technical aspects of online game security begin to pick back up in Chapter 5, Infested with Bugs. We spend this chapter talking about the kinds of vulnerabilities found in many games, explaining how attackers use them to build working exploits. We pay particular attention to bugs involving time and state, which, as we alluded to earlier, are the kinds of bugs we can expect to see much more of as other software evolves to become more like game software.

Chapter 6, Hacking Game Clients, really digs in and gets technical. As we move more deeply into games, we are forced to use a game or two as a particular target. We don't do this to single out any one game; instead, we do this to make our examples salient and technical. We have chosen to concentrate on World of Warcraft (WoW), a game produced by Blizzard Entertainment, mostly because it is the number one online game in the world. The kinds of techniques we demonstrate using WoW as an example can be applied by analogy to almost any online game (and to modern Web 2.0 software, for that matter). Chapter 6 begins with a discussion of the attacker's toolkit (many of the tools we describe are standard software testing tools). We then organize our discussion of game hacking techniques into four equally important areas: (1) getting over the game by using its user interface directly, (2) getting inside the game by manipulating memory, (3) getting under the game by interposing on services like video drivers, and (4) getting way outside the game by intercepting and manipulating network traffic. Chapter 6 is in some sense the heart of the book, introducing a large number of techniques commonly used by game attackers.

Chapter 6 has lots of data in it, probably too much. Sometimes it is easier to understand these kinds of techniques by seeing how they are put into practice. Toward that end, in Chapter 7, Building a Bot, we put together all of the lessons of Chapter 6. Chapter 7 is technical, with plenty of example code showing how the ideas in Chapter 6 work in concert to exploit a game.

Chapter 8, Reversing, is even more technical, focusing its attention on reverse engineering techniques that many attackers use to exploit software. Though the techniques we describe in this chapter are intense, they are by no means new. As we describe in our book *Exploiting Software* (Addison-Wesley, 2004), disassemblers and decompilers are used in computer security every day, both by good guys and by bad guys.

The final technical topic in our book is presented in Chapter 9, Advanced Game Hacking Fu. This chapter discusses what is known in the trade as total conversions and game mods. We describe the process by which some people take apart game data files in order to build their own games or combine different aspects of games in interesting ways. Though some game companies try hard to quash all discussion of total conversion, it happens anyway. We describe how.

Of course, our purpose in this book is to help those who build games understand how to do a better job with security. Chapter 10, Software Security Über Alles, provides a flyover of the new field of software security. Game developers would do well to adopt some of the best practices in common use in the financial vertical today. We also describe a set of questions that everyday gamers can ask their game companies about security. Our fervent hope is that this book will lead to more secure software—both in the game community and beyond.

The Software Security Series

This book is part of the Addison-Wesley Software Security Series of software security books for professional software developers. The series includes the following titles:

- *Exploiting Online Games: Cheating Massively Distributed Systems*
- *Secure Programming with Static Analysis*
- *Software Security: Building Security In*
- *Rootkits: Subverting the Windows Kernel*
- *Exploiting Software: How to Break Code*
- *Building Secure Software: How to Avoid Security Problems the Right Way*

More books in this series are planned for the future. Contact Addison-Wesley or Gary McGraw for more information. Also see the Web site <http://buildingsecurityin.com>.

Contacting the Authors

The authors welcome e-mail contact from readers with comments, suggestions, bug fixes, and questions. Contact us through the book's Web site: <http://www.exploitingonlinegames.com>.

Acknowledgments

Compared to writing *Exploiting Software*, writing this book was a breeze. Our collaboration was stronger than ever, fueled by pirate rum and a desire to get this book into your hands. Many people helped, both directly and indirectly. We'll take the blame for errors and omissions, but we want to share the credit with those who helped us.

A number of kind people provided reviews for early drafts of this book: Richard Bejtlich, Pravir Chandra, Brian Chess, Greg Cummings, Jim DelGrosso, Michael Gegick, Marcus Leech, Amit Sethi, and Ken van Wyk. Kathy Clark-Fisher provided the most detailed reviews and a complete edit to boot, and for that we're eternally grateful.

We also owe a great deal of gratitude to our publisher, Addison-Wesley, especially our editor, Karen Gettman, and her assistant, Romny French. Jessica Goldstein has also been great even though this is not one of her books. Chrysta Meadowbrooke banished several hobgoblins and made our sentences parse. Thanks for the support and encouragement as we bulldozed our way through.

Greg's Acknowledgments

I acknowledge my beautiful firebrand wife Penny, and all other wives and partners of gamers, from whom video games have taken so much.

Gary's Acknowledgments

My company Cigital continues to thrive and prosper. Under the apt leadership of John Wyatt, we are back on track with impressive growth and superb execution. I like working at Cigital because of the smart people I am surrounded by on a daily basis. To be sure, the problem of making software behave is challenging, but with great creativity and flair Cigital continues to demonstrate thought leadership second to none.

Special thanks to the executive team and the Board for allowing me the freedom to think and write: Jeff Payne, John Wyatt, and members of the Cigital Board. The Cigital Principals, purveyors of the Justice League blog <http://www.cigital.com/justiceleague>, keep me sharp and expand my technical horizons on a daily basis. Thanks to Pravir Chandra, Scott Matsumoto, Sammy Migues, Craig Miller, and the unflappable John Steven for making work a joy.

I owe a great debt of gratitude to Ryan MacMichael, Cigital's Web guru. Ryan takes my crazy ideas and makes them real. Thanks to Ryan, Brandi Ortega, and Kathy Clark-Fisher (editor of *IEEE Security & Privacy* magazine), the Silver Bullet Security Podcast <http://www.cigital.com/silverbullet> continues to thrive.

Much of Cigital's success as a business can be directly attributed to the hard work of the Managing Principals. Thanks to Richard Brown, Jim Casey, Drew Kilbourne, John Reilly, and Garry Yeates for treating our customers right. Also thanks to Pat Higgins for keeping me on airplanes.

Cigital's Software Security Group (SSG) pushes the limits of applied software security on a daily basis. Special shouts to Paco Hope, the Canuck, Eric the French guy, and Will Kruse. I am also supremely pleased to be working with Susyn Conway and Lynn Nolitt on a daily basis. Thanks for the oxygen, Susyn. And of course I could not even begin to function without Tahsin Imam (the all-powerful T) and Chris Johnson to keep my nose pointed in the right direction. There are many others at Cigital who deserve mention, and I must say that I enjoy working with you all.

My coauthor Greg Hoglund was a blast to work with during this project. Our collaboration is stronger than ever. Though our book sessions tended to degenerate into postadolescent, rum-filled pirate runs, we still got things done. Thanks to Greg for providing the technical backbone of this book, identifying the topic, and asking me to write it with him. If you like the depth of technical material in this book, blame Greg.

Like all of my books before, this one has been indirectly shaped by my friends in the security community. Thanks to Mike Ackerman, Ross Anderson, Annie Anton, Becky Bace, Steve Bellovin, Matt Bishop, Brian Chess, Bill Cheswick, Crispin Cowan, Drew Dean, Dorothy Denning, Jeremy Epstein, Dave Evans, Ed Felten, Dan Geer, Virgil Gligor, Li Gong, Peter Honeyman, Mike Howard, Steve Kent, Paul Kocher, Carl Landwehr, Patrick McDaniel, Greg Morrisett, Peter Neumann, Jon Pincus, Bill Pugh,

Marcus Ranum, Greg Rose, Avi Rubin, Fred Schneider, Bruce Schneier, Gene Spafford, Kevin Sullivan, Roger Thornton, Phil Venables, David Wagner, and Dan Wallach.

Thanks to DARPA, the National Science Foundation, and the Advanced Technology Program for supporting my research work over the years. Cigital customers I interact with on a weekly basis and who have influenced my view of security in the real world include Lance Johnson (Visa), Jon Alibur (Fidelity), Marty Colburn (NASD), James Routh (DTCC), Kathy Memenza (Marriott), Mike Ackerman (Morgan Stanley), and Jerry Brady (Morgan Stanley).

Most important of all, thanks to my family. Love to Amy Barley, Jack, and Eli. Thanks to my dad, my grandma Ruth, my brothers Walt and Chris, and Nora and Simone for their love. Thanks to the 54-footed menagerie that inhabits our farm: ike and skillet, soupy, ghosty and soupy jr, sage and guthrie, lewy and lucy, the one remaining "girl" (soon to be joined by a new flock), picasso and petunia (the new peacocks), chin-chin and chilli, and moustache the bunny. Special thanks to my dear friends rhine and april, cyn and ant, doug and laura, and gina and joe for seeing me through the great leg debacle of 2007. The music and the friendship make my life complete.

About the Authors

Greg Hoglund is a largely self-taught computer hacker who, like many others of his generation, stepped into the industry at the right time and place to make a career out of it. Because a decade ago computer security was so new, there was no formal curriculum for teaching software exploit. In fact, direct, deeply technical discussion of attacks remains rare to this day. Hoglund found he had a special skill in structuring and explaining complex information about attacks and attack patterns so that other people can understand it. Success in this area led naturally to training and writing.

An entrepreneurial spirit combined with a strong self-motivation to "do his own thing" led Greg to found a number of security companies, including Cenzic and BugScan. He is currently involved in his third start-up, HBGary, Inc. <http://www.hbgary.com>—a company that specializes in using software to catch bad guys using covert monitoring and forensics. HBGary services primarily U.S. Department of Defense organizations.

Greg's primary interests in computer security center on exploiting bugs and reverse engineering low-level software. After many years of applying his knowledge to low-level operating systems code, Greg's interest in hacking was rekindled when he came across the concept of hacking online games. He has applied his skills to game hacking for the last few years, with a primary focus on Blizzard Entertainment's World of Warcraft game (as is evident from this book and his other published material on the Net). He has also spent time hacking Asheron's Call II, EVE Online, and Vanguard.

Hoglund has coauthored two deeply technical bestselling books, *Rootkits: Subverting the Windows Kernel* with Jamie Butler (Addison-Wesley, 2005) and *Exploiting Software: How to Break Code* with Gary McGraw (Addison-Wesley, 2004). He also operates the popular Web site <http://www.rootkit.com>.

In his day-to-day work, Greg obtains and executes multimillion-dollar security contracts with the U.S. government. He also teaches advanced classes on rootkit development several times a year. Greg aspires to develop a new game someday, and he wants to become more involved in game security issues. He is married to Penny Hoglund and has an eleven-year-old daughter and three dogs. When not flying around the country working, Greg likes to be in Carmel, California, at his beach house. He also strangely enjoys being frustrated about something or another going wrong with his sailboat.

Gary McGraw is the CTO of Cigital, Inc. <http://www.cigital.com>, a software security and quality consulting firm that has provided services to some of the world's best-known companies for a decade. Dr. McGraw is a globally recognized authority on software security and is featured frequently as a keynote speaker at events coast-to-coast as well as internationally. His strategic advice counsels business executives and top management, technology developers, and IT and operations staff in industries such as finance, hospitality and gaming, and e-commerce. He sits on the Board of Directors of Cigital, chairs Fortify Software's Technical Advisory Board, and serves as an advisor to Raven White. Gary also speaks at academic conferences and participates in academia by advising the Computer Science departments of the University of Virginia and the University of California, Davis. He is a member of the Dean's Advisory Council of the School of Informatics at Indiana University. Among his federal government credentials is serving as a prime contributor on the National Cyber Security Summit Alliance study *Security Across the Software Development Lifecycle* in 2005.

Dr. McGraw has, quite literally, written the book on software security, with six of them bestselling in their field. He coauthored the groundbreaking *Building Secure Software* with John Viega (Addison-Wesley, 2001), introducing ideas that were expanded and made actionable in *Software Security: Building Security In* (Addison-Wesley, 2006). His other titles include *Java Security* (Wiley, 1996), *Securing Java* (Wiley, 1999), *Software Fault Injection* (Wiley, 1998), and *Exploiting Software* (Addison-Wesley, 2004); he is also editor of the Addison-Wesley Software Security Series. He has authored over ninety peer-reviewed scientific publications, writes a monthly security column for darkreading.com, and is often quoted in the press. He holds a dual Ph.D. in cognitive science and computer science from Indiana University and a B.A. in philosophy from the University of Virginia. He serves as a member of the IEEE Security and Privacy Task Force and the IEEE Computer Society Board of Governors. He also produces the monthly Silver Bullet Security Podcast for *IEEE Security & Privacy* magazine.

When not performing as a technologist, scientist, author, and speaker, Gary is an active musician, playing the violin since the age of three. He has been doing improvisation since college; his other instruments include mandolin and guitar. He plays occasional gigs and records original music with the band Where's Aubrey <http://www.wheresaubrey.com>, the band's repertoire ranging from old-time folk music to modern jazz. Gary and his wife, Amy Barley, live with their two sons and an assorted menagerie on a farm on the banks of the Shenandoah River with vistas of the Blue Ridge Mountains.

Why Games?

Computer games are huge. Tens of millions of people play them, all over the world. Microsoft reports that gaming is the third most common activity on its platforms, just after browsing the Web and reading e-mail. In 2005, the gaming market was estimated at over $6 billion worldwide growing at a rate of over 10% per year. People like games.

The first computer game was created in 1952 when A. S. Douglas developed Tic-Tac-Toe for the Electronic Delay Storage Automatic Calculator (EDSAC), a British computer. Today, there are many kinds of computer games, ranging from stand-alone games on a PC (think Pac-Man) to massively multiplayer online games (think World of Warcraft), and everything in between (think online poker and DOOM). Over 10 million people played massively multiplayer online games (MMOs) worldwide in 2006, and the number is doubling every two years.[1] The analyst firm IDG estimates that 2.9 million people in the United States actively subscribe to MMOs.

The most popular MMOs are role-playing games (RPGs). RPGs are very much in the spirit of Dungeons and Dragons. Today, more than fifty active MMORPGs exist worldwide. In them, gamers develop characters that inhabit huge virtual worlds. Quests are undertaken. Friends and enemies are

---

1. A graph of the growth of MMOs can be found at
<http://mmogchart.com/Chart4_files/ Subscriptions_21524_image001.gif>.

made. Bits become valuable. A quick search on eBay for "World of Warcraft gold" <http://search.ebay.com/world-of-warcraft-gold> shows that this is so. It turns out that a *de facto* exchange rate from virtual game money to real money already exists!

Even more money is involved in online poker games than in MMOs. On any given day, tens of thousands of people play online poker against each other on the many popular online poker sites, playing games like Texas hold 'em. Poker game sites make their money by charging a "rake" or percentage of the kitty. (The players themselves can make money as well by beating their opponents. Some people play online poker professionally.) Some of the more popular online poker sites report annual profits in the billions. At least two such companies went public in 2005 <http://www.businessweek.com/bwdaily/dnflash/feb2005/nf20050225_9794_db039.htm>.

All computer games share an Achilles' heel—they're made of software. By manipulating, changing, tweaking, and otherwise exploiting the software that makes up a computer game, malicious gamers can cheat. When cheating involves hacking the high-score file for Tetris on the PC in your kitchen, there doesn't seem to be much point to it. But when cheating can set you up to win real money at online poker, or make money by selling your "vorpal sword of heinousity" to another player through eBay, or sell pretend gold pieces to third-party clearinghouses in the real world, the whole thing changes.

Many people exploit online games every day. Some are criminals who do it for a living, others are legitimate gamers gone bad. Still others are people too busy to devote as much time to a game as they would like.

In order to fix the precarious security situation in online gaming, game developers and game companies need to do a better job with software security. The first step in improving online game security is to get a realistic handle on what is really going on. Just how are games exploited, anyway?

That's what this book is about—exploiting online games. We'll be very explicit, showing you code for cheats from simple game macros to complex rootkit-based hacks—no holds barred. We'll also discuss countermeasures and provide straight talk about their effectiveness and their sometimes drastic implications.

We think that online games make a very interesting petri dish for software security. Software pervades modern life and has moved far beyond the domain of entertainment. But even in entertainment, lots of money is at stake. In some sense, the security story in the gaming world may be a harbinger of things to come in the rest of the online world.

Online Games Worldwide

The most popular computer game in history is World of Warcraft, called WoW by insiders <http://www.worldofwarcraft.com>. WoW was developed and is sold by Blizzard Entertainment (a division of Vivendi). WoW is an MMORPG with over 8 million users in several different countries.[2] WoW client software is available in English, Korean, German, French, Chinese, and, most recently, Spanish.

At any one time, over 500,000 people are playing WoW together on a distributed farm of game servers. Their characters inhabit a virtual world called Azeroth (see <http://www.blizzard.com/wow/townhall/worldmap .shtml>). As shown in Figure 1–1, WoW accounts for slightly more than half of MMO subscriptions worldwide.

From a security perspective, two things make WoW particularly interesting. The first is that the game is played on central server clusters (called realms), which players connect to over the Internet using their PCs. Every modern MMORPG uses this architecture. It almost goes without saying that this network-based, distributed architecture comes with a number of inherent security risks. The second major factor is that the WoW economy is strikingly large and that there are many convenient ways to transfer real money out of the game. For example, until very recently you could sell your character or some of your virtual items on eBay for real money (see Chapter 3). This makes WoW a much more interesting target than less popular MMORPGs and is one of the reasons we focus our attention on it.

Many gamers take MMORPGs very seriously. In June 2005, a Chinese gamer in Shanghai was convicted of killing a competitor in a disagreement over a virtual sword. According to MSNBC, "Qiu Chengwei, 41, stabbed competitor Zhu Caoyuan in the chest after he was told Zhu had sold his 'dragon saber,' used in the popular online game, *Legend of Mir 3*."[3] Qiu is now serving a life sentence.

Professional gamers and gaming sweatshops have also emerged, with players discovering vulnerabilities, developing exploits, building macros, and then creating banks of computers called *farms* to create wealth that is

---

2. The number 8 million comes from a Blizzard press release <http://www.blizzard.com/ press/ 070111.shtml>. Of these users, 2 million are in the United States; 3.5 million are in China.
3. See the entire story at <http://www.msnbc.msn.com/id/8143073/>.

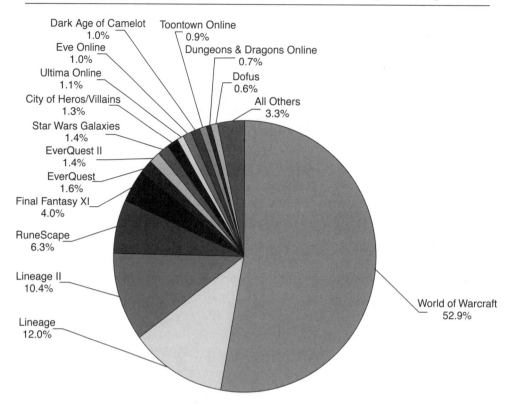

Dark Age of Camelot 1.0%
Toontown Online 0.9%
Eve Online 1.0%
Dungeons & Dragons Online 0.7%
Ultima Online 1.1%
Dofus 0.6%
City of Heros/Villains 1.3%
All Others 3.3%
Star Wars Galaxies 1.4%
EverQuest II 1.4%
EverQuest 1.6%
Final Fantasy XI 4.0%
RuneScape 6.3%
Lineage II 10.4%
Lineage 12.0%
World of Warcraft 52.9%

Figure 1–1 Market share for MMOs by subscription—June 2006. (From Woodcock, Bruce Sterling. "An Analysis of MMOG Subscription Growth, Version 21.0" <http://www.mmogchart.com>; used by permission.)

then transferred or otherwise sold to others.[4] Wealth is created by attaining virtual items or virtual money as the game is played. Farms provide computer equipment loaded with games for mandatory use by exploited laborers working for a ringleader. Clearinghouses launder virtual money or other items back into the game for use by other players. In extreme cases, this is organized crime.

Sometimes players uncover bugs that can be used to exploit a game. These bugs are so lucrative that one man operating out of Canada was able to make U.S. $700,000 in one year by duplicating currency in Star Wars Galaxies, a popular MMORPG. He then bought a house with the money,

---

4. An interesting article about gold farms in Lineage II, WoW, and Star Wars Galaxies can be found at <http://www.1up.com/do/feature?cId=3141815>.

and to emphasize the source of his good fortune, his doorbell plays the theme song for *Star Wars*.[5]

Hackers are also interested in getting early access to unopened areas of virtual worlds that are supposed to be off-limits to gamers until they are officially launched. Software exploits are used to break into those areas.

Locked in a virtual arms race, game minders monitor cheating activities and, on occasion, ban players from the game.

Online gaming is growing by leaps and bounds. As noted earlier, MMO use is doubling every two years, but even more impressive is the growth of online poker, which was projected to end 2006 with more than $1 billion in revenue (see Chapter 3 for more).[6] As more people choose to play, more money will be involved, and the incentive to cheat by hacking, duping, leveling up, phishing, and otherwise exploiting game software will likewise rise.

Crime already exists in the virtual world. It will only become more common.

The Lure of Cheating in MMORPGs

Given the opportunity in life, many people cheat, especially if they believe they will never get caught. The perceived anonymity of the Internet makes cheating even more attractive. Factor in the ability to make some quick cash, and you have a formula for trouble. Money is probably the number one driver for cheating. (Chapter 3 is all about money and online games.)

Cheating is not always done to make money, however. Even those players who genuinely want to play an online game as intended have reasons to cheat. It takes months of serious playing in an MMORPG to build a character to a sufficiently high level to make gaming fun. For example, training up on a single skill in the game EVE Online can take six months in real time. Leveling up more quickly is another impetus for cheating (especially for busy people with a life outside of gaming). A related impetus is acquiring rare items or the in-game currency to buy them with.

Cheat Codes

Cheating comes in several forms. Sometimes cheating can be as simple as locating your character at a certain spot in the game world where monsters appear in order to kill them every time they show up. Less violently, you can

---

5. See Chapter 3 for more.
6. Online poker playing in the United States is likely to drop because of the Unlawful Internet Gambling Enforcement Act passed by the U.S. Congress in 2006.

cheat by creating crafts or growing food with your character over and over and over. As we show in Chapter 2, this kind of cheating gets much more complicated when these activities are automated with programs.

Sometimes it's hard to draw the line. For example, some people consider the act of writing simple macros to carry out repetitive activities a weak form of cheating. Macros for any number of actions, from scanning the horizon for enemies to aiming and firing, can be found all over the Internet (see <http://www.cheatcc.com/> and <http://cheatcodes.com> for two examples).

More powerful macros, like the farming macro we present in Chapter 2, can basically play the game for you while you do something else. Most gamers agree that using these programs is cheating. For obvious reasons, many hard-core gamers abhor cheating.

We describe a number of basic cheating techniques in Chapter 2. More advanced techniques are the subject of later chapters.

Criminal Cheating

We introduced the notion of professional farmers who create gold and other items to sell to gamers earlier in the chapter. Services that can level up your character for you are also common. While neither of these activities seems like cheating on the face of it, the use of such services often violates a game's terms of use (see Chapter 4). Some people deem these activities criminal, even though there often aren't any specific laws against them. The worst kinds of things that commonly happen involve legal action by game companies against the service providers (who are most often sued for damages and economic hardship). The gamers who take advantage of the services are usually not prosecuted or sued but are simply banned from the game.

Cheats come closest to actual crime when they are used to make a great deal of money. A large underground economy exists in discovering, exploiting, and then selling cheats to others. Rumors abound in the underground of individuals who make thousands of dollars on a weekend by using a dupe bug (to copy items surreptitiously) and even of small teams making seven figures during the first year of a new game release. Online poker players regularly use databases that track the relative skill of each player, including hands lost and won, and they use this information to find "weak tables" where they can clean house. In at least one case, security researchers at Cigital cracked the shuffling algorithm for an online poker site and were able to predict the complete shuffle and thereby all of the players' hands in advance (see Chapter 2).

Turning Bits into Cash: From Exploits to Items

Turning virtual belongings from an MMO into actual real money is very easy. As we show in Chapter 3, legitimate trading companies like IGE turn a blind eye toward the origin of many items. That means making money from an MMO is as easy as acquiring an item and selling it to a middleman.

Players can also cut out the middleman and sell directly to each other. A number of gamers traditionally used eBay for this until eBay stopped all trading in virtual items in 2007. A player can auction off a game item on an auction site, get paid into a PayPal account, and then meet the buyer somewhere in the game to give up the item to the buyer's character. Buyer beware (of course).

Exploits that take advantage of software defects in the game are much more valuable in the underground gaming economy than game currency and virtual items are. These vulnerabilities can be turned into macros and then sold to gold farms or others who use the macros to create wealth. Exploits and defects are like mints for printing money.

Games Are Software, Too

MMOs are made out of software, and all software has defects. As we describe in our book *Exploiting Software*, both implementation bugs and design flaws are vulnerabilities that can be exploited by hackers (see Chapter 5 of this book for our current take on bugs and gaming software). All of the tools and techniques in the attacker's toolkit can be and are applied to MMO software. Many of the ideas we describe in this book are as old as the hills, but they do have one thing in common—the techniques explained here all leverage the fact that MMOs are simply software programs.

Basic Game Architecture

Most MMOs follow the same basic architecture. A central bank of servers (sometimes many banks) is constructed to allow communications with gamers in real time over the Internet. Gamers use programs called clients on their own Internet-connected PCs. Many times this client software must be purchased through a retailer, but sometimes the client software is given away for free. Figure 1–2 shows an illustration of basic game architecture.

To make a client work with the central servers, most MMOs require a subscription model.

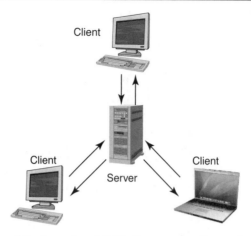

Figure 1–2 Basic architecture of an MMO. Gamers use client software on their own PCs to connect to a central game server.

The Game Client

Game clients are software programs that run on a gamer's PC. Client software takes input from the user and communicates with the central servers over the Internet. The client software usually displays a view of the virtual world showing location, other players, messages, and so on. Figure 1–3 shows a screenshot from WoW. This is a typical game client view.

Client-Side State

Things happen in games, especially those with thousands of players interacting in real time. The game has an engine in the middle that takes all of the user input and updates the game as time unfolds. The game has state in the same sense that any computer program has state. The state of a system is defined as the collection of the current values of all memory locations, all secondary storage, and all registers and other components of the system.[7]

The problem is that the Internet today is not fast enough to allow all of the game state to reside on the server and to be instantaneously pushed down to all clients in parallel. To solve this problem and to make the game action appear to be seamless, game designers allow the client software to preserve and manage some state.

Though there are good reasons to allow the client to preserve state, any client-side state presents serious security risks. As we describe in Chapter 2, client-side state is one of the primary targets for attackers.

---

7. See *Computer Security: Art and Science* by Matt Bishop (Addison-Wesley, 2005).

Figure 1–3 Client software from WoW allows a user to interact with the game. The client software runs on a gamer's PC and communicates with a central server. (From <http://compactiongames.about.com>; used with permission.)

Another serious security issue involves time. Advanced attacks on distributed systems often involve manipulating state over time.[8] When communication with a server is essential, race conditions and other attacks that take advantage of time are important to consider. One of the most commonly used duping attacks against WoW involved a race condition made available when a server was rebooted on its regular schedule.

Analogies to Other Applications

Many software applications involve complex interactions of clients and servers over time. Some of the most important are online auctions run by financial houses for things like Treasury bonds and more pedestrian auctions run for everyday people on eBay. Over the years, distributed real-time applications have undergone rigorous security analysis and substantial

---

8. See Chapter 12 of *Software Security: Building Security In* by Gary McGraw (Addison-Wesley, 2006).

redesign to mitigate risk. Some of the lessons learned by the auction builders should be applied to MMOs.

Hacking Games

By now we've established a clear motive for exploiting online games. Much money can be made, gaming software was not really designed with security in mind, and games are in widespread use. The good news is that at least some game developers are aware of the problem and have begun to think about security while they design their games. The White Hat Corner presents nine rules about game development and security identified by guru game developer Matt Pritchard.

Who Hacks Games?

Game hacking is almost as old as games themselves. As online games emerged with the popularization of the Internet in the 1990s, a number of game hackers gained prominence. Many of the first game programmers were classic hackers in the MIT sense of the word—technologists interested in learning as much as they could about how the games really worked. Eventually, these hackers created systems that could be used to cheat.

An excellent history of cheating in the online game Counter-Strike can be found in Wikipedia <http://en.wikipedia.org/wiki/Cheating_in _Counter-Strike>. This article discusses a Russian hacker calling himself Vasily (the author of the hook.dll program) and a Swedish high school student who went by the handle XQZ (and created an aimbot collection called XQZ2). These two were among the first game exploiters.

White Hat Corner

Game developer and guru Matt Pritchard wrote an article available on Gamasutra <http://www.gamasutra.com/features/20000724/pritchard_pfv.htm> entitled "How to Hurt the Hackers: The Scoop on Internet Cheating and How You Can Combat It." In the article, he presents nine rules about online cheating, meant to be used by game developers.

Rule #1: If you build it, they will come—to hack and cheat.

Rule #2: Hacking attempts increase with the success of your game.

Rule #3: Cheaters actively try to keep developers from learning their cheats.

Rule #4: Your game, along with everything on the cheater's computer, is not secure.

The files are not secure. Memory is not secure. Services and drivers are not secure.

Rule #5: Obscurity is not security.

Rule #6: Any communication over an open line is vulnerable to interception, analysis, and modification.

Rule #7: There is no such thing as a harmless cheat or exploit. Cheaters are incredibly inventive at figuring out how to get the most out of any loophole or exploit.

Rule #8: Trust in the server is everything in a client-server game.

Rule #9: Honest players would love for a game to tip them off to possible cheating. Cheaters want the opposite.

Reprinted here with permission.

Today, groups of hackers calling themselves clans work together to compromise games. One such group is the TKC (short for Teamkill and Cheat) Community <http://www.tkc-community.net>). These loose affiliations of players develop and trade exploits among themselves, mostly for reasons of prestige. Clans keep cheats secret so that they will continue to work. A cheat in the open (including the ones covered in this book) is often a cheat with a countermeasure.

Why Hack Games?

Hackers create cheats for simple reasons: money, fame, and glory.

In the Black Hat Corner, the cheat author Vasily discusses his motives and justifications for cheating. Interviews and manifestos can be found all over the Internet. As an example, members of the TKC Community mention a number of reasons for hacking games in their FAQ at <http://tkc-community.net/Main/modules.php?name=TKFAQ>. They start with this little gem:

Cheating Philosophy

As with real life, there are many different types of people present in online gaming, with many different tastes. Some are content with a game as it was intended for play by the developers, while others are not. We do not agree with the notion that if one is not satisfied with a game the way it was developed, that a player should look for another game to play. When a game does not meet one's expectations, or has lost its former appeal, the use of game modification techniques is encouraged to create a better gameplay experience for the player. This same belief applies to unintended coding vulnerabilities as well.

Then they go on to present a list of reasons why someone might want to hack online games (and join their group):

- To Prolong the Gaming Experience
- Companionship
- To Challenge Ourselves
- Amusement
- Offline Hecklers
- For Attention
- Non-Conformity
- Kiss Ass
- Revenge
- Advertisement
- Get an Edge
- By Accident
- To Spy

Over time, as the economies of online games have developed and become tied in with the real economy, the original motive for cheating—gaining status—has shifted to making money. Early cheaters were basically showing off their hacking skills and building up a technical reputation. Some even tried to help the game builders (but were reportedly turned down). Most early cheats were eventually eradicated once discovered by game companies. As a result, more recent cheats are kept under close wraps and sold and traded carefully between clans.

How to Hack Games

One of our goals with this book is to show you in as detailed a manner as possible how game hacks work. That means there will be plenty of code in this book. In fact, some of the things we intend to show you get downright hairy. We're forced to show you lots of code because simply describing a technique in philosophical terms is often unsatisfying and vague. To understand game hacking properly, there is no alternative to getting your hands dirty.

There is a catch. Getting your hands dirty by working your way through real game hacks requires an actual target. We choose to use WoW for many of our explicit examples for two reasons. The first is that WoW is the most popular MMORPG on the planet, and a majority of players have no clue what some of their gaming compatriots are doing to cheat. The second is that many of the classic techniques of game hacking have already been leveled against WoW, and we can easily show you the results. For example, when there are open source game hacking tools available (and they are abundant for WoW), we show them to you.

Black Hat Corner

The following is a quote taken from an interview with Vasily (the author of hook.dll, used to exploit the early game Counter-Strike), in which he discusses his motives. The original interview can be found at <http://www.cached.net/?go=main/featurearticle/ single/96>.

> styles.no: Do you ever feel bad about being one of the leading men behind the CS-cheating-plague?

Vasily: Honestly I don't see any reason why I should feel bad. I didn't release any cheat to public, I just gave it to a few famous persons. [. . .] Yes, my position in this is well-known, I'm not against the cheating in computer games. I do not care about it—in my opinion it is not a problem at all and if it is a problem for someone, he has to sit and reconsider his life carefully. There is a lot of things you should be proud of fighting for rather than cheating. Terrorism, racism, discrimination, misery, unemployment, crime. According to UN reports, every day thousands of children are starved. Every day people in Israel, Palestine and other hot spots are dying of the war. Cities and states are attacked by terrorists. You still tell me that cheating in computer games is a most serious problem which should be solved immediately coute que coute? You must be kidding!

Here's a quick overview of what we intend to cover in this book on the technical front. We start off fairly light with coverage of what we call game hacking 101 techniques in Chapter 2. We begin with a farming bot that uses rudimentary techniques. The idea behind Chapter 2 is to provide some vocabulary and a list of game hacking approaches. We cover bots, GUI hacks, proxies, memory hacking, debuggers, randomness, and rootkits. Chapter 2 also covers countermeasures and shows the lengths that some game companies will go to in order to prevent cheating. We'll dive into some code that watches the watcher, so that you get a real feel for what is happening on your PC when you install a game client.

The next chunk of technical material comes in Chapter 5, which is about bugs and flaws in games and why these make excellent game hacking targets. One of the most interesting things about our work on MMORPG security is that the kinds of security vulnerabilities we discuss are becoming more and more common in domains outside of gaming. In fact, MMORPG defects are a harbinger of things to come. Massively distributed software programs that actively manipulate state for thousands of interacting processes using central servers always have very complex time and state issues. In fact, discussion of software-intensive military systems at the U.S.

National Academy of Sciences referred to online games as an important example to understand and study.[9]

Things start to get deeper from a technical perspective in Chapter 6, which explains game client hacking in some detail. We use the metaphor of "getting around the game" to build categories of techniques, explaining what it means to go over, in, under, and way outside the game. There is lots of code in Chapter 6, making the techniques we describe abundantly clear.

The only problem with Chapter 6 is its smorgasbord approach to game hacking techniques. Chapter 7 addresses that problem head on by combining a number of the techniques introduced in Chapter 6 into a sophisticated bot program. Chapter 7 steps through bot fundamentals and ends by describing some working debugger-based bot code.

The deepest, darkest techniques in the book are introduced in Chapter 8. Chapter 8 is all about reverse engineering a game. Turns out that a basic handle on reversing is necessary if you want any hope of building new techniques by analogy to the ones on display in Chapters 6 and 7. Chapter 8 is a basic introduction to reversing, showing you some useful heuristics we have developed over the years.

Total conversions and other game mods are in some sense the apex of game hacking. Chapter 9 shows you how these kinds of things are done. Once again, there is no shortage of code demonstrating exactly what we mean.

So enjoy your romp through this book, but don't be surprised when you need to get out your keyboard and your compiler to get things straight.

How Much Game Hacking Happens?

Nobody is sure exactly how rampant cheating is in online games. If the game companies know, they aren't telling. They do, however, selectively ban suspected cheaters from their servers. In 2005, Blizzard Entertainment banned over 1,000 players from WoW for that reason.[10] The game company Valve has also banned players. But getting back into the game is often as simple as buying another copy with a different serial key and in some sense starting over.

Game companies are ambivalent about cheating until it affects play for noncheaters in an obvious manner. In Chapter 3, we describe an inflation problem in Ultima Online as one example of how an inherent tolerance threshold can be crossed. In some cases, game companies use anticheating

---

9. For more on the software-intensive systems study, see <http://www7.nationalacademies.org/cstb/project_producibility.html>.
10. See the article "World of Warcraft Players Banned for Selling Gold" at <http://www.gamesindustry.biz/content_page.php?aid=7392>.

mechanisms as differentiators to attract gamers. Many gamers abhor cheaters and will switch games to avoid them. In other cases, small-scale cheating (such as farming) is tolerated and maybe even encouraged. (Don't forget that sweatshop farmers must purchase legitimate licenses for their workers to create value, and that means the game company is realizing revenue.) Ultimately, the cheating acceptance tradeoff is one that must be carefully negotiated by game companies.

The Big Lesson: Software as Achilles' Heel

Over the past ten years, software security has emerged as an important discipline. We can apply the lessons we learn by studying vulnerabilities and exploits in online games directly to other kinds of software. The fact that tens of millions of people play MMOs online may help to make the "invisible" software security problem easier to perceive.

One reason MMORPGs are important is that they are a bellwether for other kinds of modern software. Online games are the future of software today—massively distributed systems with hundreds of thousands of users interacting in real time on a set of common servers. Problems with time and state, many of which are directly exploitable security vulnerabilities, are common in online games and are becoming more critical in other kinds of software (see Chapter 5). We have lots to learn about security engineering and massively distributed systems. MMORPGs are pushing the limits and can teach us important lessons.

The idea of building better software by building security in from the beginning has been explored by a number of large enterprises that rely on software (see Chapter 10). The most well-publicized software security initiative is Microsoft's Trustworthy Computing Initiative. A large number of financial institutions are also undergoing software security initiatives, but they are less public about what they're doing.

To learn more about software security, see the other titles in the Addison-Wesley Software Security Series. If you can get only one book, pick up a copy of *Software Security: Building Security In* <http://www.swsec.com>.

There is no reason that MMOs and other online games cannot be built to be more secure than they are today. Ignoring the problem or threatening people who talk about vulnerabilities is no substitute for building more secure games. If you are concerned about online game security in games that you play, contact your favorite game companies today and ask what they are doing about software security.

2

Game Hacking 101

Software piracy has long been a problem in the computer games business—ever since games moved from stand-alone machines in the 1970s to PCs in the 1980s. Game makers, justifiably, have gone to great lengths to thwart piracy. In the past, game makers added various countermeasures to their software to make games harder to crack. The main purpose was to prevent rampant copying so that people who wanted to play the game had to buy it. In the end, these games were always cracked—but in some cases, the countermeasures delayed the release of a cracked version by days or even weeks. This delay earned real revenue for the game companies because delaying a crack for even a week translated into hundreds of thousands of dollars.

Antipiracy countermeasures made some economic sense in the over-the-counter paradigm, in which a gamer purchased a copy of the game from a retailer and installed the copy locally on his or her PC. But things have changed. Many modern games have moved online, and with the advent of game consoles connected to the Internet, this trend is likely to accelerate.[1] That means companies now have two revenue sources to protect: the

---

1. The hugely popular Nintendo Wii, which debuted in late 2006, will certainly accelerate this trend.

original game price in the retail channel, and a monthly subscription revenue stream for online access.

In this chapter, we'll describe a number of cheating techniques that have become mainstream and discuss new techniques that have emerged to prevent piracy and cheating. Unfortunately, some of the new security monitoring approaches have grave privacy implications that require vigilance on the part of gamers.

Defeating Piracy by Going Online

One easy way to prevent simple piracy like copying is not to distribute anything to copy. That is, if a majority of your game resides on a central server, it can't be easily copied. By and large, game companies have adopted this strategy to prevent trivial game cracking (recall the client-server model from Chapter 1). Modern games almost all require gamers to play the game online using only supported servers. These online servers, at the very least, can check a local copy of the game client (running on the gamer's PC) for a legitimate serial number or some other key.

Of course, online games also require an online account, implying that some kind of user or gamer authentication is required to play the game. Note that this is a much clearer way to tie a game to a particular gamer than existed in the previous paradigm. Tracking gamer behavior is an important tactic in the fight against cheating.

As we briefly describe in Chapter 1, gaming is big business. For example, Blizzard Entertainment, the developers of World of Warcraft, not only charge over $30 for the game client but also require a gamer to pay $14 per month to log into the online servers. WoW has over 8 million users all paying these fees. You do the math.

Or Not . . .

Of course, the server model is not completely foolproof. A number of clever developers realized some time ago that it is possible to create new, possibly free, servers for gamers to connect to, thus sidestepping the subscription model. The question is, is this piracy?

When three programmers wrote an open source version of Blizzard's server software called BnetD, Blizzard sued—and won. See Chapter 4 for more.

Tricks and Techniques for Cheating

There are many ways to cheat in an online game. Some of them don't require much in the way of computer programming skills at all. Colluding as a group in an online poker game against an unsuspecting fellow player is an example from the "just takes a telephone" camp. On the other hand, some cheats require deep programming skills.

In this chapter, we'll introduce you to some basic cheating concepts:

- Building a bot
- Using the user interface (UI)
- Operating a proxy
- Manipulating memory
- Drawing on a debugger
- Finding the future

The end results of many of these approaches are now available for purchase online at a number of spurious Web sites. One example is the Pimp My Game Web site at <http://www.pimpmygame.org/>. The Web site, similar to many others like it, boasts the following:

> We give our users the chance to get Exploits, Bots, Hacks, Macros, Patches, Cheats and Guides for all usual MMORPGs and FPS Games that we support. Get them from our own downloads section and forums where you can discuss and debate. You will become more successful in your Game!

Of course, we're more interested in understanding what goes on behind the curtain of these "Exploits, Bots, Hacks, Macros, Patches, Cheats, and Guides" than we are in buying them.

Building a Bot: Automated Gaming

If you Google "online game bots," you'll amass impressive millions of hits. Most of the hits are for sites that offer to sell you a bot. But what is a bot really?

Bots are stand-alone programs that play a game (or part of a game) for you. The term originates from first-person shooter (FPS) games developed for the PC. The term derives from a ro*bot* that simulates another player in the game. You might play a game of chess against a bot, or you might battle a bot in an FPS game like DOOM.

Today, the term *bot* is applied widely to a range of programs, from those as simple as a keyboard mapping that allows you to script together several common actions to those as complex as a player based on artificial intelligence (AI) that plays the game by following simple reasoning rules. In the FPS world, people use bots to perform superhuman actions (e.g., perfect aim). In the MMORPG realm, players use bots to automate the boring parts of play. We provide an example of a macro later in the chapter that controls a character in WoW, thus making that character a bot (temporarily at least).

In all cases, bots perform certain tasks better than humans. Maybe their understanding of chess logic is superior, or maybe they outplay human characters by knowing more about game state than a human can track, or maybe they just do repetitive tasks without getting bored. But whatever they're programmed to do, bots give cheaters an unscrupulous advantage.

Bots have even been used to rob other characters in a game. According to an article in the *New Scientist*:[2]

> A man has been arrested in Japan on suspicion of carrying out a virtual mugging spree by using software "bots" to beat up and rob characters in the online computer game Lineage II. The stolen virtual possessions were then exchanged for real cash. The Chinese exchange student was arrested by police in Kagawa prefecture, southern Japan.

In a slightly less obvious fashion, online poker bots have been used to win poker games for their masters. Though professional-level play is not yet possible (because solving the problem involves creating legitimate AI that can pass the Turing test[3]), poker bots are good enough to win on basic tables with some regularity.[4]

In final analysis, bots have a mixed reputation. Some serious gamers deride them as a cancer ruining games and the gaming industry for everyone. Others see bots as extremely useful tools for delegating the boring aspects of play to a computer program. Still others see bots as a great way to make a living.

Game companies often deploy technical and legal countermeasures to detect and stop bot activity. Sometimes they keep play statistics about characters and notice when certain values go out of range (e.g., flagging

---

2. "Computer Characters Mugged in Virtual Crime Spree," by Will Knight (August 18, 2005; see <http://www.newscientist.com/article.ns?id=dn7865>).
3. For more on the Turing test, see <http://en.wikipedia.org/wiki/Turing_test>.
4. You can find an article from MSNBC about poker bots at <http://www.msnbc.msn.com/id/6002298/>.

things when a character quadruples its wealth in one hour). Another common countermeasure is to ask a character questions to see how humanlike its responses are.[5] The *Korea Times* reports that in the MMORPG Lineage, at least 150 game minders monitor the game for use of bots and then ban players using them. The report states that 500,000 accounts had been suspended between 2004 and April 2006 because of bot activity.[6]

Using the User Interface: Keys, Clicks, and Colors

Games have outstanding UIs these days. Consider the UI from WoW shown in Figure 2–1. For an impressive and diverse collection of UIs for MMORPGs, see <http://xune-gamers.tripod.com/id3.html>.

Figure 2–1 A WoW screenshot, demonstrating the state of the art in online game user interfaces.

---

5. In this case, the perfect MMORPG bot would need to be able to pass the Turing test.
6. See <http://times.hankooki.com/lpage/culture/200605/kt2006052116201765520.htm>.

As you can see, UIs include parts of the screen that a user can interact with by using standard input devices. There are buttons, text windows, and pictures. You play the game by interacting with the UI—it's your window on what's going on.

Cheaters use the UI to cheat. Let's say a game has three buttons, A, B, and C, that you're only allowed to click manually yourself. By some game companies' definition, if you were to install a software automation tool (such as a quality assurance testing tool) that automatically clicks the mouse on x- and y-coordinates to drive these buttons, you would be cheating.

In many cases, EULA allowances and their associated enforcement mechanisms *restrict how you use the software*. That is, you're allowed to click on buttons yourself, but a program that you write is not. You can learn much more about EULAs in Chapter 4.

Controlling someone's use of the game like this seems rather extreme until you consider the economic impact of automated game play. In most cases, automated game play is realized by using special tools and scripts typically referred to as *macros*. For example, in WoW, monsters appear at specific locations on a periodic basis. You can easily write a macro that causes the in-game character to stand in that location and automatically kill the monster every time it appears (thus gaining experience points and virtual gold). Of course, you can do this manually yourself, waiting around all day for the monster to appear, but given that the monster appears only once every 10 minutes, that plan will commit you to a very long and boring night. Why not write a macro to wait around for you? Ultimately the question is, how can automating such a boring and repetitive activity be considered cheating?

WoW, and many MMORPGs like it, are so afflicted with repetitious game play that the players have invented a term to describe it: *grinding*. That is, doing awful, repetitive things all day with your character just to gain experience is likened to a mule going around and around on a treadmill, grinding grain into flour day in and day out. For some reason, players *enjoy* this self-inflicted misery and will pay $14 a month for the privilege of doing it. Why?

As it turns out, there is deep-seated human psychology at play here, and it has to do with living a double life, as well as the fact that grinding away like this brings economic reward. Whenever you kill that monster, it drops in-game play money and gives you other rewards, such as more experience, skills, and ultimately levels.

If you write a macro to do this grinding for you by manipulating the UI, you can go away to work, or sleep, and come back later and have the sum of all the gold pieces and experience for all the repetitive monster kills waiting for you. Thus, the macro earns you in-game money and simultaneously increases your character's power—but without the associated boredom of actually paying attention. What a great idea! It's so great, in fact, that thousands of players do it all the time. There is even a special term used to describe players who play this way—they are called *farmers*.

The simple bot that we include later in the chapter uses UI manipulation to control a grinding character.

Operating a Proxy: Intercepting Packets

Interacting with a game through the client software by going through the UI is a straightforward cheating technique that is not hard to code. There are many more sophisticated methods, of course. One method involves operating a proxy between the game client and the game server. This proxy can intercept packets and alter them in transit. In other words, a proxy-based cheating scheme carries out what is in security circles known as an attacker-in-the-middle attack[7] (Figure 2–2).

There are many ways to carry out an attack like this. Monitoring the network wire is one way. Getting between a program and the system dynamic link libraries (DLLs) it is using is another. Basically, any place where messages are passed around by the target program is susceptible to this kind of interpositioning.

Proxy attacks have a long history. Some of the first network-based proxy attacks were devised and used against FPS games. In these games, a fair amount of data about game state is passed around between the client software and the server. Sometimes these data are not displayed for the player to see, but they are available to the software the player is using. A proxy cheat sniffs the network packets, analyzes them, and adjusts various parameters that should not be known by the player. A classic example comes from the FPS game Counter-Strike, where proxy cheats have been used to improve aim drastically (an essential characteristic in the shoot-'em-up world).

Proxy-based cheats in FPS games are usually held very close to the vest. That's because those who use them are interested in evading detection even

---

7. This kind of attack is most often called a man-in-the-middle attack, but we find that terminology sexist.

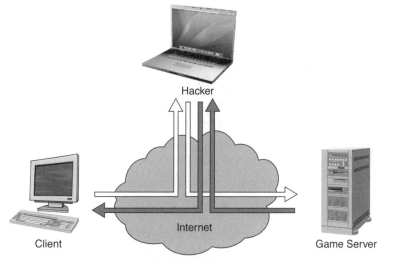

Figure 2–2 A picture of an attacker-in-the-middle attack. In this picture, the hacker interposes between the client and the server and can both monitor and manipulate traffic as it goes either direction.

in complicated social situations. Being outed at a LAN party for a visually detectable cheat could lead to bodily harm of the meat-space variety! Proxy-based aimbots are thus carefully designed to be effectively used in social situations and may involve statistical fuzzing of calculations to simulate not-quite-perfect aim.[8]

Sophisticated proxy-based attacks attempt to change data as they move between the server and the client. An obvious countermeasure is to encrypt the data so that unintelligible gibberish is all that can be seen going by. However, encryption costs cycles, and the balance is payable in a less-realistic gaming experience that is a major resource hog. Security always trades off against something; it never comes for free.

To use a proxy attack, cheaters configure the proxy with the address of the server they are using. In most cases, the FPS client runs on another machine entirely and connects through the proxy to the server. This situation is very similar in nature to a standard network sniffing situation, the only difference being that packets can be manipulated as they go by.

The real trick is being able to construct a useful model of the game from the traffic going by. The model will do things like track player locations.

---

8. See the history of aimbot cheating in the game Counter Strike on the Wikipedia site at <http://en.wikipedia.org/wiki/Cheating_in_Counter-Strike>.

When a packet with a marked command such as "fire the truly impressive blunderbuss of flatulence" goes by, the proxy software determines who is where and who must die and makes it so. It may need to do some weapon movement to cause this to happen so that the blunderbuss is properly aimed. (Remember, the weapon and/or player movement needs to seem natural and reasonable—a complete back flip with a triple gainer followed by a shot between the eyes may be a tip-off that something is fishy.)[9]

Proxy attacks are just as useful for non-FPS games as well. In fact, the most sophisticated attacks against MMORPGs use a very similar idea, interposing on machine state through manipulation of interrupts. You can read more about those attacks in Chapter 6.

Manipulating Memory: Reading and Writing Data

Manipulating game state through interposition as described in the previous subsection is a hands-off cheating technique. The game software is not directly manipulated, only its input and output are. More hands-on techniques get into the game program itself, reading and writing memory, changing values, and generally messing around with game state directly in the software.

One obvious target for manipulation is the drivers that control graphics rendering on the PC. Once again, FPS games led the way in cheating. The Counter-Strike game is a classic FPS. Like many games, it makes extensive use of drivers to control graphics, sound, and networking. Cheaters target the OpenGL and Direct3D drivers to do their dirty work. The Counter-Strike hack called XQZ was one of the first to alter drivers. The creators of Counter-Strike built an anticheat engine called Cheating-Death that was able to detect when OpenGL drivers had been replaced. The arms race was on.

Historically, the reason that drivers are easy to manipulate is that Microsoft Windows doesn't include an easy way to determine whether a driver is legitimate or nefarious. All of this is changing with the release of Vista and its driver signing capability (though don't believe for a minute that this is a security silver bullet). Prior to Vista, finding these cheats on any given computer was difficult even when full access was provided to the machine (and, in fact, even when rootkit technology was involved).

Another common form of client-side manipulation involves the use of classic hooking techniques to interpose on DLLs and other system libraries.

---

9. For more on proxy attacks in FPS games, see <http://www.gamasutra.com/features/20000724/ pritchard_pfv.htm>.

Many of these techniques are in common use in software exploits (see our book *Exploiting Software* for more). All modern operating systems use runtime-loadable libraries (Win32 uses DLLs; Linux and Mac OS X use standard UNIX-shared object libraries such as `glibc.so`), and as such, all are susceptible to hooking attacks.

In some games, client-side communication is accomplished through DLL calls, all of which are easily intercepted. Modern software almost always makes extensive use of outside libraries, which in this particular case leads directly to the risk of rampant cheating.

Once again, an arms race of sorts has emerged, with classic hacks (such as the `loadd11` library for Counter-Strike[10]) leading to hook-proof anticheats leading to sneakier hooks leading to hook detection mechanisms.

Drawing on the Debugger: Breakpoints

Debuggers are another common attack tool used by those who exploit software. There's nothing quite as powerful as a kernel-level debugger with the ability to stop processes in mid stride. Many cheaters use debugger techniques to set breakpoints or other triggers. These triggers can look for certain messages (e.g., a secret key press) or the use of particular functions (e.g., an easily thwarted DLL) and then carry out various nefarious activities.

Modern attacks of the sort that we describe in Chapter 6 often involve the use of sophisticated interrupt-driven state manipulation. More on that later.

Finding the Future: Predictability and Randomness, or How to Cheat in Online Poker

Many games involve an element of chance, poker being among the most obvious. The problem is that producing unpredictable randomness is nontrivial given the way computers work. Much work in software security has gone into improving randomness (which as you might imagine is also necessary for good cryptography).

Here's a good example of how poor pseudorandom number generators (PRNGs) can be broken in practice.[11] In 1999, the Software Security Group at Cigital discovered a serious flaw in the implementation of Texas hold 'em

---

10. See <http://www.answers.com/topic/cheating-in-counter-strike>.
11. This attack was first described in *Building Secure Software* by John Viega and Gary McGraw (Addison-Wesley, 2001). The text here is adapted from that account.

poker distributed by ASF Software, Inc. The exploit allowed a cheating player to calculate the exact deck being used for each hand in real time. That means a player who used the exploit knew the cards in every opponent's hand as well as the cards that made up the flop (cards placed face up on the table after rounds of betting). A cheater could "know when to hold 'em and know when to fold 'em" every time. A malicious attacker could use the exploit to bilk innocent players of actual money without ever being caught.

The flaw exists in the shuffling algorithm used to generate each deck. Ironically, the shuffling code was publicly displayed in an online FAQ with the idea of showing how fair the game is to interested players (the page has since been taken down), so it did not need to be reverse engineered or guessed.

In the code, a call to `randomize()` is included to reseed the random number generator with the current time before each deck is generated. The implementation, built with Delphi 4 (a Pascal IDE), seeds the random number generator with the number of milliseconds since midnight according to the system clock. That means the output of the random number generator is easily predicted. As it turns out, a predictable random number generator is a very serious security problem.

The shuffling algorithm used in the ASF software always starts with an ordered deck of cards and then generates a sequence of random numbers used to reorder the deck. In a real deck of cards, there are 52! (approximately 2^{226}) possible unique shuffles. The seed for a 32-bit random number generator must be a 32-bit number, meaning that there are just over 4 billion possible seeds. Since the deck is reinitialized and the generator reseeded before each shuffle, only 4 billion possible shuffles can result from this algorithm, even if the seed had more entropy than the clock. Yet 4 billion possible shuffles is alarmingly less than 52!.

The flawed algorithm chooses the seed for the random number generator using the Pascal function `randomize()`. This particular `randomize()` function chooses a seed based on the number of milliseconds since midnight. There are a mere 86,400,000 milliseconds in a day. Since this number was being used as the seed for the random number generator, the number of possible decks now reduces to 86,400,000—alarmingly less than 4 billion.

In short, there were three major problems, any one of which would have been enough to break the system.

- The PRNG algorithm used a small seed (32 bits).
- The PRNG algorithm used was noncryptographic.
- The code was seeded with a poor source of randomness (and, in fact, reseeded often).

The system clock seed gave the Cigital group members an idea that reduced the number of possible shuffles even further. By synchronizing the program with the system clock on the server generating the pseudorandom number, they were able to reduce the possible combinations down to a number on the order of 200,000 possibilities. After that move, the system is broken, since searching through this tiny set of shuffles is trivial and can be done on a PC in real time.

The tool Cigital developed to exploit this vulnerability requires five cards from the deck to be known. Based on the five known cards, the program searches through the few hundred thousand possible shuffles and deduces which one is a perfect match. In the case of Texas hold 'em poker, this means the program takes as input the two cards that the cheating player is dealt, plus the first three community cards that are dealt face up (the flop). These five cards are known after the first of four rounds of betting and are enough to determine (in real time, during play) the exact shuffle.

Figure 2–3 shows the GUI for the exploit. The Site Parameters box in the upper left is used to synchronize the clocks. The Game Parameters box in the upper right is used to enter the five cards and initiate the search. The figure is a screenshot taken after all cards have been determined by the program. The cheating attacker knows who holds what cards, what the rest of the flop looks like, and who is going to win in advance.

Once the program knows the five cards, it generates shuffles until it discovers the shuffle that contains the five known cards in the proper order. Since the `randomize()` function is based on the server's system time, it is not very difficult to guess a starting seed with a reasonable degree of accuracy. (The closer you get, the fewer possible shuffles you have to look through.) After finding a correct seed once, it is possible to synchronize the exploit program with the server to within a few seconds. This *post facto* synchronization allows the program to determine the seed being used by the random number generator and to identify the shuffle being used during all future games in under one second.

The ASF poker software was particularly easy to attack. However, most uses of linear congruential PRNGs (such as `rand()`)are susceptible to this kind of attack. These attacks always boil down to how many outputs an

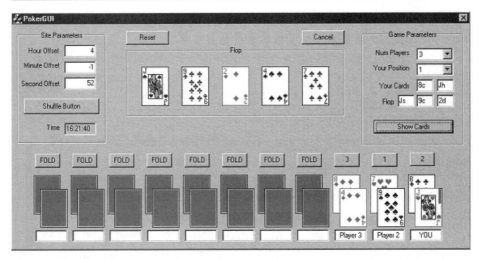

Figure 2–3 Cigital's Internet poker exploit can predict the outcome of a poker hand by taking advantage of a broken shuffling algorithm.

attacker must observe before enough information is revealed for a complete compromise. Even if you only select random numbers in a fairly small range, thus throwing away a large portion of the output of each call to rand(), it usually doesn't take very many outputs to give away the entire internal state.

Many games other than poker make use of randomness. Any game that is completely predictable can be won by a simple program that knows how to predict what will happen next! As more and more money is poured into gaming, these kinds of randomness problems turn into cash cows for attackers.

The Bot Parade

Since bots are such pervasive cheaters' tools, it is worth spending some time pondering a few examples. Three large-scale categories of bots are combat macro bots (used to cheat in MMORPG games), aimbots (a particular type of combat macro bot used commonly in FPS games), and poker bots.

Combat Macro Bots

Many games, especially MMORPGs, have simple scripting languages that can be used to interact with the game. These languages allow a number of basic activities to be strung together into a macro. Sometimes games don't include a scripting language off the shelf, but third-party programs that run with the game provide scripting capability.

Scripts are very useful for automating simple tasks. Here is an example of a macro that works with WoW.[12] Web sites filled with macros like this one are easy to find on the Internet.

Macro

TargetFreeEnemy   **Last Updated: June 22nd, 2006**

Updated since last WoW Patch

This macro cycles through all enemies around you and stops when it hits an untapped enemy (non-faction, i.e., non-horde and non-alliance). Very useful while grinding undead currently! (Stops after cycling through 30 enemies as to not hang your computer when none are available.) (This macro assumes you're Alliance, if you're not, replace "`Horde`" with "`Alliance`" to make it work for you as well.)

Code Start:
```
/script TargetNearestEnemy(); local i = 1;
if(UnitExists('target')) then while(UnitExists('target') and
(UnitFactionGroup('target') == 'Horde' or
UnitIsTapped('target')) and i < 30) do TargetNearestEnemy();
i = i+1; end;end;
```
Code End:

Here is another example. This macro works with Star Wars Galaxies.[13]

Date Added: August 2, 2004

Ok, this is an AFK combat macro designed for the in-game macro system. If you want to take it a step further, you can run a HAM Checker macro (checks your HAM and heals you when needed) with AC Tool.

To run this macro, set up a droid running a patrol pattern in a square pattern around a spawn. Angle your camera in so it faces the spawn (and go watch tv or sleep.

The macro is:

```
/ui action targetGroup0;
/follow;
```

---

12. The WoW macro is from <http://ui.worldofwar.net/listmacros.php?type=2>.
13. The Star Wars Galaxies macro is from <http://rpgexpert.com/2789.html>.

```
/ui action cycleTargetOutward;
(if you're a Brawler, insert /follow here)
/attack;
(insert specials here)
/pause XXX;
(amount of time to kill it)
/follow;
/pause 2;
/loot;
/harvest hide;
/macro AFKCombat;
```

This macro is slightly more interesting than the first example because it works unattended. In fact, its simple description makes this clear. Some gamers draw a big distinction between attended use of macros and unattended use. They believe that unattended use is cheating.

Some games go so far as to outlaw the use of macros (see Chapter 4 for more on legal moves to prevent cheating). The game Asheron's Call includes the following legalese:

> Use of unauthorized third-party software or macros with the Software may be prohibited in the sole discretion of Turbine. Specifically, you may not use third-party software which allows your character to gain experience points or items by engaging in combat without being at the keyboard, ready to respond to Turbine staff on demand (this activity is commonly called a "Combat Macro"). Logging off as soon as an admin appears (visible or invisible) or when an admin tries to speak with you will be taken into consideration in determining the use of Combat Macros.[14]

One of the most well-known and widely used macro systems in gaming is Lin2Rich <http://lin2rich.com/>. Lin2Rich is actually an advanced bot environment. It works alongside your client (i.e., you use it in tandem with the regular game client), sending packets directly to the game server according to the way it is configured. Lin2Rich can be configured to send a set of commands to the server when a certain event happens. For example, if you click certain buttons at particular times or begin to rest at a particular time and place, you can program the cheating client to send particular commands to the game. Because of the way it works, detecting Lin2Rich by monitoring player behavior is difficult.

---

14. You can find more on the Asheron's Call legalese at <http://turbine.fuzeqna.com/asheronscall/consumer/kbdetail.asp?kbid=305>.

Aimbots

Aimbots are bots used in FPS games. The idea is simple: Aim better than your opponent and win. Superhuman aim achieved through programming is generally considered cheating (though some FPS games have built-in aimbots that can be used).

Aimbots come in a variety of flavors. Some only aim. Some aim and shoot. Some move, aim, and shoot. The first aimbots were created for Quake and Counter-Strike. An interesting FAQ about Unreal Tournament and cheats can be found at <http://www.digdilem.org/ut/aimbot.php>.

Black Hat Corner: ZelliusBot Readme File

========ZelliusBot UT2004 Edition ver 1.0===========

—About—
My leet aimbot with lots of useful features :D Works on UT2004 Demo & UT2004 retail ver. 3186. My bots feature base is aimed towards ease of tracking down crybabies and huge-ego clanmembers :)

—Installation—
1. Copy ZelliusBot.u & Zelliusbot.ini to your UT's 'System' folder
2. Open up your UT2004.ini, navigate to the [XInterface.ExtendedConsole] and edit the ServerInfoMenu so its value is: ZelliusBot.ZelliusServerInfo. It should look like ServerInfoMenu=ZelliusBot.ZelliusServerInfo. If Serverinfo line aint already there, just add it.
3. Open up your User.ini and bind 'serverinfo' to a key of your choice. e.g., z=serverinfo
4. Wait until you've joined a game and press your serverinfo key, if all goes well the Zelliusbot status should appear on your HUD.

—Usage—
Use your number row keys to toggle various commands. You can change your selected toggling keys by editing your ut2004.ini statements like AutoTauntKey.

You can get the various number codes for each key by setting bShowKeyNumbers to True, joining a game and taking note of the numbers that are displayed when you press a certain key.

—Notes—
This bot will not aim while in UT2004 vehicles
Compile in the UT2003 development environment.

Experiment in game or read the uscript to figure out how everything works.

If you encounter a 'shooting at wall' problem when an enemy comes into sight increase your FireDelayTime.

Unload the bot when the match is ended, if you still get a invalid game file error on map change type 'reconnect' in the console.

—Thanks—

Thanks go to tenbucks, moonwolf, play2win, lamer, spunky and many others for lots of testing and feedback.

Thanks go to [ELF]HelioS for his help with ping code, HUD and his textures (from helios ut bot).

Thanks go to DrSiN[Epic] for leaving multiple gaping holes in UT2004.

I hope you have lots of fun!

~Zellius

One popular aimbot called ZelliusBot works by reprogramming initialization files in Unreal Tournament. The Black Hat Corner includes some text from the readme file that comes with ZelliusBot.

In most cases, aimbots come packaged with other features such as the ability to travel through walls. One early aimbot for Counter-Strike was XQZ. XQZ combined several capabilities into an easy-to-use package. It was eventually released to the public. XQZ at first replaced and then later hooked the OpenGL DLL. XQZ included features that allowed users to use it stealthily during LAN parties without detection. Counter-Strike is still filled with spinoffs from XQZ.

In its first instantiations, the XQZ aimbot was invoked when a button on the keyboard or mouse was pressed. Pressing the button resulted in the aimbot controlling the aiming crosshairs.

Care must be taken when developing and using aimbots to ensure that their superhuman potential does not become a giveaway. For example, using an aimbot that perfectly tracks a strangely moving adversary, shooting it over and over in the exact same spot, is called slaving. Decoupling the aim and shoot features is sometimes necessary. As we mentioned earlier, more advanced aimbots can add statistical noise to their actions.

Poker Bots

Now that online poker has topped $1 billion in revenue, it's not surprising that much activity has been invested in creating automated bots to play poker. Fortunately, poker is a reasonably hard game that can't easily be automated. However, poker bots do exist, and they are improving rapidly.

Of course, if poker bots get too good, they will undermine the game itself. Nobody wants to lose consistently to a bot! Especially when money is involved.

Rumors abound of a new generation of sophisticated poker bots that can beat newbies with some regularity. Some even say that above-average players can be beaten as well. Of course, just as in other kinds of gaming, the game companies want to discourage the use of bots. They make use of player monitoring and look for suspicious patterns of play, sometimes adapting their games to defeat bots.

Still, some people are making their living by selling poker bots commercially. A number of programs are available at the WinHoldEm Web site <http://www.winholdem.net/>, ranging from a $25 standard package of hand analysis software to a $200 version that includes bot play capability.

Once again we find ourselves in the midst of a classic arms race. Simple bots pop up, antibot measures out them, the bots improve, and so on. Of course, most online casinos don't allow bots, but enforcing that rule is difficult.

The entire online poker phenomenon is confusing to many security professionals. The biggest problem is collusion between players. Cheating by discussing hands in an out-of-band conversation is very difficult to detect. Banning this activity is easy from a legal perspective, but enforcing the ban may not be possible.

Some believe the inability to control poker bots and out-of-band communication will be the demise of online poker. We'll just have to wait and see.

Lurking (Data Siphoning)

Much valuable gaming data can be gleaned simply by watching other players play the game and learning how they behave. This is true for sports, of course, where watching your opponents play in order to understand their play is an invaluable aid. The same kind of technique works for online gaming, from actions in an MMORPG to hands in online poker.

Online Statistics

Services like Thottbot help users collect and use statistics about the game.[15] For example, Thottbot can tell you exactly where to find the vorpal sword of heinosity, provide you with a map to it, and let you know what your chances are of obtaining it once you're there. Thottbot works by sucking up as much information as it can from cooperating gamers and then republishing that information after it has been properly organized. For more on Thottbot, see Chapter 3.

Poker Statistics

Online poker is just as big as if not bigger than MMORPGs, though the recently passed legislation in the United States will put a big crimp in the market.

A number of third-party vendors create and sell software packages to help analyze hand history data and build a database of information about players and their tendencies. Serious poker players use these statistics to check for weaknesses in their play and uncover weaknesses in the play of others. Using these tools is extremely common, and all serious players (including an entire class of professional online poker players) use them.

As usual, academics and mathematicians have entered the fray. One interesting paper titled "Mathematical Statistics and Online Poker" by Jason Swanson can be found at <http://www.math.wisc.edu/~swanson/instructional/stats_poker.pdf>. Be forewarned, though—this paper includes real math!

Figure 2–4 shows the GUI from a typical online poker third-party application. This application helps a player understand poker statistics and what to do next. It generates statistics, win percentages, hand probabilities, and useful tactical information for the game of Texas Hold 'em Poker.

In any game that involves money, it should be clear that your adversary will tool up. Online poker cheats and stats trackers are destined to become much better over time. Perhaps one day the bots will be good enough to beat even the best humans consistently.

---

15. Thottbot <http://www.thottbot.com> is an online database of WoW information.

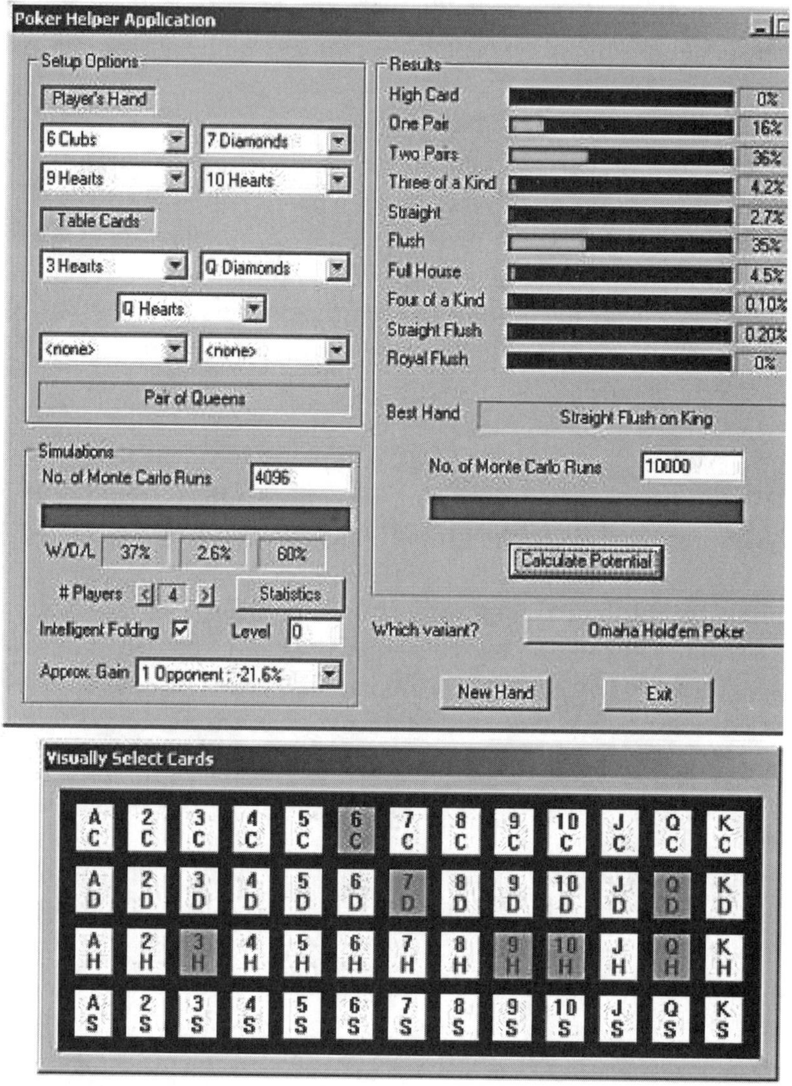

Figure 2–4 An online poker helper application. (From <http://www.frayn.net>; reproduced with permission.)

Auction Manipulation

Cheaters also like to cheat in auctions. Though only tangential to online gaming, online auctions share many of the same "instant riches" lure that online games do. Considering some of the tactics that cheaters in online auctions resort to may provide some insight on cheaters in general.

Probably the most obvious tactic in auction manipulation is shill bidding. The idea behind shill bidding is to place a bid on an item only to inflate the final value. Of course, it's also against the law and a felony in the United States (you see, shill bidding existed long before online auctions). Auction houses like eBay track IP numbers to try to defeat shill bidding. They also monitor bidding activity over time to look for suspicious patterns. Sound familiar?

Another common cheating technique in online auctions is interfering in a transaction through out-of-band communication. This can take place through e-mail or any other channel. Colluding in an auction can be just as unfair as colluding in a poker game, and just as hard to detect.

A third form of cheating involves interposing near the end of an auction to try to intercept payment. By simply dashing off a quick e-mail to the winner as if the attacker were the seller and asking for payment, the attacker can sometimes dupe the poor winner into paying the wrong person. Traceable payment systems help make this attack less prevalent than others.[16]

Finally, there's a way to cheat in head-to-head auctions, applicable when things begin to heat up at the end. The competing parties (A and B) may be bidding against each other for the last few minutes, when A carries out an attack to deny service to B. One simple technique involves A attempting to log in as B unsuccessfully several times in a row so that B is temporarily locked out of the account.

Tooling Up

By now we have described a number of common "game cheating 101" attacks. We've even shown you how simple macros work. But explaining how these things work is not quite the same as seeing how they are constructed. Toward that end, we present a simple macro for WoW. *Warning*: Use of this macro is cheating and is against the rules. Your character may be banned from the game if you use this macro.

Note that these kinds of tools are in common use every day. in all kinds of games. It's not just in WoW that cheating happens.

---

16. For more on online auction cheating, see <http://www.dummies.com/WileyCDA/DummiesArticle/id-2679.html>.

AC Tool: Macro Construction

There are a number of popular macro construction tools on the Internet. These include macro express (which costs money), AC Tool, AutoHotKey, AutoIt3.0, LTool-0.3, and xautomation. All of the ones mentioned here have been nicely collected on a wiki at <http://wiki.atitd.net/tale2/Macros>.

AC Tool is particularly popular. You can download it for free from <http://www.actool.net>. Once you have installed AC Tool, you can create macros for WoW using its macro language. The FAQ on the AC Tool Web site describes the tool as follows:

> AC Tool is a utility that allows you to list a series of keystrokes and mouse clicks in advance and send them to Asheron's Call at a later time. The list of keystrokes and mouse clicks is called a macro or a script.

Here is a simple grinding/farming macro (called Hoglund's WoW_Agro Macro) designed to be used with AC Tool. This macro controls a character that camps out waiting for monsters to appear and kills them when they do. We'll interleave commentary with the code so you can understand what's happening.

```
// ————————————————————
// hoglund's WoW_Agro Macro
// ————————————————————
//RESOLUTION: 1024x768
//PUT ALL FILES IN YOUR AC TOOL\MACROS FOLDER.

SETActiveWindow World of Warcraft
delay 4 sec

// put all your 'globals' here
Constants
        gPCHealth = "NoValue"
        // the current health of the PC ( HIGH | MEDIUM | LOW |
CRITICAL )
        gMobHealth = "NoValue"
        // the current health of the current targeted mob ( HIGH |
MEDIUM | LOW | CRITICAL )
        gPCPosture = "Standing"
        // current/starting posture of the PC character
        gMachineState = "START"
        // global machine state, core of the system
        gSelectedTarget = "NoTarget"
        pc_name = xanier
```

The first part of the code sets up global variables, most importantly the currently selected target, the name of the character being automated, and the current state of the state machine. This script implements a classic architecture that many macros follow—that is, it is designed to operate as a state machine. This means that the script maintains a single state variable while automating the character. States can have mnemonic labels such as "attacking," "healing," or "running away for dear life." Only one state can be active at any one time, and there are rules for transitioning from one state to another.

```
// hot keys
keyExecAttack = 1
// set your F1 key to attack before using this MACRO
keyExecPickup = {F2}
```

The part of the script above indicates which keys need to be used in order to automate the game. When the F2 key is pressed, the character picks up items, and when the number 1 key is pressed, the character attacks. This kind of key binding is very common in macros like this. Simple macros operate the software using only keystrokes and mouse movements—there is nothing invasive that exploits the game software directly. More advanced methods of cheating are nowhere near as simple.

```
// screen coordinates
coord_MobHPMin          = 262, 50
coord_MobHPFull         = 370, 50

coord_SafeHP            = 200, 50
//if green at or above this mark, you're fine
coord_HalfHP            = 146, 50
//half hp if lower than this mark
coord_LowHP             = 116, 50
//low hp if at or lower than this mark
coord_DeadHP            = 96, 50
//you're dead :(
coord_temp              = 0,0

// colors
color_AliveGreen        = 150
color_AttackRed         = 147
```

```
// temp stuff
TempTarget                 = NoValue
//holds the value for target before placing into list
tCount                 = 1
//used to traverse the targetList index
Total                  = 1
//used to find the ListCount
redDifference          = 0
blueDifference         = 0
greenDifference        = 0
numAttacks             = 0
Returned               = 0
aCount                 = 0
```

End

The section of the script above is quite fascinating. It designates x- and y-coordinates on the screen. Furthermore, it designates exact color thresholds for pixels. This information is used to sample pixels on the screen at precise x- and y-coordinates. The pixels in question happen to correspond to locations where health and enemy health are displayed on the screen for the game user. This information, along with the color threshold, is then used to determine whether the character is at full health, is partially damaged, or is in critical condition—all via sampling pixels on the screen and figuring out color matches while the macro runs.

```
////MAIN LOOP
While 1=1
   Processmessages      //required for AC Tool operation
   Call Lazy8_Main      //the main lazy8 machine handler
End
///END MAIN LOOP

////////////////////////////////////////////////////
// the main lazy8 machine handler
////////////////////////////////////////////////////
Procedure Lazy8_Main

      //KeyDown /whisper $pc_name Lazy8_Main {RETURN}
      //KeyDown /whisper $pc_name current state: $gMachineState
{RETURN}
```

You see this sort of thing all over the place in the macro; the `whisper` command prints a message on the screen and is used to output debug messages while the macro is under development. You can see the results of a whisper call in the screenshot in Figure 2–5.

```
        // perform effective switch() on machine state
        //
        // START
        if $gMachineState = "START"
        Call LazyStart
        end

        // IDLE
        // bored, we need to do something
        if $gMachineState = "DRAWING"
        Call LazyDraw
        end

        // END
        // game over, man
        if $gMachineState = "END"
        call LazyEnd
        end
End //end Lazy8_Main

Procedure LazyStart
        KeyDown /stand {RETURN}
        delay 100
        // go directly to draw agro mode
        Set gMachineState = "DRAWING"
End

Procedure LazyDraw
        KeyDown /whisper $pc_name LazyDraw {RETURN}

        //Call LureIfNoMonster

        //target last agro, this targets nearest also
        KeyDown {TAB}
        Delay 400

        Call EnsureAttackMode

        // hero strike
        KeyDown 2
        Delay 400


End
```

In the above section of the macro, we perform a pixel test to determine whether the character is currently in "agro" mode—that is, attacking a monster. If not, we call a routine to target the nearest monster and begin attacking. The script presses the 2 key in order to perform a hero strike—a powerful form of attack in the game.

```
// run forward and back to lure agro
Procedure Lure
        KeyDown {UP} 3 sec
        KeyDown {DOWN} 3 sec
End

// put the PC into attack mode
Procedure EnsureAttackMode
        LoadRGB 34,64
        Compute $redDifference = Abs ( $color_AttackRed -
{RGBRED} )
        if $redDifference < 80
                KeyDown /whisper $pc_name im currently in attack
mode {RETURN}
        else
                KeyDown /whisper $pc_name im attempting to start
attack mode {RETURN}
                KeyDown $keyExecAttack 150
        end
End

// perform a random move if no monster is targeted
Procedure LureIfNoMonster
        Call util_GetMobHealth
        if $gMobHealth = "DEAD"
                KeyDown /whisper $pc_name Rest in Peace! .. luring
{RETURN}
                Call Lure
        else
                KeyDown /whisper $pc_name still going... {RETURN}
        end
End
```

The section of the macro above is used to "draw agro" from nearby monsters. Essentially this amounts to getting the monster's attention by moving nearby. Such movement causes the monster to attack the character. Once the attack occurs, the character can attack the monster and kill it.

```
/////////////////////////////////////////////////
// END - kill the engine
/////////////////////////////////////////////////
Procedure LazyEnd
        KeyDown /whisper $pc_name LazyEnd {RETURN}

        //TODO
End


/////////////////////////////////////////////////
// Utility Function
// Get target mob health
/////////////////////////////////////////////////
Procedure util_GetMobHealth
        //KeyDown /whisper $pc_name util_GetMobHealth {RETURN}

        LoadRGB $coord_MobHPMin
        Compute $greenDifference = ABS ( $color_AliveGreen -
{RGBGREEN} )

        //KeyDown /whisper $pc_name sample monster {RGBRED}
{RGBBLUE} {RGBGREEN} {RETURN}

        if {RGBRED} = 0 AND {RGBBLUE} = 0 AND $greenDifference < 80
                Set gMobHealth = "ALIVE"
                //KeyDown /whisper $pc_name monster is still alive
{RGBGREEN} {RETURN}
        else
                // we never found any green
                Set gMobHealth = "DEAD"
                KeyDown /whisper $pc_name monster is dead {RETURN}
        end

End
```

This section of the macro detects whether or not the target monster is dead yet. Like monitoring character health, this is done through the simple technique of sampling pixels. In this case we pull a sample at the location that displays the monster's health bar.

And that's it, a complete macro for automating the attraction and killing of monsters in WoW. By running this macro, a character can accumulate experience and gold without human intervention.

Figure 2–5 shows a screenshot taken while the WoW_Agro macro is running. Notice the pile of dead monsters near the character. You should

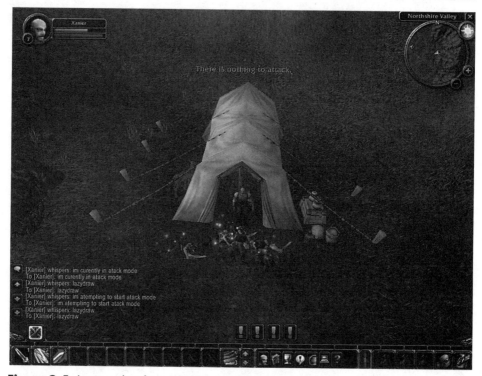

Figure 2–5 A screenshot from WoW showing what happens when the WoW_Agro macro runs. Virtual bodies pile up as the macro runs all night long.

note that running a macro like this is against the rules and can cause you to be banned from the game. The WoW character's name displayed on the screen, Xanier, is no secret. Blizzard banned Hoglund's Xanier account just before the character was to reach level 60 (which at the time was the ultimate level for a WoW character). In this case, Hoglund was a little too flagrant with his cheating. Hoglund had spent over $400 on game-card registered accounts by this point. All of the accounts were banned for various reasons.

Time for another pesky question: Why is farming with a macro cheating? Some would argue that Blizzard made the game boring in the first place, so fair is fair.

Countermeasures

For obvious reasons, gaming companies are most interested in keeping bots out of games. Scientists have even begun to study the problem and publish work about it. For example, the paper "Preventing Bots from Playing

Online Games" by Philippe Golle and Nicolas Ducheneaut appears in *ACM Computers in Entertainment.*[17]

One clever idea suggested for ensuring that humans (rather than bots) are playing games has been used successfully to combat spam. It's called a reverse Turing test. The Turing test is a test from the AI field meant to determine whether the entity at one end of a conversation is a human. A reverse Turing test works by asking questions to ensure that the answering target (in this case, a gamer) is a human. In many cases, this involves displaying a convoluted picture that only a human can properly decode (Figure 2–6). This technique is often referred to as *captcha*, short for Completely Automated Public Turing Test to Tell Computers and Humans Apart.

Often, gamers self-police and try to ferret out and expose bots among themselves. This can happen through the invocation of a game's chat function (something that game masters also employ as a tactic to find bots). The chat countermeasure works in many games, from MMORPGs to online poker. Poker bots are not very good at small talk!

Monitoring in real time (possibly using chat) is often accompanied by monitoring history as well. Looking for behavior that is nonhuman in nature—maybe superhuman aim, or maybe obsessive behavior such as killing monsters over and over in the same spot—is often a tip-off that a bot may be involved. Game masters make use of history to uncover cheating as a standard tactic.

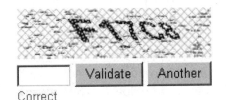

Figure 2–6 A classic reverse Turing test based on human perception. (From <http://www.brianpautsch.com/Blog/2005/12/1/Captcha>; used by permission.)

---

17. The paper is also available from the PARC Web site at <http://www.parc.xerox.com/research/publications/files/5445.pdf>.

Spyware

Anticheat tools have been around almost as long as game servers have. Public outcry on open servers led to the first such tools. Game companies running private servers carry on the tradition to this day.

The first service devoted to this is called PunkBuster, run by a Texas company named Even Balance, Inc. The PunkBuster service started in 2000. The first versions relied on simple techniques such as variable checking and process validation authorized through a server. This was followed by a number of server-based checks. Today, PunkBuster is integrated into a number of online games.

The PunkBuster Web site lists the following "features" of the product.[18]

- Real-time scanning of memory by PB Client on players' computers searching for known hacks/cheats
- Throttled two-tiered background auto-update system using multiple Internet Master Servers to provide end-user security ensuring that no false or corrupted updates can be installed on players' computers
- Frequent status reports (highly encrypted) are sent to the PB Server by all players and the PB Server raises a violation when necessary which causes the offending player to be removed from the game and all other players are informed of the violation
- PB Admins can also manually remove players from the game for a specified number of minutes or permanently ban if desired
- PB Servers can optionally be configured to randomly check player settings looking for known exploits of the game engine
- PB Admins can request actual screenshot samples from specific players and/or can configure the PB Server to randomly grab screenshot samples from players during gameplay
- An optional "bad name" facility is provided so that PB Admins can prevent players from using offensive player names containing unwanted profanity or racial slurs
- Search functions are provided for PB Admins who wish to search player's keybindings and scripts for anything that may be known to exploit the game

---

18. Quoted from the PunkBuster Web site at <http://www.evenbalance.com/index.php?page=info.php>.

- The PunkBuster Player Power facility can be configured to allow players to self-administer game servers when the Server Administrator is not present entirely without the need for passwords
- PB Servers have an optional built-in mini http web server interface that allows the game server to be remotely administered via a web browser from anywhere over the Internet

Note that some of these features are extremely invasive, such as the one that scans client PCs! This kind of scanning often involves the installation of spyware on a gamer's PC.

PunkBuster was originally conceived as a way to stop client-side hacks in Counter-Strike. But today PunkBuster concentrates on helping to protect and police other games.

As it turns out, PunkBuster was a harbinger of invasive techniques to come.

The Warden: Defeating Cheaters by Crossing the Line

Today, WoW has a two-pronged strategy to defeat cheaters. The first approach is to make rules against cheating and ban those characters caught cheating. This is carried out by publishing the terms of use, which are administered according to the legally binding EULA. Nothing is wrong with that.[19] (For more on the legal situation, see Chapter 4.) The second approach is to keep an eye on every PC running the WoW client and try to determine whether it is being used to cheat. This spying thing is a problem.

If monitoring someone's PC sounds like spying to you, that's because it is. WoW's embedded Warden reads all sorts of data from the gamer's PC. Hoglund's Warden discovery in fall 2005 set off a controversy over privacy, security, and just what lengths security measures should go to in order to stop cheating. And it's part of the reason that we decided to write *Exploiting Online Games*.

Besides monitoring the WoW process space and keeping track of DLLs running in that space, the Warden pokes around into other processes, doing things like reading the window text in the title bar of *every window* and doing a scan of the code loaded for *every process running* on your computer (which it then compares against known cheat code). Blizzard claims not to

---

19. Note that this is not a law, it is a contract, and there is no due process. Game companies can ban your character at any time.

have any designs to use the data it digs up for purposes other than security, but nothing is really stopping the company from doing whatever it wants on a gamer's PC, and it has already crossed the invisible line by poking around outside the game's process area. We don't trust them.

This is a clear invasion of privacy. So much so that the Electronic Frontier Foundation (EFF) has even weighed in with an opinion <http://www.eff.org/deeplinks/archives/004076.php>. Though the EULA does call out that Blizzard may monitor PC activities with the Warden (without specifying what the Warden actually does), this information is buried in the small print that almost nobody ever reads. In informal conversations with WoW players, we have found that none of them were aware that they had agreed to such monitoring. Some of them were concerned enough to stop playing.

Worldwide, 8 million people play WoW (usually about 500,000 at any one time). And *every single one* of these players has granted Blizzard the right to scan their computer programs and memory—which Blizzard does.

The Warden process scans for an arbitrary list of things such as open processes, URLs, and so on, controlled at Blizzard's discretion, and mails the information it finds back to Blizzard any time the game program is running. Figure 2–7 shows an example of content being sent back to Blizzard by the Warden as determined by a program we wrote called the

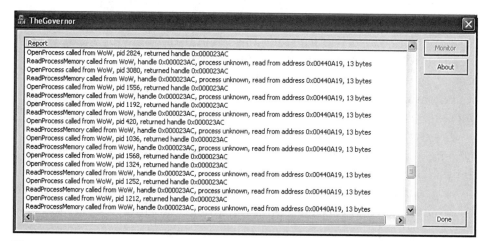

Figure 2–7 The Governor program, which we created, reports on the activities of the WoW Warden. The Warden acts as a spy for Blizzard and keeps an eye on your PC by calling into open processes and reading memory to see what it finds, then reporting that information back to Blizzard for analysis.

Governor. You can think of the Warden as 8 million copies of what the game companies call "legitimate spyware." We think the term *spyware* is apt without a modifier.

Of course, Blizzard isn't the only company that does monitoring like this—many other game companies do it, too. Sony even tried to install a monitor when music CDs were inserted into a PC but did it so poorly that the company landed in hot water. Reaction to the unmasking of programs like the WoW Warden and Sony's rootkit has been intense.

The Black Hat Corner reprints a blog entry outing the Warden as spyware. This story spread worldwide.

Black Hat Corner: WoW Warden as Spyware

In the fall of 2005, one of us (Hoglund) discovered the WoW Warden and outed it to the technical community. Hoglund's original posting to the rootkit.com blog (available at <http://www.rootkit.com/blog.php?newsid=358> with follow-up threads and discussion) touched off a firestorm. Here's the post.

4.5 million copies of EULA-compliant spyware
Oct 05 2005, 19:07 (UTC+0)

Hoglund writes:

I recently performed a rather long reversing session on a piece of software written by Blizzard Entertainment, yes—the ones who made Warcraft, and World of Warcraft (which has 4.5 million+ players now, apparently). This software is known as the 'warden client'—it's written like shellcode in that it's position independent. It is downloaded on the fly from Blizzard's servers, and it runs about every 15 seconds. It is one of the most interesting pieces of spyware to date, because it is designed only to verify compliance with a EULA/TOS. Here is what it does, about every 15 seconds, to about 4.5 million people (500,000 of which are logged on at any given time):

The warden dumps all the DLL's using a ToolHelp API call. It reads information from every DLL loaded in the 'world of warcraft' executable process space. No big deal.

The warden then uses the GetWindowTextA function to read the window text in the titlebar of every window. These are windows that are not in the WoW process, but any program running on your computer. Now a Big Deal.

I watched the warden sniff down the email addresses of people I was communicating with on MSN, the URL of several websites that I had open at the time, and the names of all my running programs, including those that were minimized or in the toolbar. These strings can easily contain social security numbers or credit card numbers, for example, if I have Microsoft Excel or Quickbooks open w/ my personal finances at the time.

Once these strings are obtained, they are passed through a hashing function and compared against a list of 'banning hashes'—if you match something in their list, I suspect you will get banned. For example, if you have a window titled 'WoW!Inmate'—regardless of what that window really does, it could result in a ban. If you can't believe it, make a dummy window that does nothing at all and name it this, then start WoW. It certainly will result in warden reporting you as a cheater. I really believe that reading these window titles violates privacy, considering window titles contain a lot of personal data. But, we already know Blizzard Entertainment is fierce from a legal perspective. Look at what they have done to people who tried to make BNetD, freecraft, or third-party WoW servers.

Next, warden opens every process running on your computer. When each program is opened, warden then calls ReadProcessMemory and reads a series of addresses—usually in the 0x0040xxxx or 0x0041xxxx range—this is the range that most executable programs on windows will place their code. Warden reads about 10–20 bytes for each test, and again hashes this and compares against a list of banning hashes. These tests are clearly designed to detect known 3rd party programs, such as wowglider and friends. Every process is read from in this way. I watched warden open my email program, and even my PGP key manager. Again, I feel this is a fairly severe violation of privacy, but what can you do? It would be very easy to devise a test where the warden clearly reads confidential or personal information without regard.

This behavior places the warden client squarely in the category of spyware. What is interesting about this is that it might be the first use of spyware to verify compliance with a EULA. I cannot imagine that such

> practices will be legal in the future, but right now in terms of law, this is the wild wild west. You can't blame Blizz for trying, as well as any other company, but this practice will have to stop if we have any hope of privacy. Agree w/ botting or game cheaters or not, this is a much larger issue called 'privacy' and Blizz has no right to be opening my excel or PGP programs, for whatever reason.
>
> —Greg

The Governor

Hoglund was upset enough by the Warden to write a program called the Governor that gamers can use to determine exactly what the Warden is doing.

We believe that having the Governor around is useful, especially if you're interested in what WoW software might be doing on your PC. A listing of part of the Governor is included here. You may download a copy of the software and the libraries required to build it from the book's Web site or at <http://www.rootkit.com/vault/hoglund/Governor.zip>. As we did earlier, we have interspersed the code with commentary to make it easier to understand.

```
// The Governor
// Oct 16, 2005 - Greg Hoglund
// www.rootkit.com

#include "stdafx.h"
#include "GovernorDLL.h"
#include <windows.h>
#include <stdio.h>
#include <stdarg.h>
#include <process.h>

HANDLE g_hPipe = 0;
CRITICAL_SECTION g_pipe_protector;

void PatchFunctions();
```

The code here is used in a DLL—a type of code object that can be
loaded directly into a program. In this case, the WoW program is *forced* to
load this DLL via a process known in software security parlance as *DLL
injection.* The injected DLL is actually just a normal DLL, but it is forced to
load after the WoW game client has already started and logged into the
WoW server.

```
BOOL APIENTRY DllMain( HANDLE hModule,
                       DWORD  ul_reason_for_call,
                       LPVOID lpReserved )
{
        switch (ul_reason_for_call)
        {
        case DLL_PROCESS_ATTACH:
                InitializeCriticalSection(&g_pipe_protector);
                g_hPipe = StartPipe("\\\\.\\pipe\\wow_hooker");
                SendText(g_hPipe, "GovernorDLL Loaded.");
                PatchFunctions();
                break;
        case DLL_THREAD_ATTACH:
                break;
        case DLL_THREAD_DETACH:
                break;
        case DLL_PROCESS_DETACH:
                SendText(g_hPipe, "GovernorDLL Unloaded.");
                ShutdownPipe(g_hPipe);
                break;
        }
        return TRUE;
}
```

The DLL opens a named pipe—a form of communication port—when it
is loaded. Later, the named pipe will be used to report on the Warden's
activity.

```
//
// Send text down the pipe
//
void
SendText (HANDLE hPipe, char *szText)
{
        if(!hPipe) return;
```

```
char *c;
DWORD dwWritten;
DWORD len = strlen(szText);
DWORD lenh = 4;

EnterCriticalSection(&g_pipe_protector);

// send length first
c = (char *)&len;
while(lenh)
{
      //char _g[255];
      //_snprintf(_g, 252, "sending header %d", lenh);
      //OutputDebugString(_g);

      if (!WriteFile (hPipe, c, lenh, &dwWritten, NULL))
      {
            LeaveCriticalSection(&g_pipe_protector);
            ShutdownPipe(hPipe);
            return;
      }
      lenh -= dwWritten;
      c += dwWritten;
}

// then string
c = szText;
while(len)
{
      //char _g[255];
      //_snprintf(_g, 252, "sending string %d", len);
      //OutputDebugString(_g);

      if (!WriteFile (hPipe, c, len, &dwWritten, NULL))
      {
            LeaveCriticalSection(&g_pipe_protector);
            ShutdownPipe(hPipe);
            return;
      }
      len -= dwWritten;
      c += dwWritten;
}
```

```
                LeaveCriticalSection(&g_pipe_protector);
}

HANDLE StartPipe(char *szPipeName)
{
        HANDLE hPipe;
        TCHAR szBuffer[300];

        //
        // Open the output pipe
        //
        hPipe = CreateFile (szPipeName, GENERIC_WRITE, 0, NULL,
                        OPEN_EXISTING, FILE_FLAG_WRITE_THROUGH,
                        NULL);
        if (hPipe == INVALID_HANDLE_VALUE)
        {
                _snprintf (szBuffer, sizeof (szBuffer),
                    "Failed to open output pipe(%s): %d\n",
                    szPipeName, GetLastError ());
                    OutputDebugString(szBuffer);
                return NULL;
        }

        return hPipe;
}

void ShutdownPipe(HANDLE hPipe)
{
        //cleanup
        if (hPipe)
        {
                FlushFileBuffers (hPipe);
                CloseHandle (hPipe);
        }
        // make sure it stops being used
        g_hPipe = 0;
}
```

Some of the Warden hooking files are displayed below in order to enhance
your understanding of what's going on. Remember, we're only showing you
the essential parts of the Governor system here.

```
// The Governor
// Oct 16, 2005 - Greg Hoglund
// www.rootkit.com

#include "stdafx.h"
#include <windows.h>
#include <stdio.h>
#include <string.h>
#include <winsock2.h>
#include "GovernorDLL.h"
#include "detours.h"
#include <psapi.h>

///////////////////////////////////////////////////////////////////
// These are functions used by the Warden to spy on other processes
///////////////////////////////////////////////////////////////////
```

The functions below are all used by the WoW Warden. Here, we use the public Microsoft *Detours* library to intercept calls made to these functions.[20] This move allows us to report on any program that attempts to use these calls, including the Warden, through our named pipe.

```
DETOUR_TRAMPOLINE(BOOL __stdcall Real_GetWindowTextA( HWND hWnd,
LPSTR lpString, int nMaxCount), GetWindowTextA);
BOOL __stdcall Mine_GetWindowTextA( HWND hWnd, LPSTR lpString, int
nMaxCount)
{
        int len = Real_GetWindowTextA( hWnd, lpString, nMaxCount);
        if( len != 0)
        {
                // WoW found some window text, let's report it
                char _t[255];
                _snprintf(_t, 252, "GetWindowTextA called from WoW,
returned %d bytes, %s ", len, lpString);
                SendText(g_hPipe, _t);
        }

        return len;
}
```

---

20. You can find out more about the Microsoft Detours library and download the code from <http://research.microsoft.com/sn/detours>.

```
DETOUR_TRAMPOLINE(BOOL __stdcall Real_GetWindowTextW( HWND hWnd,
LPWSTR lpString, int nMaxCount), GetWindowTextW);
BOOL __stdcall Mine_GetWindowTextW( HWND hWnd, LPWSTR lpString,
int nMaxCount)
{
        int len = Real_GetWindowTextW( hWnd, lpString, nMaxCount);
        if( len != 0)
        {
                // WoW found some window text, let's report it

                char _t[255];
                _snprintf(_t, 252, "GetWindowTextW called from WoW,
returned %d bytes", len);
                SendText(g_hPipe, _t);
        }

        return len;
}
```

Now we can identify when the Warden is opening windows on the computer, even windows that belong to other programs (e.g., your instant
messaging program). The Governor reports not only which window the
Warden opened but also what text it read. This technique has been used to
watch the Warden program read sensitive and presumably private information, including the e-mail addresses of the contacts in your instant messen-
ger program.

```
DETOUR_TRAMPOLINE(int __stdcall Real_WSARecv(
   SOCKET s,
   LPWSABUF lpBuffers,
   DWORD dwBufferCount,
   LPDWORD lpNumberOfBytesRecvd,
   LPDWORD lpFlags,
   LPWSAOVERLAPPED lpOverlapped,
   LPWSAOVERLAPPED_COMPLETION_ROUTINE lpCompletionRoutine),
WSARecv);

int __stdcall Mine_WSARecv(
   SOCKET s,
   LPWSABUF lpBuffers,
   DWORD dwBufferCount,
```

```
    LPDWORD lpNumberOfBytesRecvd,
    LPDWORD lpFlags,
    LPWSAOVERLAPPED lpOverlapped,
    LPWSAOVERLAPPED_COMPLETION_ROUTINE lpCompletionRoutine)
{
        int res = Real_WSARecv(s, lpBuffers, dwBufferCount,
                               lpNumberOfBytesRecvd,lpFlags,
                               lpOverlapped,lpCompletionRoutine );
        char _t[255];
        _snprintf(_t, 252, "WSARecv returned %d, %d bytes
received", res, *lpNumberOfBytesRecvd);
        SendText(g_hPipe, _t);

        return res;
}

DETOUR_TRAMPOLINE(DWORD __stdcall Real_CharUpperBuffA( LPTSTR
lpString, DWORD cchLength), CharUpperBuffA);
DWORD __stdcall Mine_CharUpperBuffA( LPTSTR lpString, DWORD
cchLength)
{
        DWORD len = Real_CharUpperBuffA( lpString, cchLength );
        if( len != 0)
        {
                // WoW is processing some text, let's report it

                char _t[255];
                _snprintf(_t, 252, "CharUpperBuffA called from WoW,
string %s", lpString);
                SendText(g_hPipe, _t);
        }

        return len;
}

DETOUR_TRAMPOLINE(HANDLE __stdcall Real_OpenProcess( DWORD
dwDesiredAccess, BOOL bInheritHandle, DWORD dwProcessId ),
OpenProcess);
HANDLE __stdcall Mine_OpenProcess( DWORD dwDesiredAccess, BOOL
bInheritHandle, DWORD dwProcessId )
{
        HANDLE h = Real_OpenProcess( dwDesiredAccess,
bInheritHandle, dwProcessId );
```

```
            if( h != 0)
            {
                    // WoW is opening a process, let's report it

                    char _t[255];
                    _snprintf(_t, 252, "OpenProcess called from WoW, pid
%d, returned handle 0x%08X", dwProcessId, (DWORD)h);
                    SendText(g_hPipe, _t);
            }

            return h;
}

DETOUR_TRAMPOLINE(BOOL __stdcall Real_ReadProcessMemory(
                            HANDLE hProcess,
                            LPCVOID lpBaseAddress,
                            LPVOID lpBuffer,
                            SIZE_T nSize,
                            SIZE_T* lpNumberOfBytesRead ),
ReadProcessMemory );

BOOL __stdcall Mine_ReadProcessMemory( HANDLE hProcess, LPCVOID
lpBaseAddress, LPVOID lpBuffer, SIZE_T nSize, SIZE_T
*lpNumberOfBytesRead )
{
        BOOL ret = Real_ReadProcessMemory( hProcess,
lpBaseAddress, lpBuffer, nSize, lpNumberOfBytesRead );
        if( ret && ((DWORD)hProcess != -1) )
        {
                // WoW is reading a process, let's report it
                char szProcessName[MAX_PATH] = "unknown";


                GetProcessImageFileName(hProcess, szProcessName,
MAX_PATH);


                char _t[255];
                _snprintf(_t, 252, "ReadProcessMemory called from
WoW, handle 0x%08X, process %s, read from address 0x%08X,
%d bytes",
                        hProcess,
                        szProcessName,
                        lpBaseAddress,
                        nSize);
```

```
            SendText(g_hPipe, _t);
    }

    return ret;
}
```

The last two functions above leave no guesswork as to Warden activity. They clearly report whenever the Warden opens another process and it reads the memory of that process. Our spy versus spy system is complete.

```
void PatchFunctions()
{
        DetourFunctionWithTrampoline( (PBYTE)Real_GetWindowTextA,
(PBYTE)Mine_GetWindowTextA);
        DetourFunctionWithTrampoline( (PBYTE)Real_GetWindowTextW,
(PBYTE)Mine_GetWindowTextW);
        DetourFunctionWithTrampoline( (PBYTE)Real_CharUpperBuffA,
(PBYTE)Mine_CharUpperBuffA);
        DetourFunctionWithTrampoline( (PBYTE)Real_OpenProcess,
(PBYTE)Mine_OpenProcess);
        DetourFunctionWithTrampoline( (PBYTE)Real_ReadProcessMemory,
(PBYTE)Mine_ReadProcessMemory);

        //DetourFunctionWithTrampoline( (PBYTE)Real_WSARecv,
(PBYTE)Mine_WSARecv);
}
```

This last part of the code actually installs the "detours" we defined against the selected functions. You can easily modify the source code to monitor additional calls, and you can apply this code against any program you want, including other games. We encourage you to experiment with this functionality. Perhaps you will discover other games and applications that are spying on users.

Where Do You Stand?

Online MMORPG forums and Web sites have been abuzz with the spyware controversy ever since Hoglund described the Warden. Some people believe that complaining about such spyware is silly and that if someone is so worried about it, he or she can just choose not to play. We disagree. We've also heard the opinion that maybe the blame belongs to Microsoft since its operating system allows arbitrary programs to collect the kind of information the Warden collects. What we worry about is the intention here. Regardless of whether you *can* invade privacy, should you?

What Blizzard is doing in the name of security is unacceptable, and it needs to stop. The tradeoff between personal liberty and security is an essential tradeoff that must be carefully negotiated. Citizens in a free society must guard their freedoms vigilantly or risk tyranny in the name of security. Historically, monitoring activities lead very quickly to abuse and present an unacceptably slippery slope. Blizzard does not need to read our e-mail, surf our URLs, or look into our non-Blizzard processes. Allowing the company to do so gives up too much ground for not enough return. Once everyone is doing this, there will be no more privacy on a "personal" computer.

Hoglund says it best in an open message to Blizzard posted at <http://www.rootkit.com/newsread.php?newsid=371>:

> Blizzard, it is within your right to attempt to make your computer game the way you wish it to be, and to attempt to catch cheaters. But, reading the memory of other processes and windows that are not part of the World of Warcraft game client is a violation of privacy. Making a violation of privacy legal in your EULA and TOS does not make it also moral. It remains a violation of privacy. Please refactor your policy in regards to scanning memory, and limit the warden to integrity checking of the game client's memory space, and please stop opening other processes and reading windows that do not belong to you.

If we stand by and let a game company poke around on our PCs in the name of security, what do you suppose they will do next?

Cheating

As we have shown in this chapter, there are many widespread ways to cheat in online games. Some of the techniques we describe are several years old. As more and more money is at stake, more gamers are likely to be tempted to cheat. Cheating is bad. Cheating technology is improving.

Big questions remain regarding anticheating technology, though. Are back door programs, rootkits, and invasive scanners really necessary for piracy detection? When does such a countermeasure cross the line between legitimate copy protection and invasion of privacy? What rights to your computer must you give up in order to play an online game?

Consider, for example, that Blizzard's Warden scanning program isn't really used to detect pirates—it's really used to detect cheaters. Blizzard, of course, gets to define precisely what it means by cheating—it is their game, after all. Among other things, cheating in this case means any use of software automation tools like the WoW_Agro macro we showed in this chapter to play the game.

It seems that the war on cheating has led to collateral damage in the form of privacy. Yet we have only begun to describe what's happening in the gaming world.

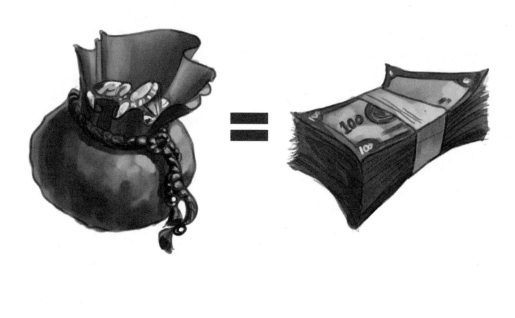

## 3

Money

Millions of people play games online, and most of them pay money to do so. In fact, so much money is involved that online game economies have emerged that academics say rival the size of some small countries.

Spending a few cycles thinking about money in online games can give us a better understanding of why some people cheat and what kinds of resources are likely to be brought to bear to stop them as game companies defend their business. When there's money to be made—and there's certainly money to be made playing online games—cheaters come out of the woodwork. When there's money to be lost due to rampant cheating or gamers becoming annoyed with the game—and the dollars in question are significant—game companies will go to great lengths to protect their territory.

How Game Companies Make Money

MMORPG game companies make money in two ways. The first is by selling copies of their games directly to gamers. The second way is to charge online players a subscription fee (usually on a monthly basis).

Let's think about these two revenue streams in terms of WoW for a minute. With more than 8 million players, if on average the WoW client software costs $20 retail, that's $160 million. This is how much money could have been lost every year in the old days when game software was completely compromised (or cracked) and distributed for free. Problems with the "game on a disk" model provided one technical reason that the client-server model caught on. Recall from Chapter 2 that by storing a majority of state on the server, the modern client-server model puts a serious crimp in the idea of cracking games directly.

So far, we've come up with $160 million or so. But it gets much more interesting once we factor in the subscription model revenue stream. In the case of WoW, that stream is $14 per month per player, which sums to $112 million per month. Multiply this princely sum by 12, and we have a whopping $1.344 billion per year! Much more serious money, and this estimate considers only one MMORPG![1]

Microsoft estimates that the total value of the gaming market on the company's platforms was approximately $6 billion worldwide in 2005, evenly split between retail sales and online game subscriptions. The analyst firm DFC reports that by 2010, the wider gaming market will double to $12 billion (a 14% compound annual growth rate).

The game companies are raking it in. Clearly, they want to protect this source of income. Not only that, but they also want to make sure that a majority of their players remain satisfied with their gaming experience so they will continue to subscribe.

Cheating is a direct threat to this large business. It's no wonder the game companies work hard to thwart it.

Poker

Online poker is similarly huge. Figure 3–1 shows the estimated growth in online poker (both in terms of players and in terms of money) over a multiyear period. Online poker companies have taken advantage of this growth to go public, with staggering results.

One real damper on all of this growth will be the kibosh put on online poker by the U.S. Congress in fall 2006. After 2006, U.S. citizens will by law have a very hard time gambling online with real money. There is the rest of the world, however. You can see the impact of the U.S. law in the stats of Figure 3–1.

For 2005, revenues from online poker were estimated at $200 million per month.[2]

---

1. Recall from Chapter 1 that WoW has just over 50% market share for MMORPGs.
2. For an analysis of poker revenues, see <http://www.digitaljournal.com/news/?articleID=4388>.

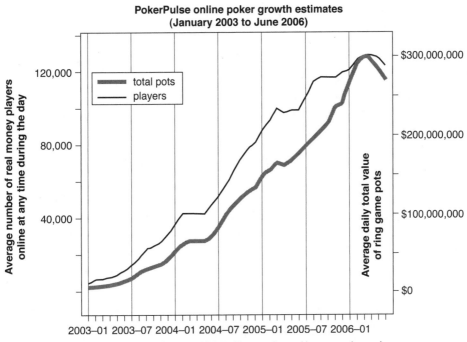

PokerPulse online poker growth estimates (January 2003 to June 2006)

Figure 3–1 Poker stats through June 2006. (From <http://www.pokerpulse.com>; reproduced with permission.)

With this kind of money at stake, it's not surprising that players are looking for any advantage over their adversaries. Because everything is automated with machines, tracking poker play online is easy. Using the handy "hand histories" feature available on most online poker sites, a player can track every action in a game, revealing a wealth of statistical information.

Virtual Worlds: Game Economics and Economies

Academics have studied MMOs for years. Several projects are under way to document and understand MMO player sociology (for two examples, see the PlayOn project at PARC <http://blogs.parc.com/playon/> and the Daedalus Project <http://www.nickyee.com/daedalus/>). Sociology is fine, but in our opinion, the most interesting work involves understanding the economics of MMOs.

In one early study, academic Edward Castranova (now a professor at Indiana University) determined that the gross domestic product of the

MMO EverQuest exceeded that of many real countries.[3] As reported in *The Walrus* magazine:

> The Gross National Product of EverQuest, measured by how much wealth all the players together created in a single year inside the game . . . turned out to be $2,266 U.S. per capita. By World Bank rankings, that made EverQuest richer than India, Bulgaria, or China, and nearly as wealthy as Russia.

It was the seventy-seventh richest country in the world. And it didn't even exist.[4]

Though Castranova's estimation of EverQuest's GDP is probably too high, it is clear that the virtual worlds of online games do, in fact, create wealth out of nothing. Well, not really out of nothing—out of the time that players invest in them.

Professor Steven Levitt of the University of Chicago (and the author of *Freakonomics*) uses online poker to teach economics <http://www .pokernomics.com/>. He is using the reams of data collected by online poker tracking companies (and players who track their own hands) in a large-scale analysis. One of his goals is to understand what kinds of strategies work and what kinds fail. Of course, his work might lead to better ways to play poker . . . and make money.

Connections to the Real Economy

Virtual world economies have not remained walled off from the real economy. Connections exist at many levels. The most obvious connection is the time gamers invest (which has obvious real-world economic value). Following closely on the heels of time is the revenue game companies generate in the real economy. But there's more. Virtual items such as pretend gold pieces or swords made exclusively of bits also have real value.

Most sizeable MMOs have exchange rates between virtual gold and hard currency. The Web site GameUSD.com <http://gameusd.com> tracks exchange rates over time. Figure 3–2 shows exchange rates in the first half of 2005 for WoW gold to U.S. dollars.

---

3. Castranova's popular sociology paper "Virtual Worlds: A First-Hand Account of Market and Society on the Cyberian Frontier" (December 2001) can be found at <http://papers .ssrn.com/sol3/papers.cfm?abstract_id=294828>.

4. See *The Walrus* magazine for a complete article on game economics at <http://www .walrusmagazine.com/article.pl?sid=04/05/06/1929205&mode=nested&tid=1>.

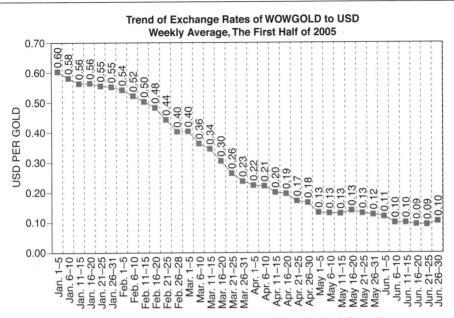

Figure 3–2 Exchange rates between WoW virtual gold and U.S. dollars. (From GameUSD.com <http://www.gameusd.com/>; used with permission.)

Like real economies, MMO economies can suffer from economic instability and other macroeconomic problems. Some game companies even employ economists to help them understand and manage their emergent economies. One of the earliest successful MMOs, Ultima Online, experienced massive inflation that led to a currency crisis in 1997. Interestingly, it turns out that the inflationary pressure came from a software exploit that allowed players to "dupe" gold (i.e., create copies of gold pieces from scratch with no work). Duping is akin to counterfeiting.

In any case, groups of academics are using MMOs for research purposes, focusing on which kind of economic model makes the most sense: centralized economy, free market, welfare state, and more. It turns out that game designers and game minders make critical decisions regarding the economics of their games all the time, much like central bankers do in the real world.

Just as there is crime in real economies, there is crime in virtual economies. Some activities are only marginally criminal (or at least against the rules of the game; see Chapter 4). For example, gamers are often expressly forbidden from selling their characters or other objects that they acquire in the game world, but this hasn't stopped a rich middle market from developing.

Middlemen

Game economies are certainly rich enough that they have spawned an entrepreneurial class of professionals. One early entrepreneur, Robert Kiblinger, was an Ultima Online player who went on to found UO Treasures <http://www.uotreasures.com/>. UO Treasures is a classic middleman, buying virtual characters and items and later reselling them at a profit. This kind of activity is known in the industry as real money trading (RMT).

According to the book *Play Money*, the record sum for a single virtual item in a game was $100,000 paid in October 2005 for an "Asteroid Space Resort" in the Project Entropia game.[5] Julian Dibbell, the gamer author of *Play Money*, estimates that the worldwide annual sales of virtual goods approaches $880 million and continues to grow. However, the popular virtual reality game Second Life may soon change these numbers for all time. Second Life is pushing the limits of virtual economics by explicitly allowing and supporting active trade in virtual items in its world. In fact, unlike most virtual creations in game worlds, Second Life creations belong to the creator instead of to Linden Lab (the game company). This is a novel approach to intellectual property among games. As you might imagine, this has led to some interesting legal situations. Several lawsuits are currently pending over Second Life transactions and the value of virtual property.

The largest RMT middleman outfit is Internet Gaming Entertainment, known to gamers as IGE <http://www.ige.com/>. IGE was founded by child actor Brock Pierce and Alan Debonneville and in August 2005 had about 420 employees. Interestingly, IGE runs its currency trading operations in Hong Kong. IGE claims that, "Some experts believe that the market for virtual assets will overcome the primary market—projected to reach $7 billion by 2009—within the next few years."[6] According to *Wired* magazine, IGE has a stable of more than 100 suppliers, all hard-core players who sell their surplus to IGE.[7]

Like all economies, MMOs harbor a dark side. First, companies like IGE provide easy access to real money for would-be game hackers. The problem is that middleman companies are not often very diligent about the origin of the various game items they trade in. They're just as happy to buy and sell gold that has been created through duping as they are to buy and sell

---

5. *Play Money* by Julian Dibbell (Basic Books, 2006).
6. "Our Business" (see <http://www.ige.com/about>).
7. "When Play Money Becomes Real," by Daniel Terdiman (April 7, 2004; see <http://www.wired.com/news/games/0,2101,62929,00.html>).

legitimate level 60 characters created over months of constant gaming. (Rumor has it that the Star Wars Galaxies hacker we mentioned in Chapter 1 used IGE to launder his duped money.) *Wired* magazine reports that entrepreneurs in Russia pay workers a small base salary ($100 per week) to create in-game money that is then sold to IGE. Very productive workers can make even more real money. The disparity between developing countries' economies and first-world economies is what makes a scheme like this work.[8]

The line between creating virtual money by paying hourly workers versus using automated bots is very thin, but it seems to be important. *Wired* reports:

> Automation . . . is generally considered cheating, and is frowned upon. IGE CEO Brock Pierce said the company cracks down on suppliers whose volumes imply they're using bots. That leaves the other method: cheap labor.

Other gamers are less tolerant of this kind of play, however, and have been known to gang up and kill the hourly farmers.

Less legitimate game services companies come and go with some regularity. Some, like the now defunct BlackSnow Interactive (BSI), open sweatshops where low-wage hourly workers constantly "play" characters in order for them to gain experience and level up. BlackSnow was created to level up Dark Age of Camelot characters. Mythic, the company that created the game, eventually forced them to close down.

In early 2007, eBay announced a ban on trading in online game items. This is very likely to have a huge positive impact on the middleman market. According to news reports, eBay's share of the market was multiple millions. CNET reports, "While there is no universally agreed-upon value for the RMT market, it is assumed to be worth somewhere between $250m and $880m a year."[9]

Playing for Profit

The market for middlemen also includes a mercenary class of people willing to play characters or simply play games for a fee. Conceivably, a wealthy gamer could pay someone to play their character when they're not available to do so. In fact, according to the gaming Web site Gamasutra.com, IGE has

8. "Boring Game? Outsource It," by Laila Weir (August 24, 2004; see <http://www.wired.com/news/digiwood/0,1412,64638,00.html>).
9. "eBay Bans Auctions of Game Goods," by Daniel Terdiman (January 30, 2007; see <http://news.cnet.co.uk/software/0,39029694,49287317,00.htm>).

entered this business as a middleman between gamers who want to level up and those people willing to play someone's character for money.[10]

A number of Web-based games offer cash prizes for playing games (along with virtual versions of simple games like backgammon, chess, or checkers). See <http://www.games4dollars.com/home.php> for one example. Puzzle contests are also popular. Most of these games have very small stakes and use PayPal or other digital cash intermediaries for payment systems. Whether this kind of activity is legal depends on where you live. In the United Kingdom, almost anything goes. In the United States, different states have different rules. Some states outlaw contests or sweepstakes like this, including Arkansas, Arizona, Delaware, Florida, Iowa, Louisiana, Maryland, and Tennessee.[11] And with the U.S. federal government stepping in to regulate online poker, who knows what the future holds.

Thottbot

Thottbot is both an application and a Web site <http://www.thottbot.com/>, now owned, like many other game consolidation Web sites, by IGE. Thottbot amasses and collects vast amounts of information about the WoW world. Gamers install the Thottbot plug-in (called Cosmos), which communicates raw information to the Thottbot application. This information is then organized into an extensive database that players can use to improve their play.

The Thottbot database includes an extensive inventory that itemizes a large percentage of the virtual property that exists in the WoW universe. This database includes information on mobs (i.e., nonplayer characters, monsters, objects that can own or transport merchandise). Thottbot collects information by mining a large number of WoW clients for the data.

The Thottbot application tracks which character or mob has what and makes this information available to players who have installed the helper application on their PCs. The plug-in reads information from the database and displays helpful statistics about what's going on around your character. In some sense, it works like a very well informed assistant. Of course, while it's helping, it's also busy collecting information to send back to the Thottbot server.

---

10. "IGE: Inside the MMO Trading Machine," by Simon Carless (August 25, 2006; see <http://www.gamasutra.com/features/20060825/carless_02.shtml>).
11. "Gaming for Money: Online Games of Skill," by Dave Spohn (see <http://internetgames.about.com/cs/playingformoney/a/playformoney1.htm>).

The Thottbot assistant provides services, such as delivering a map showing players how to get items they may want and marking that map with probability percentages so they can decide their course of action.

This is clearly useful information for a gamer willing to know more about the game than other players not using the service. And it's also useful for sweatshop players, who can make the best use of their labor when directed by a system like Thottbot.

This has led some people to question the links between Thottbot and IGE. We know that IGE owns Thottbot. And we know that Thottbot reads your inventory and other data to know what gamers who use the system have. This information could be used in many ways, from price fixing to arbitrage to market maximization.

IGE also purchased Allalhazam and OGaming, which are similar in nature to Thottbot. This kind of consolidation is met with mixed reviews by hard-core gamers who wonder whether the IGE philosophy will pervade the gaming world (many gamers disagree vehemently with the very idea of selling characters or items).

Criminal Activity

Sweatshops, like the one run by BSI or the IGE subcontractor from Russia, are most common in third-world countries, especially in the Far East. These businesses often run directly counter to the terms of use that players agree to when they license the game (for more on these legal agreements, see Chapter 4). Nevertheless, they persist. Sometimes when they get big enough to make it onto the radar of gaming companies, something gets done about it.

Middleman companies, like IGE, seem much more legitimate and claim to offer services to gamers in an above-board manner. But IGE and other middlemen are obvious targets for laundering money, both virtual and real. Pumping black-market dollars through an online game to "clean" them makes sense given the large sums of money and the millions of transactions involved. Likewise, selling virtual items created through cheating turns the cheating into a black-market business.

For the record, we do not condone cheating in online games or any other criminal activity. However, this phenomenon exists and is fairly widespread. The more online gaming grows, the more deeply entangled with criminal activity it will become. We can combat this activity only by understanding exactly how it occurs.

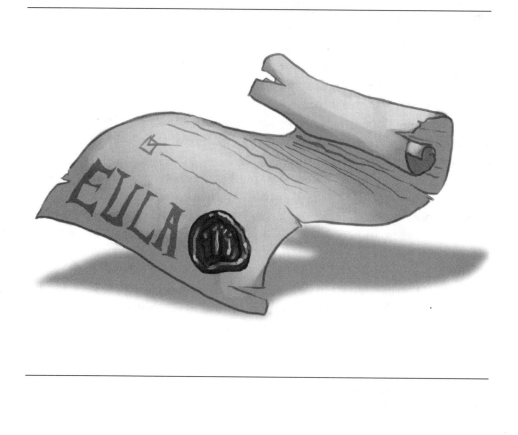

4

Enter the Lawyers

We are not lawyers. Nor do we play lawyers on TV. Sometimes we talk to lawyers when we do expert witness work, but that's only when we're being paid lots of money. Suffice it to say that the opinions in this chapter should not be taken as legal advice of any kind. If you want a legal opinion, don't ask a geek!

Regardless of all that, the world of online games is filled with lawyers these days. That's because MMORPG distributors have two weapons they can use against cheaters: making rules with legal documents and enforcing rules with technology. The first weapon involves lots of lawyers.

Legality

In the old days of computer gaming, a game came on a CD and ran only on your PC. In that case, legal agreements were set up to limit liability for the game maker and prevent piracy on the part of the gamer. The biggest problem in those days was cracking of the content protection mechanisms and the subsequent release of a "free" version of the game.

As we have established, most modern online games use a client-server architecture (see Chapter 1). Originally, the server was meant only to connect players of a mostly client-based game such as a first-person shooter

(FPS) game or maybe as an online license checker. Only recently has a majority of game state and game processing been relegated to the server (as is the case in MMORPG games like WoW).

Players of FPS games have for many years gathered at LAN parties where they would hook up their machines and play against one another. Once FPS manufacturers started protecting their client-side games with server-side technology, hooking the client games together on a LAN became more challenging. To avoid the hassle of server-side license checking, some programmers took it upon themselves to produce workarounds. Eventually, similar workarounds were applied to MMORPGs as well.

When three programmers wrote an open source version of Blizzard Entertainment's server software, Blizzard sued—and won. The suit is summarized on the Electronic Frontier Foundation (EFF) Web site as follows (the EFF defended the developers).

> At issue in this case was whether three software programmers who created the BnetD game server—which interoperates with Blizzard video games online—were in violation of the Digital Millennium Copyright Act (DMCA) and Blizzard Games' end user license agreement (EULA).
>
> BnetD was an open source program that let gamers play popular Blizzard titles like Warcraft with other gamers on servers that don't belong to Blizzard's Battle.net service. Blizzard argued that the programmers who wrote BnetD violated the DMCA's anti-circumvention provisions and that the programmers also violated several parts of Blizzard's EULA, including a section on reverse engineering.[1]

The open source server software BnetD worked fine and was easy to understand. Blizzard's problem was that buyers of the game who didn't want to pay the secondary online subscription fee to connect to commercial servers didn't have to. Blizzard thought that was unfair and a misuse of its intellectual property.

On the other hand, the programmers felt that they wanted to play the game just like they had played similar other games in the past—with their friends at a LAN party—or over the Internet on a shared server. They felt that Blizzard was double-dipping by charging for the game client as if it were a stand-alone game and also requiring online subscription service fees.

---

1. The EFF Web site devoted to this case can be found at <http://www.eff.org/IP/Emulation/Blizzard_v_bnetd/>.

Blizzard didn't see it this way. To Blizzard the open source server opened the door for people to make illegal copies of the game client and play without having a key check or an online account. Blizzard contended, and the court ultimately found that the open source server was created for pirates, not for legitimate players.

So just what do these EULAs and the DMCA say, anyway? With this chapter, we'll begin our foray into the legal jungle with a look at copyright law in the United States.

Fair Use and Copyright Law

The conception of fair use is unique to the United States and is now codified in section 107 of the copyright law.[2] The Copyright Act, title 17 of the U.S. Code, sets forth a number of limitations on the rights of a copyright holder in sections 107 though 118. According to the Copyright Office:

> Section 107 contains a list of the various purposes for which the reproduction of a particular work may be considered "fair," such as criticism, comment, news reporting, teaching, scholarship, and research. Section 107 also sets out four factors to be considered in determining whether or not a particular use is fair:
>
> 1. the purpose and character of the use, including whether such use is of commercial nature or is for nonprofit educational purposes;
> 2. the nature of the copyrighted work;
> 3. amount and substantiality of the portion used in relation to the copyrighted work as a whole; and
> 4. the effect of the use upon the potential market for or value of the copyrighted work.

Of course, the law is always subject to interpretation, and many cases have been argued around the line between fair use and infringement.

A large body of copyright law exists. In fact, the Copyright Office itself says, "The Copyright Office can neither determine if a certain use may be considered 'fair' nor advise on possible copyright violations. If there is any doubt, it is advisable to consult an attorney." That's darn good advice, but what about games?

---

2. The U.S. government Copyright Office has a Web site explaining fair use at <http://www .copyright.gov/fls/fl102.html>.

As far as most nonlawyers are concerned, in the past, if you purchased copyrighted material, you typically had the right of fair use—meaning you could use the copyrighted material pretty much any way you wanted to as long as your uses were personal and you were not reselling or sharing derivative works (or the original content).[3] Naturally, some gamers argue that if they pay for a game, they have the right to play it on their own servers. But times have changed with the introduction of the Digital Millennium Copyright Act.

The Digital Millennium Copyright Act

In late 1998, the U.S. Congress enacted the DMCA. Its purpose is "to amend title 17, United States Code, to implement the World Intellectual Property Organization Copyright Treaty and Performances and Phonograms Treaty, and for other purposes."[4] The law criminalizes both the production and distribution of technology meant to circumvent copyright protection mechanisms. In other words, it restricts certain activities surrounding digital rights management (DRM) and other security technologies that are meant to enforce copyright laws. It also heightens penalties for copyright infringement on the Internet. The European Union has a very similar law in place called the EU Copyright Directive (EUCD).

The DMCA is not without controversy. Many people believe that it goes too far to uphold the rights of copyright holders, even to the point of stifling competition. Ironically, the *raison d'être* for the DMCA (bolstering DRM with the law) may be itself eroding. Princeton Professor Ed Felten argues that "as the inability of DRM technology to stop peer-to-peer infringement becomes increasingly obvious to everybody, the rationale for DRM is shifting" and that eventually debate over DRM will shift away from copyright enforcement.[5]

The DMCA is relevant to our purposes here because together with the EULA, it has been used to restrict certain activities when it comes to online games.

---

3. For a much more in-depth treatment of this issue, see <http://fairuse.stanford.edu/>.
4. A complete copy of the DMCA can be found on several U.S. government Web sites, including on <http://thomas.loc.gov/cgi-bin/query/z?c105:H.R.2281.ENR:>.
5. Professor Felten made this argument at an invited talk at Usenix Security in 2006 and later blogged about the ideas at <http://www.freedom-to-tinker.com/?p=1052>.

The End User License Agreement

The EULA is the kind of license typically used for software. It's really a legal contract between the software producer and the end user, stating how the software will be used. EULAs often place restrictions on use and make disclaimers meant to limit liability.

As you might imagine, there are many different kinds of EULAs. Some require a click to activate (often over the Internet). Some go into force when a CD is taken out of its packaging. Of course, the terms and restrictions in EULAs differ as well.

Both EULAs and the DMCA are directly relevant to online gamers. Today, the DMCA is being used to uphold restrictions on use placed in the EULA and can now include the requirement to pay and play using the vendor's online service.

Before you click Agree on a EULA, you must understand what you are agreeing to. The fine print may surprise you.

A EULA can place all kinds of seemingly strange restrictions on the use of the material being licensed. We'll discuss some of these examples in upcoming subsections.

- A EULA can state where and when you can use the software or that if you install it once, you can never install it again.
- A EULA can also state that the software is allowed to install a rootkit back door on your computer (see Sony's EULA).
- A EULA can grant the online service full access to your memory (see Blizzard's EULA).
- A EULA can grant full access to your hard drive and allow the vendor to download all your files (see Gator's EULA).
- A EULA can even state that, once you have accepted the EULA, you also accept all future unwritten EULAs that the vendor has yet to release (see Apple Computer's EULA).

Open-ended, egregious EULAs abound with language like this—and they are very common.

Some people believe that the idea of EULAs has not been appropriately tested in court and thus the EULAs can't be valid. This is a misunderstanding of contract law. The only way in which EULAs have been challenged successfully in the past has to do with whether the contract terms were objectionable. In some cases, only certain terms are found objectionable. In other cases, they are most certainly not. As a result, EULAs sometimes hold up in court, and other times they don't.

Sony BMG's EULA: Rootkits Galore

Sony got into big trouble for installing rootkits on the machines of unsuspecting CD buyers (see the sidebar Sony Goes to the Dark Side).[6] But the company's EULA clearly stated its intent. That doesn't make what Sony did right, but it does change its legal status.

Here is a piece of the EULA that came with Sony CDs that installed the rootkit.[7]

> As soon as you have agreed to be bound by the terms and conditions of the EULA, this CD will automatically install a small proprietary software program (the "SOFTWARE") onto YOUR COMPUTER. The SOFTWARE is intended to protect the audio files embodied on the CD, and it may also facilitate your use of the DIGITAL CONTENT. Once installed, the SOFTWARE will reside on YOUR COMPUTER until removed or deleted. However, the SOFTWARE will not be used at any time to collect any personal information from you, whether stored on YOUR COMPUTER or otherwise.

Among other things, the EULA continues by describing the software that is installed (the rootkit). The real question is this: How many people read that EULA and completely understood it before pressing Accept and listening to the CDs they had installed in their CD drives? We bet that number is small.

Fortunately, this EULA language didn't stop Sony BMG from being sued in at least 15 class action lawsuits after news of the rootkit hit. The class action suit filed in New York district court was settled shortly after it was filed. In the end, the suits were all consolidated, and Sony BMG compensated the buyers of the infected CDs (giving them MP3 files of the songs in exchange) and created uninstall software for the various rootkits it distributed. The company also agreed to continue to halt the manufacture and distribution of CDs with the two rootkits on them. Hopefully the people at Sony learned their lesson.

One lesson that we can learn is that just because something is in the EULA, that doesn't make it legal. In this case, Sony crossed the line, and the law ended up protecting consumers.

---

6. For more on the Sony rootkit debacle, see Gary McGraw's *IT Architect* article "Is Sony BMG Run by Malicious Hackers?" (January 2006) at <http://www.itarchitect.com/shared/article/showArticle.jhtml?articleId=175001534>.

7. The complete EULA has been preserved for posterity at <http://www.sysinternals.com/blog/sony-eula.htm>.

Sony Goes to the Dark Side*

Sony is really interested in making sure that you don't rip digital copies of its music—so interested that the company will go so far as to root your box to make sure you can't. There are many reasons why this is an awful development. These include the morally questionable use of spyware as a security feature, the fact that malicious hackers can use this spyware to further compromise machines, and the invasion of privacy this poorly conceived security mechanism promulgates. But the worst possible effect of the Sony rootkit spyware may be imposed on your IT staff. Put simply, this mess is going to be hard to clean up.

Mark Russinovich of Sysinternals discovered that XCP2, a CD protection scheme peddled by British-based First4Internet and licensed and used by Sony/BMG, monitors computer use and disallows users from ripping CDs <http://www.sysinternals.com/blog/2005/10/sony-rootkits-and-digital-rights.html>. When an XCP2-protected CD is inserted into a Windows PC, Windows Autorun copies a small piece of software onto the computer. From then on, if the user attempts to rip a protected CD, the software replaces the music with static.

Copy protection software is nothing new, so what makes this a rootkit? The software deliberately cloaks itself from normal diagnostic tools and some security products by hiding certain processes, rewriting the interrupt address table, and interposing on various kernel-level system calls. This makes XCP2 hard to find. It is also very difficult to remove.

Running a large network of PCs has always been difficult, but imagine trying to administer a large network of PCs all of which are running "invisible" rootkits. One of the basic ideas that rootkits employ is stealth. That is, they attempt to hide their very existence from system administrators and others responsible for security. This makes rootkits a very dangerous weapon indeed (rootkits are well deserving of their place at the apex of the attacker's toolkit). When supposedly legitimate processes adopt this bad behavior, they make administering a machine almost impossible! That's because finding processes hidden away like XCP2 is difficult and time consuming. Multiply this by the number of machines in your enterprise and you can begin to appreciate the problem.

But it gets worse. The Sony rootkit technology not only hides the antiripping process, it will hide any specially tagged process just as well. According to Russinovich, XCP2's stealth mechanism will hide any file, directory, Registry key, or process whose name begins with "sys". This means that malicious software can take advantage of the existence of the Sony rootkit to avoid detection. In fact, the first malware attempting to take advantage of the Sony rootkit emerged several days after the story broke. Rumors have also emerged of gamers using the code to hide game hacking programs from the detection system used by the online game World of Warcraft.

In addition, the Web-based uninstaller trumpeted to the press (and made very difficult to find and use by actual owners of Sony CDs) is linked specifically to one and only one machine. That is, it will uninstall only on one infected PC. Corporate IT will not appreciate that at all. Plus, according to Ed Felten <http://www.freedom-to-tinker .com/>, the Web version of the uninstaller opens a serious security hole on any computer that it's run on. Toxic waste, anyone? So corporate IT departments need to first determine whether this invisible software exists on their machines and then safely remove it. Both of these activities are time consuming and may lead to difficulties on some machines.

XCP2 may also affect a PC's normal operations. The program scans all running processes on the system every two seconds, querying basic information about the files and consuming up to 2% of system resources (due to sloppy coding). Users have reported serious impacts on PCs infected with the XCP2 rootkit, most of which impacts were extremely mysterious until Sony was outed and the source of the problems— music CDs—became clear. Some antivirus mechanisms and personal firewalls apparently go berserk when faced with XCP2.

According to the *Washington Post*, "a class-action lawsuit has been filed on behalf of California consumers who may have been harmed by anti-piracy software installed by some Sony music CDs. A second, nationwide class-action lawsuit is expected to be filed against Sony in a New York court." Shame on Sony. Let's hope the right side prevails.

---

*Portions of this sidebar appeared originally in the January 2006 *IT Architect* column, "Is Sony BMG Run by Malicious Hackers?" by Gary McGraw <http://www.itarchitect.com/shared/article/ showArticle.jhtml?articleId=175001534>.

Blizzard's EULA: All Your Memory Are Belong to Us

As we described in Chapter 2, WoW players are subject to monitoring by the Warden program (installed and maintained by Blizzard). This activity is covered directly in Blizzard's EULA. In particular, Blizzard's EULA grants Blizzard permission to trawl around in your PC's memory. Here is an interesting snippet from that EULA.[8]

---

8. A complete copy of the Blizzard EULA can be found at <http://www.worldofwarcraft .com/legal/eula.html>.

5. Consent to Monitor. WHEN RUNNING, THE GAME MAY MONITOR YOUR COMPUTER'S RANDOM ACCESS MEMORY (RAM) FOR UNAUTHO-RIZED THIRD PARTY PROGRAMS RUNNING CONCURRENTLY WITH THE GAME. AN "UNAUTHORIZED THIRD PARTY PROGRAM" AS USED HEREIN SHALL BE DEFINED AS ANY THIRD PARTY SOFTWARE, INCLUDING WITHOUT LIMITATION ANY "ADDON," "MOD," "HACK," "TRAINER," OR "CHEAT," THAT IN BLIZZARD'S SOLE DETERMINATION: (i) ENABLES OR FACILITATES CHEATING OF ANY TYPE; (ii) ALLOWS USERS TO MODIFY OR HACK THE GAME INTERFACE, ENVIRONMENT, AND/OR EXPERIENCE IN ANY WAY NOT EXPRESSLY AUTHORIZED BY BLIZZARD; OR (iii) INTERCEPTS, "MINES," OR OTHERWISE COLLECTS INFORMA-TION FROM OR THROUGH THE GAME. IN THE EVENT THAT THE GAME DETECTS AN UNAUTHORIZED THIRD PARTY PROGRAM, THE GAME MAY (a) COMMUNICATE INFORMATION BACK TO BLIZZARD, INCLUDING WITHOUT LIMITATION YOUR ACCOUNT NAME, DETAILS ABOUT THE UNAUTHORIZED THIRD PARTY PROGRAM DETECTED, AND THE TIME AND DATE THE UNAUTHORIZED THIRD PARTY PROGRAM WAS DETECTED; AND/OR (b) EXERCISE ANY OR ALL OF ITS RIGHTS UNDER THIS AGREEMENT, WITH OR WITHOUT PRIOR NOTICE TO THE USER.

Remember, just because the EULA names an activity and you (uninten-tionally) agree to it, that does not make the activity legal. Some EULA clauses have been known to fall in court.

While we're on the subject, it is also worth noting that the Blizzard EULA has a clause that forbids online sale of items accumulated in the game:

3. Ownership
a. All title, ownership rights and intellectual property rights in and to the Game and all copies thereof (including, but not limited to, any titles, computer code, themes, objects, characters, character names, stories, dialog, catch phrases, locations, concepts, artwork, character inventories, structural or landscape designs, animations, sounds, musical composi-tions, audio-visual effects, storylines, character likenesses, methods of operation, moral rights, any related documentation, and "applets" incorporated into the Game) are owned or expressly licensed by Licensor. The Game is protected by the copyright laws of the United States, international copyright treaties and conventions, and other laws.

Looks like that plan for getting rich by building and selling WoW characters may not work. Alas.

When the Blizzard EULA is violated (and the Warden is often the program that notices this), Blizzard usually cancels your game account. Be forewarned.

Gator's EULA: A Permanent Unwelcome Visitor

The Gator Corporation was once an adware company. The company sold an online wallet and form filling program that also tracked Web surfing behavior and displayed pop-up ads. The underlying program used what Gator called GAIN technology to track user behavior. That is, Gator used spyware. Gator has now become Claria, and the company no longer supports Gator.

The Gator spyware came with a EULA that ran for a reported 63 pages.[9] Buried deep in the EULA was this humdinger:

> You agree that you will not use, or encourage others to use, any unauthorized means for the removal of the GAIN AdServer, or any GAIN-Supported Software from a computer.

Gotta love that. You weren't allowed to remove it. Nice. Even spyware removal programs were not authorized to remove the Gator AdServer.

Gator also prohibited the use of packet sniffers to determine exactly what it was doing when it phoned home with your personal surfing data:

> Any use of a packet sniffer or other device to intercept or access communications between GP and the GAIN AdServer is strictly prohibited.

All your data are belong to Gator. It's nice to see some ideas go away.

Microsoft FrontPage 2002's EULA: Be Nice, Because You Have To

At one time, Microsoft apparently tried to use its EULA for FrontPage (a Web site development tool) to control bad press it was getting. The EULA that came in the box reportedly said:

> You may not use the Software in connection with any site that disparages Microsoft, MSN, MSNBC, Expedia, or their products or services, infringe any intellectual property or other rights of these parties, violate any state, federal or international law, or promote racism, hatred or pornography.

---

9. For more on Gator's EULA, see <http://www.benedelman.org/news/112904-1.html>.

The thought police want to know what you're doing with that magic marker they gave you.[10]

A Virus with a EULA: Malware Gets Legal

In 2002, a piece of malware called the FriendGreetings electronic greeting card was released that spread in a virus-like fashion, mailing copies of itself to everyone in a victim's Outlook contacts file. But the virus writer was apparently protected from prosecution by including a EULA that specifically allowed the virus-like behavior to take place. If the user clicked Agree, the virus did its dirty work and the writer was off the hook.[11]

This is truly a story of a EULA gone bad!

Apple Computer's EULA: To Infinity and Beyond

Reportedly, Apple Computer's EULA is an evolving document. By agreeing to the EULA, you agree to any future additions or changes to the EULA. Sounds a bit open-ended to us! Here's what the EULA says:[12]

> Apple reserves the right, at any time and from time to time, to update, revise, supplement, and otherwise modify this Agreement and to impose new or additional rules, policies, terms, or conditions on your use of the Service. Such updates, revisions, supplements, modifications, and additional rules, policies, terms, and conditions (collectively referred to in this Agreement as "Additional Terms") will be effective immediately and incorporated into this Agreement. Your continued use of the iTunes Music Store following will be deemed to constitute your acceptance of any and all such Additional Terms. All Additional Terms are hereby incorporated into this Agreement by this reference.

The EULA Parade

One thing is clear—when you agree to a EULA, you are contractually obligated to limit your use of the licensed software as stated. It pays to know what you're agreeing to before you agree to it! Read those EULAs

---

10. The "Stop Before You Click" Web site at <http://seeri.etsu.edu/affect.htm> includes a number of pointers.

11. "Greeting Card Virus Licensed to Spread," by Robert Lemos (November 13, 2002; see <http://news.com.com/2100-1001-965570.html>).

12. See section 20 at <http://www.apple.com/support/itunes/legal/terms.html>.

The EFF on Bad EULA Clauses

In the online article "Dangerous Terms: A User's Guide to EULAs," Annalee Newitz discusses a handful of the "countless terms written into EULAs that could potentially harm consumers." We reproduce her list here (with permission from the Electronic Frontier Foundation) without the relevant commentary. See the original article at <http://www.eff.org/wp/eula.php>.

Common EULA terms that harm consumers:

1. "Do not criticize this product publicly."
2. "Using this product means you will be monitored."
3. "Do not reverse-engineer this product."
4. "Do not use this product with other vendor's products."
5. "By signing this contract, you also agree to every change in future versions of it. Oh yes, and EULAs are subject to change without notice."
6. "We are not responsible if this product messes up your computer."

from now on. If you're particularly worried about a EULA you appear to be bound by, you might read the EFF article "Dangerous Terms: A User's Guide to EULAs" (see the sidebar The EFF on Bad EULA Clauses).

But the real question is whether EULA allowances like the ones we described are really required to stop software pirates. Are they, or is there more here than meets the eye? You have to admit that the requirement to play online using a given server is a most excellent tactic for curbing piracy. But how do you feel about game companies sifting through personal information on your PC? What do you think about companies mining data on your computer? How do you feel about a video game that installs a rootkit? When is the DMCA and its accompanying sidekick EULA not about copyright protection anymore? These are the sorts of legal questions facing online gamers today.

Forbidding Reverse Engineering

The DMCA expressly forbids reverse engineering for the purposes of defeating copy protection mechanisms. The purpose as stated in the law is to enforce copyright law. The question is whether or not it is legal to reverse engineer software such as a game client. Is copyright being violated if a hidden API is exposed? What about faulty security design?

Note that the DMCA includes exceptions for computer security research in order to protect researchers and academics. Nonetheless, this is a very murky area of law.

Forbidding Game Hacking

No one has yet established a legal definition for game hacking. Nevertheless, hack, cheats, mods, and sometimes even network sniffing are often called out in a EULA or in the terms of use (as we explain soon).

Property Rights

Property rights are another aspect of online gaming in which the law is not yet clear. Though Blizzard tries hard to make things clear through its public posturing, there really is no clear precedent for dealing with virtual property. Blizzard says things like, "The World of Warcraft Terms of Use clearly states that all of the content in World of Warcraft is the property of Blizzard, and Blizzard does not allow 'in game' items to be sold for real money. Accordingly, Blizzard Entertainment will take any and all actions necessary to stop this behavior. Not only do we believe that it is illegal, but it also has the potential to damage the game economy and overall experience for the many thousands of others who play World of Warcraft for fun."[13]

But a recent lawsuit filed against Linden Lab the purveyors of Second Life, may change all that. Marc Bragg, a lawyer from Pennsylvania, became upset after a virtual land deal went bad and Linden Lab confiscated his virtual property. Of note is the fact that Second Life explicitly allows members to legally own the content they create. This has led to a large online economy with active trading in real estate, clothes, cars, and other pretend stuff.

Of note in the Second Life case is the technique that Bragg used to accumulate some of his property. He noticed that the Second Life online auction system was using tags in a URL to track which piece of property was being auctioned. By changing the tag (a classic attack described in our

---

13. "IGE: Inside the MMO Trading Machine," by Simon Carless (August 25, 2006; see <http://www.gamasutra.com/features/20060825/carless_03.shtml>).

book *Exploiting Software*), Bragg effectively bid on land not yet up for sale publicly. This should be an interesting case to watch.

In any case, all of the time and effort you invest in an online game may disappear in a puff of logic if you fall afoul of the game maker.

The Terms of Use

Another legal tool at the disposal of game companies is the terms of use agreement. These TOU documents (sometimes called terms of service [TOS] agreements) often accompany a EULA for any client-server game and restrict the uses of the game on the server side. The EFF says, "Many terms are shared between EULAs and TOS agreements. But typical TOS agreements also include terms that forbid vaguely defined forms of behavior and communication."[14]

TOU documents are also filled with interesting language, just as EULAs are. The Battle.net TOU document from Blizzard, for example, states the following:[15]

> A. You are entitled to use Battle.net for your own personal use, but you shall not be entitled to. . . .
>
> (ii) copy, photocopy, reproduce, translate, reverse engineer, modify, disassemble, or de-compile in whole or in part any Battle.net software; . . .
>
> (iv) host or provide matchmaking services for any Blizzard software programs or emulate or redirect the communication protocols used by Blizzard as part of Battle.net, through protocol emulation, tunneling, modifying or adding components to the Program, use of a utility program, or any other technique now known or hereafter developed, for any purpose, including, but not limited to, network play over the Internet, network play utilizing commercial or non-commercial gaming networks, or as part of content aggregation networks without the prior written consent of Blizzard or exploit Battle.net or any of its parts for any commercial purpose, including, but not limited to, use at a location such

---

14. See the EFF document "Dangerous Terms: A User's Guide to EULAs" at
<http://www.eff.org/wp/eula.php>.
15. See the Blizzard TOU document at <http://www.battle.net/tou.shtml>.

as a cyber cafe, arcade, or other location where users are charged a fee, whether hourly or otherwise, to use Battle.net;

    (v) use any third-party software to modify Battle.net to change game play, including, but not limited to cheats and/or hacks;

Note that TOU agreements can be just as open-ended as EULAs are. Here is an example claim from a Microsoft TOU:[16]

12. USE TERMS. Microsoft reserves the right to change the terms under which SUPPORT and Remote Access and the SOFTWARE are provided. Your continued use of SUPPORT or this website will be deemed to be your acceptance of any changes to the terms.

The Ban

TOU documents often call out the right of the game licensee to terminate the license at any time. Here is a passage from the Blizzard TOU:

B. In the event that you violate any of the foregoing provisions, Blizzard may at its option and without notice to you
(i) temporarily suspended your access to Battle.net; or
(ii) immediately terminate your access to Battle.net;

Banning is the most common action game companies take when they suspect cheating.

WowMapView Goes Down

On January 10, 2006, Jack Snyder (an "Anti-Piracy Investigator") from the Entertainment Software Association (ESA) sent a cease and desist letter regarding the open source WowMapView project to both Szego Zoltan, the leader of the project, and to SourceForge (a popular location where open source projects are posted). Though it is not clear that the project was doing anything illegal, this letter was enough to cause the project to be abandoned and to cause SourceForge to take it down. This is a common result.

    Strong-arm tactics and threats have clearly worked for game manufacturers in the past, so it should not come as a surprise if tactics like this are used again.

    A snippet from the e-mail runs as follows.

---

16. See the Microsoft TOU document at <http://support.microsoft.com/tou/>.

ESA is providing this letter of notification pursuant to the Digital Millennium Copyright Act and 17 USC § 512 (c) to make Sourceforge.net aware of material on its network or system that infringes the exclusive copyright rights of one or more ESA members. This notice is addressed to you as the agent designated by Sourceforge.net to receive notifications of claimed infringement, as so reflected in the current records of the U.S. Copyright Office. Under penalty of perjury, we hereby affirm that the ESA is authorized to act on behalf of the ESA members whose exclusive copyright rights we believe to be infringed as described herein.

ESA has a good faith belief that the Internet site found at http://wowmapview.sourceforge.net and http://wowmapview.sourceforge.net/wowmodelview/ continues to infringe the rights of one or more ESA members by offering for download one or more unauthorized access programs of one or more game products protected by copyright, including, but not limited to: World of Warcraft

The unauthorized access programs of such game product[s] appearing on, or made available through, such site are listed and/or identified thereon by their titles, variations thereof, or depictions of associated artwork (any such game titles, copies, listings and/or other depictions of, or references to, any contents of such game product, are hereinafter referred to as "Infringing Material"). Based on the information at its disposal on January 10, 2006, ESA believes that the statements in this Notice are accurate and correctly describe the infringing nature and status of the Infringing Material. [emphasis theirs]

According to our sources, Blizzard has never taken any of these cases to court, with the exception of the BnetD case that we described earlier in this chapter. In that case, the claim was very narrow and involved only the online license checking apparatus. In all other cases, the use of an infringement notice has always been enough to cause game enthusiasts to shut down all operations and abandon software projects.

Being Sued != Breaking the Law

Game companies have also been known to file lawsuits to thwart game hacking. It is important to understand that being sued is not the equivalent of breaking the law. You can be sued even if you break no law at all. That's what makes our litigious society great!

In the sidebar WowMapView Goes Down, we briefly discuss what commonly happens when a lawsuit is threatened.

Stealing Software versus Game Hacking

Many of the laws involved with online gaming were originally intended to help control piracy (i.e., direct copying and distribution of software programs belonging to someone else). The situation with more complex online games that use a client-server model is much more complicated.

Online game hacking is not really very much like software cracking of old. Yet legal precedents are all set to deal with software cracking and piracy. What will happen when the courts begin to realize this is anyone's guess.

5 Infested with Bugs

Bugs and flaws in software account for a majority of computer security risks.[1] This is true for banking applications, and this is also true for online games. So many security-related bugs exist in software, and they're so pervasive, that software tool vendors like Fortify Software <http://www.fortify.com> have created special tools just to look for them. Not only that, but scientists have published reams of papers on taxonomies for bugs, all of which disagree with each other.

One popular taxonomy is the "seven pernicious kingdoms" described in McGraw's book *Software Security: Building Security In.*[2] Briefly, here are the seven kingdoms:

1. Input validation and representation
2. API abuse
3. Security features
4. Time and state
5. Error handling
6. Code quality

---

1. For a discussion about the difference between bugs (found at the implementation level in software) and flaws (found at the architectural level), see *Software Security: Building Security In*, by Gary McGraw (Addison-Wesley, 2006).
2. Also see <http://vulncat.fortifysoftware.com>, where a number of examples are posted.

7. Encapsulation

*. Environment[3]

Note that these kingdoms (analogous to kingdoms in biology tax-onomies) are listed in order of pervasiveness in the world. That is, input validation and representation problems such as buffer overflow, SQL injection, and cross-site scripting are the most common kinds of bugs, followed by misuse of APIs in languages and libraries, followed by mistakes in security features, and so on.

Probably the most interesting bugs fall into the time and state kingdom, clocking in at number four. This category of bugs is interesting mostly because it is also a harbinger of what to expect in the future. Timing and synchronization problems are already a major issue. But as distributed

---

Pernicious Kingdom Four: Time and State

Distributed computation is about time and state. That is, in order for more than one component to communicate, state must be shared (somehow), and all that takes time. Playing with time and state is the biggest untapped natural attack resource on the planet right now.

Most programmers anthropomorphize (or, more accurately, only solipsistically ponder) their work. They think about themselves—the single omniscient thread of control manually plodding along, carrying out the entire program in the same way that they themselves would do it if forced to do the job manually. That's really quaint. Modern computers switch between tasks very quickly, and in multi-core, multi-CPU, or distributed systems, two events may take place at *exactly the same time*. Defects rush to fill the gap between the programmer's model of how a program executes and what happens in reality. These defects are related to unexpected interactions between threads, processes, time, and information. These interactions happen through shared state: semaphores, variables, the filesystem, the universe, and, basically, anything that can store information.

One day soon, this kingdom will be number one.

Reprinted by permission from *Software Security: Building Security In*, by Gary McGraw (Addison-Wesley, 2006).

---

3. Careful readers will notice that there are really eight pernicious kingdoms. We like to say there are seven plus or minus one.

systems and multithreaded languages become more common, problems with synchronizing and tracking state will become only more common. (See the snippet from *Software Security* in the sidebar Pernicious Kingdom Four: Time and State.) Because of the way online games are designed, they are rife with time and state problems.

Time and State Bugs in Games

As we describe in Chapter 1, online games are a prime example of massively distributed programs. The big problem of moving state around when thousands of client processes are interweaving on a common server, over the network, in real time, leads precisely to the number one software security risk for online games—the race condition.

Race conditions and other problems with state are the primary source of bugs in online games. They are exacerbated by laggy network connections (which tend to warp time in interesting ways—sort of like black holes). By their very design, large online games require vast amounts of data storage distributed over many servers. Some servers may store accounting information for billing, while others store player statistics and inventory, and yet others store the current state of an online world.

Technically, the truth of the matter is that most MMOs don't really involve a single monolithic online world, but rather have many duplicate shards of what only seems to be a world. Copies of the online world WoW uses, for example, tend to limit the number of users to 50,000 players per server. EVE Online is a single online world, but that virtual world is distributed across such a large universe (think solar systems) that no one server ever gets overloaded.

The problem with multiple world shards is boundaries. Race conditions are found on the borders between software states—such as the state of being logged in and the state of being logged out. If everything happens atomically, that is, you go from being logged in to being logged out in one fell swoop without gazillions of steps, things can go alright. But if multiple steps are involved, and they are not protected by semaphores in what computer scientists call critical sections, trouble can crop up.

To make this clear, consider Figure 5–1. In this simple illustration, what should be an atomic process is divided into three steps. In a race condition attack, an attacker interleaves state-changing actions between the three parts in order to screw around with the state of the world. You can protect

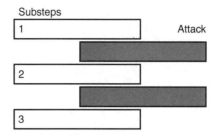

Figure 5–1 A simple race condition illustrated. The white rectangles represent three substeps of a process that should be atomic. Because they are not protected in a critical section, an attacker can interleave an attack by messing around with state between substeps (as represented by the gray rectangles).

against this by marking all three steps as a critical section and only performing them all at once without allowing interleaving. Of course, holding everything up while a critical section runs can become a serious bottleneck, so sometimes developers cut corners.

The sidebar Race Conditions 101 gives a simple example of a race condition that can happen in the real world. Who knows, maybe this has even happened to you? You see, these kinds of errors are all about time.

Race Conditions 101

What is a race condition?

Let's say that Alice and Bob work at the same company. Through email, they decide to meet for lunch, agreeing to meet in the lobby at noon. However, they do not agree on whether they meant the lobby for their office, or the building lobby several floors below. At 12:15, Alice is standing in the company lobby by the elevators, waiting for Bob. Then it occurs to her that Bob might be waiting for her in the building lobby, on the first floor. Her strategy for finding Bob is to take the elevators down to the first floor, and check to see if Bob is there.

If Bob is there, all is well. If he isn't, can Alice conclude that Bob is either late or has stood her up? No. Bob could have been sitting in the lobby, waiting for Alice. At some point, it could have occurred to him that Alice might be waiting upstairs, at which point he took an elevator up to check. If Alice and Bob were both on an elevator at the same time, unless it is the same elevator, they will pass each other during their ride.

When Bob and Alice each assume that the other one is in the other place and is staying put and both take the elevator, they have been bitten by a race condition. A race condition occurs when an assumption needs to hold true for a period of time, but actually might not; whether it does or doesn't is a matter of exact timing. In every race condition, there is a window of vulnerability. That is, there is a period of time where violating the assumption will lead to incorrect behavior. In the case of Alice and Bob, the window of vulnerability is approximately twice the length of an elevator ride. Alice can step on the elevator up until the point where Bob's elevator is about to arrive and still miss him. Bob can step on to the elevator up until the point that Alice's elevator is about to arrive. We could imagine the door to Alice's elevator opening just as Bob's door shuts. When the assumption is broken, leading to unexpected behavior, then the race condition has been exploited.

Reprinted by permission from *Building Secure Software*, by John Viega and Gary McGraw (Addison-Wesley, 2001).

In this chapter, we describe some testing scenarios and templates that you can use to find and exploit timing-related bugs in online games. To show you that this is real, we highlight some of the very real bugs found and exploited in WoW.

How to Game for Free

One good way to illustrate events that unfold over time is to use a sequence chart. Figure 5–2 shows a sequence chart for a simple state problem involving canceling your subscription.

Once you activate your account, several things happen. First, your accounting information is updated (you now owe the game company money). Second, your player account is added to a number of game databases. However, these events may not take the same amount of time. In fact, there is a window of vulnerability that opens between when your billing request arrives on the accounting server and when you are actually billed. This lag time is sometimes as long as three days. However, activation of your character is much shorter, often on the order of a few minutes. If you put on your black hat for a moment, you discover that you are in some sense "playing for free" during the window of vulnerability. You can log in and play now, and you won't be billed for three days! But wait, there's more. . . .

Let's say you get done playing at the end of the day (or more realistically, when the sun comes up and the room begins to brighten). Now, with your black hat still on your head, you log back into your online account

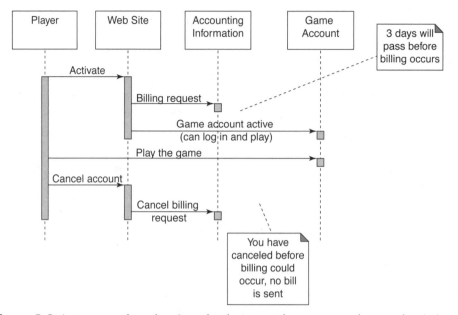

Figure 5–2 A sequence chart showing what happens when you cancel your subscription. Do you see the potential for a race condition in this sequence chart?

management system and cancel your subscription. What happens at this point is rather interesting. Your player account is not deleted as you might think. Instead it is put immediately into a suspended state. At the same time, the accounting server gets a message to mark your account as nonbillable. Since all of this happens inside the three-day window of vulnerability, you never get a bill.

After a long day's rest working at the 7-Eleven counter, you come back home and get ready for another exciting night of gaming. You reactivate your account, and the three-day time gets reset to zero and starts ticking (again). You get to play all night (again), and when the sun comes up (again), you dutifully cancel your subscription.

You can continue playing the game for free in this fashion for years and never once get billed. Of course, the pattern of behavior in your account probably sticks out like a sore thumb. "Hey, wait, this guy cancels his account ten times a month, what's going on?" But rumor has it that this "play for free" attack works on WoW, or at least it did at one time. Just for the record, we have never tested this, as we firmly believe that people should pay the subscription fee if they intend to play a game.

Using Bugs to Confuse State Boundaries

The state boundary we were gaming in the cancel/suspend example is a large one, but it is more closely related to business processes than it is to software. The good news is that there are plenty of software-related state boundaries rife with timing problems as well.

One of the most obvious software-related boundaries involves databases. Transactions that involve multiple databases are often susceptible to race conditions. Because virtual worlds are distributed across many servers, doing things like switching from one dungeon to another or flying from one continent to another often causes a player to be handed off from one server to another.

This kind of switch is a normal event in a game, and it has certainly been tested with some defined test plan by the game company's quality assurance (QA) department (not to mention plenty of players who have actually done the switch many times). But here is what happens in many QA shops. The test plan says something like "Inventory is supposed to remain constant when a player does activity47 at portal68." Then a tester logs in, goes to portal68, performs activity47, and checks to see if everything (such as, say, player inventory) is fine. This is what is known to software testers as a functional test. The problem is, this test is both boring and conventional!

You see, attackers don't often do what you're supposed to do. Instead, attackers focus on trying to do things that were never anticipated by the programmers. They do the unexpected, sometimes with insane results.

Here's an idea. Instead of gracefully walking through portal68, make sure you log out of the game while you're doing it. Pull the Ethernet cord out of the wall. Kill the game client with the task manager. When you're done, log back in and find out if anything juicy happened. Did you make it to the new continent or are you on the original side of portal68? What is the state of your character?

Let's step through some possibilities, again thinking with our black hat on. Let's say you end up on the original side of the portal. What will happen if you give some money to a player friend of yours just seconds before you kill the process, and that friend continues through the portal like normal? When you log back in this time, back on the original side of portal68, check your wallet. Was the money taken from your wallet, or did it reset itself along with your location? If it did reset (back to the original pre-give-some-away amount), does your friend have some money too on his side of the portal? If your money has doubled, you've found a duping bug—one of the most coveted bugs of all time in online gaming. Nothing like Xeroxing inventory for free!

In WoW, a number of bugs like this are known to exist around entrances to instance dungeons. That's because instances are just like continents or any other location in WoW—they are handled on specific servers, and as players join an instance they are in reality a glob of data being transferred from one back-office server to another.

In general, a single instance server is responsible for serving all particular instances of a given dungeon. For example, all deadmines instances run on the same deadmines server. However, since this is a very popular quest in the game, the server tends to become overloaded, and it gets laggy. Laggy servers are ideal for trying to crowbar a race condition out of a game.

Figure 5–3 shows a duping trick as sold (for actual money) by a company selling WoW hacks and exploits. This is a prime example of a race condition packaged as an exploit program by the vendor <http://www .wow-dupe.com>. We purchased a copy to see if it would work.

We were duped, or maybe doped, out of our $19.95 because the duping exploit didn't work when we tried it. However, the exploit as it is described sounds legit to us, and it makes a prime example of how these race conditions can be exploited.

Notice that in the screenshot shown in Figure 5–3, there is a specific description of what the user should do to cause bandwidth to be consumed

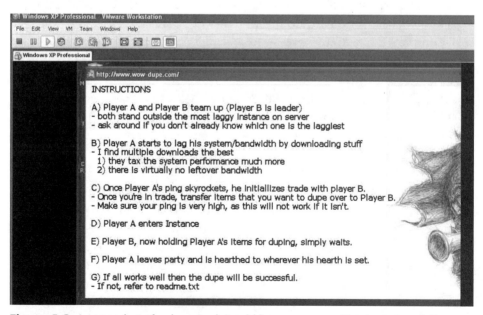

Figure 5–3 A screenshot of a dupe exploit sold by a purveyor of hacks and exploits online.

on the local Internet connection. There is a ping value meter you can use in WoW to determine how much your client program is lagging. However, if you are really interested in exploring race conditions, server lag is much more important than your local network connectivity or client lag. And server lag is not something you can control. You might simulate server lag on your client machine to see what happens by using a proxy server to delay TCP packets as they come and go. The proxy server connects to the game server and allows you to tune the delay as necessary. This gives you much better control over client lag than "downloading stuff."

Using Botnets to Lag a Game Server

As it turns out, botnets are very effective ways to induce lag on the net (see the Black Hat Corner on botnets for the basics). Thus botnets pose a very serious security risk for online games. By using a botnet to cause a given game server to lag, an attacker can set things up for a more efficient race condition exploit.

Finding the IP number of the game server is very easy. Given an IP number, a botnet controller could be contracted to carry out various activities to lag the game server; the online game thief could then carry out a race condition attack with much better success. Lag multipliers might include tricks such as logging into the server multiple times with the same account—multiple logins would be denied, it stands to reason, but processing the multiple logins certainly causes some computational delay. Countless similar lag multipliers exist. Once the server becomes lagged, race conditions are exacerbated; the exploiter can then begin duplicating items or gold, or taking advantage of whatever the exploit is, resulting in a better bottom line.

Using Bugs to Change Character States

Many activities in online games cause changes in character state. One prime contributor in WoW involves spells. An interesting technique is to cast a spell on yourself before attempting some other action. For example, you might try casting a spell on yourself that changes the way you travel and then request a flight path or travel a different way. Many ideas in this section involve doing something that "nobody would ever do," which is a classic attacker riff.

There are similar "two at once" strategies that occasionally cause interesting results. Spell interactions in WoW can be surprising, for example. Here's one. Cast the spell called Aspect of the Cheetah on your pet, then

Black Hat Corner: Botnets

Malicious hackers have been taking control of Internetworked computers for decades. Exploiting a machine involves finding a remote security vulnerability (usually in the software installed on a target machine) and exploiting that vulnerability. Early attacks based on exploiting a particular software bug called the buffer overflow would result in the creation of an interactive shell for the attacker. The payload code used during one of these attacks became known as shell code. *The Shellcoder's Handbook* by Jack Koziol et al. (Wiley, 2004) is an excellent reference explaining how such attack code works, as is our book *Exploiting Software* (Addison-Wesley, 2004).

More modern attacks install an interactive back door such as a stealthy, undetectable rootkit on the victim's machine. The book *Rootkits* by Greg Hoglund and James Butler (Addison-Wesley, 2005) explains in great detail how this technology works. One of the main purposes of installing a rootkit is to ensure that it is trivially easy to connect to and control a machine that is "0wn3d" in the future. This cuts down on the expense of rerooting a machine every time you need it to do something for you.

Entire collections of machines that are thusly rooted can be controlled by one attacker remotely. In this approach, each rooted machine is known as a *bot*, and the resulting collection of machines is a *botnet*. Once formed, a botnet can leverage the entire combined distributed computing power of thousands of machines to do the bidding of the attacker (known in hacker jargon as a *bot herder*). Botnets have been used in distributed denial-of-service attacks, massive scanning attacks, spamming, credential farming, and other attacks requiring huge computational resources.

Modern attack tools that build botnets are designed to propagate automatically, using 0day exploits to build huge networks of compromised machines.

Botnets have their uses in exploiting online games. One obvious use is to lag a server so that time-and-state–related bugs are easier to exploit.

send it far away to attack a mob, then request a flight. All of these activities are standard WoW activities, but combined in this way, interesting state interactions occur. In this particular case, instead of automatically flying, you end up gaining control of the mount and can steer it yourself. Figure 5–4 shows a frame from a YouTube video demonstrating the combination. Note that these kinds of state interactions are not limited to WoW; state combination attacks work as well against most MMORPGs.

Sometimes mutually exclusive spells or abilities cause interesting state changes. As an example, enable Aspect of the Cheetah before joining the battleground, then after joining the battleground, enable Aspect of the Hawk—you may end up with both aspects at once.[4] This is a state-tracking problem with interesting side effects. The base issue is that the game, WoW in this case, has so many interacting states that unanticipated combinations lead to interesting behavior.

Though WoW designers certainly put plenty of thought into various spell interactions, they seem to have limited their thinking to single characters. When multiple characters of different classes get involved in jointly casting spells, the combinatorial aspects get interesting and can involve surprising results that are beneficial to gamers. The combinatronics are the trick.

Some aspects of WoW allow other people to control your character. Things like mind control and transference involve having data copied into

Figure 5–4 In this picture, the player is controlling the flying creature and steering it along the ground, something that is not supposed to be possible. See the video at <http://youtube.com/watch?v=FbEOZnUF66o>.

_____

4. We found this trick at <http://www.edgeofnowhere.cc/viewtopic.php?t=328898> (posted by Snarg).

your state. Interesting tricks in this situation include things like going through different portals or having the "controller" log out. Just try things that "nobody would ever do" when you're in the special situation. For example, a spell known as Presence of Mind can be made permanent on a character by having someone mind control the character shortly after casting this spell and subsequently exiting a battleground.[5]

Sometimes games use buffers to hold various pieces of state. If these buffers don't get properly cleared, or if they don't time out, interesting things can happen. Remember, when there is lag, anything can happen.

Sometimes doing lots of things to change state quickly can be used to confuse the game and thwart the rules. One WoW trick involves using spells to change states very rapidly. For example, use Bloodrage to remove a warrior from attack mode, followed immediately by Charge (which is allowed only while not in combat). If you do this rapidly enough, you can effectively use Charge almost continuously during interplayer fighting.[6] Remember, our examples come from WoW, but the phenomenon exists in all complex games. Also note that these specific cheats will most likely be patched by the time you read this. Our point is not to discuss a specific cheat but rather to give you examples of the general problem so that you understand what cheats are like.

Pathing Bugs in Games

Time-related bugs such as the race conditions and nutty state interactions that we describe earlier are not the only kinds of bugs in online games. Other categories of problems exist, too. One category—pathing bugs—is related to space in the virtual world.

Paths are the routes that monsters (mobs) take in the game. The game often pits your character against these monsters. Many of the monsters encountered in WoW can't do any damage to you unless they are standing right next to your character in virtual 3D space. Monsters that are handicapped in this way make easy prey for pathing exploits.

Here's how pathing exploits work. The gist of the tactic is to stand in a place where the monster can't get to, but at the same time close enough to

---

5. For more, see <http://www.edgeofnowhere.cc/viewtopic.php?t=327477> (posted by Snarg).

6. Once again, see <http://www.edgeofnowhere.cc/viewtopic.php?t=324303> (posted by Snarg).

the monster that you can use a long-range attack of some kind to attack it. Given the right placement, you can eventually overcome the monster while remaining basically invulnerable the entire time. That's because the monster gets "stuck" as it tries getting to you. (Some of you may recall similar problems in the 2D world of Donkey Kong in the eighties.)

These kinds of pathing bugs are very exciting to exploit because you have to get to the location where the pathing bug exists, and this involves going either very near or maybe even through a dangerous region full of enemy monsters. Pathing bugs can also be subtle, and they are often very sensitive to your own movements as well as your position, so if you mess up and don't do things exactly right, the mob can break loose and clobber you. In these cases even cheaters feel some of the real excitement of the game.

Almost all 3D games have pathing bugs where monsters will appear to get stuck. That's because it is very difficult and tedious to design landscapes with no sticky spots where pathing bugs crop up. Nonetheless, pathing bugs are really useful only when they are combined with a macro of some kind that kills the monster automatically (say, over and over again all night). Once you get a pathing bug down, exploiting it gets boring pretty quickly. Figure 5–5 shows an example of a pathing bug found in WoW.[7]

Using Bugs to Travel in Interesting Ways

Virtual worlds in online games only seem real. In fact, they are only as solid as the models they are built on.

There are many different ways to travel in a game. Maybe you can fly. Swimming is usually possible. Perhaps you can teleport. Running and walking are usually options. And there are spells to enhance all of your travel needs. The state machine that manages travel is usually held in the client software, and at the very least, almost all of the 3D object interaction is. It should be apparent that by altering the client, you can alter how you travel. For this reason, many common exploits modify the way the client program handles travel.

By overwriting a single byte in the client code of WoW, a character can be enabled to climb mountains or even straight up walls (as we describe in Chapter 7). Gamers use this hack to get into places they are not supposed to get to in the virtual world. Using a bug like this, cheaters can stand on the Gates of Ironforge or climb up into the mountains in search of remote lakes

---

7. For more on this pathing bug, see <http://www.edgeofnowhere.cc/viewtopic.php?t=323124> (posted by Snarg).

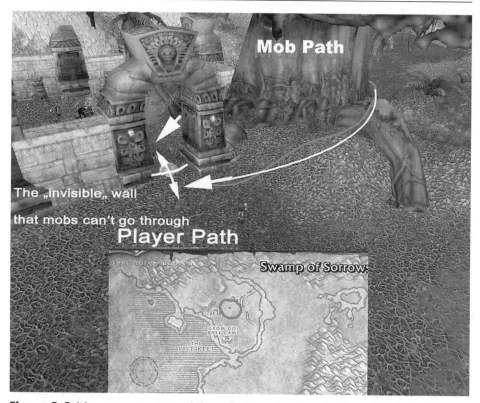

Figure 5–5 Monsters cannot travel through the archway, yet a player can, so a player can keep stepping through the portal to avoid being damaged by the monster. The monster then switches directions and tries to come around the other side, and the process repeats. (From <http://www.edgeofnowhere.cc/viewtopic.php?t=323124>.)

for fishing. More practical applications of the exploit involve taking shortcuts between two locations by going straight through hills.

Even without altering the code of the game client itself, it is possible to confuse the client about travel by invoking lots of travel-related factors at once. If your character is the victim of a fear spell, for example, the character begins running like crazy away from the spell caster. That means the client software obviously handles this travel state—and depending on where you were standing when you were "feared," you might run through walls or launch off of the end of a wall and end up falling into astral space (the area directly beneath the ground that you're not supposed to be able to get to).

All of this fear-related travel brings up another state—that of falling. Falling is also handled by the client. In fact, there is a gravity constant used for things like falling. If you fall a certain distance and hit a solid object, you die. But, in WoW at least, there is a spell that enables you to sustain no fall

Figure 5–6 The fear spell causes travel state change, through a wall, and into astral space underneath the world. In the screenshot, you can see the character is under the world in open space, and below the plane where trees are placed. To exist here may require additional modifiers such as a slow fall spell. (From "Booty Bay Cove Exploit." See the video at <http://video.google.com/videoplay?docid=-8320552955949215666>.)

damage. While under the influence of that spell, if you get a friend to "fear" you through a wall and you fall into astral space, you may well land somewhere interesting, hopefully without damage. Try falling into water as well. See Figure 5–6 for an example.

In general, all of this fancy travel work is academic considering that you can just teleport around using modifications to the x-, y-, and z-coordinates of your character (see Chapter 6).

Altering the User Interface

The user interface to most online games involves menus, colors, list boxes, enumerated values, scripts, icons, graphics, animations, and so on—all of which respond to commands that you can give directly through the GUI or maybe through scripting or specially crafted network packets. For example, chat messages are directly displayed in the user interface in WoW. But chat messages can also be sent using a crafted network packet or script macro.

Imagine that the chat window shows server messages in red and player messages in white. You, as a normal user, can't change the color of any of your chat messages. That is, they always show up in white. However, if you were to put a sniffer on the network and analyze the chat messages the server sends, you may notice escape codes that change the font color to red. You can't insert these escape codes using the in-game chat interface, but if you craft your own packets, you can insert the escape codes in question yourself.

This technique allows you to send a chat message to someone and have it appear to be a server message. Social engineering, anyone? This is just one example of how restrictions arbitrarily enforced by the client can result in possibly false expectations and perceptions on the part of unknowing users.

In WoW, for example, index numbers are used for various looting rules, which can be set by a party leader. You can't specify an out-of-range looting rule with the user interface, but you can if you use a script like this:

```
/script SetLootMethod("Master","YourCharacterNameHere","7");
```

Invoking this technique has interesting side effects. When other players attempt to leave the party, doing so initiates a user interface event for a value that is out of range. In the GUI, the illegal parameter "7" is related to color values, with the particular color value "7" being out of range. This causes an error, and the user interface will therefore not let the player leave the party—the character is trapped, so to speak. Of course, this is only a problem with the user interface. Only a player who doesn't know about this problem would be trapped for long. A more savvy trapped player (say, one who has read this book) could use a little script to get out of the trap:

```
/script LeaveParty( );
```

This technique and others like it underscore the kinds of opportunities afforded by the multiple ways to do one thing in online game GUIs. Your mileage may vary.

Modifying Client-Side Game Data

Data in the client are also at risk and subject to modification. Instance portals can be moved around, and databases associated with instance portals can be altered. We talk about this kind of attack in upcoming chapters.

Among the critical parameters the client software controls are the x-, y- and z-coordinates of many objects. Models control client-side behavior and game physics. By messing with the models, you can change things like requirements for getting into instances. You can also do things like remove doors that might otherwise block your entrance to a location.

Monitoring Drops and Respawns

Monsters in WoW and other online MMORPGs often drop interesting items when they are killed, and players are free to pick up these items. This is one way that game minders distribute things to the masses. The term *drop* can refer to anything that a monster carries, but it is usually reserved for items that have value. Monsters drop low-value items consistently and with high probability. And, as you might imagine, they drop special items of high value with much lower probability.

This behavior makes drop rates for various monsters a metric of interest. Several Web sites are devoted to tracking drop rates for all known items and monsters (see <http://www.thottbot.com> for one example). Figure 5–7 shows a screenshot of various drop rates for WoW monsters. These same sites also track locations where monsters appear in the game (Figure 5–8).

Special drops are of particular interest to gamers. They include such items as excellent weaponry or armor, special recipes, or ingredients for a magic recipe. Certain ingredients for a recipe might be hard to find in the game and thus very expensive at the market. Farming rare items can make your character a great deal of money in the game.

The problem with drops is that you never know for sure if a creature will drop something. Fortunately, in some online games, the client program may already know what a given monster might drop (and might even perform the calculation itself to determine whether the drop occurs). If this is the case, a cheater has a distinct advantage in the game because the cheater can pick and choose targets knowing in advance that a monster will drop something of value.

In WoW, things work a bit differently—only after a kill will the database be queried and a drop be calculated. However, the game client software may have access to this information ahead of time since the monster will have a copy of the special item, say, a weapon, in its inventory. In this case, the prior knowledge that the monster carries the weapon is sent to the client program. Sometimes, the weapon in question might even be visibly carried by the monster, tipping you off that it will drop.

Items dropped by Crimson Guardsman:

Name	Drops / Kills	Drop %
Lightforge Belt Lvl 53, 341 AC, +10 Str, +9 Sta, +15 Int, +6 Spi, +40 AP	6 / 240	2.50%
Pristine Black Diamond	1 / 240	0.42%
Six of Portals Use: Combine the Ace through Eight of Portals to complete the set.	1 / 240	0.42%
Stonegrip Gauntlets Lvl 55, 392 AC, +9 Str, +14 Sta, +10 def, Equip: Increased Defense +10.	0 / 240	0.00%
Aquamarine	1 / 240	0.42%
Arcane Gloves Lvl 52, 46 AC, +13 Sta, +12 Int	2 / 240	0.83%
Backbreaker Lvl 51, 43.4 DPS	1 / 240	0.42%
Burnside Rifle Lvl 51, 26 DPS	1 / 240	0.42%
Commander's Vambraces Lvl 54, 245 AC	1 / 240	0.42%
Councillor's Pants of the Owl Lvl 53, 66 AC, +17 Int, +17 Spi	0 / 240	0.00%
Crystal Sword of Stamina Lvl 52, 33.9 DPS	0 / 240	0.00%

Figure 5–7 Drop rates for a certain monster in WoW. (From <http://www.goblinworkshop.com/creatures/crimson-guardsman.html>.)

Knowledge of this sort is power.

Once a resource is taken or a monster is killed, the game server will usually mark the time that the resource was removed. Then it will periodically cycle through the world looking for respawns. This is akin to running a tasking loop on the server that looks something like this:

```
While(running)
{
        TASK t = GetTaskFromQueue( );
        t.Run( );
        Sleep(1);
}
```

The task in question can be any work the server needs to perform. One such task might be to scan for respawns. Eventually, the task runs, performing a database query such as this:

```
"SELECT * FROM mob_instances WHERE alive=0
AND killtime > (NOW - respawn_rate)"
```

Thus, a series of database rows are obtained, and the task can go about respawning all of the instances.

Figure 5–8 Locations associated with monsters with given drop rates. (From <http://www .goblinworkshop.com/creatures/ arei.html>.)

The respawn rate for some mobs may in some cases be set very low. If such a mob is selected, the resulting respawn points are high (see the query if this seems confusing). High-speed respawn points can be used in conjunction with a macro for fast experience point gathering or other kinds of drop farming.

Just Show Up

One surefire way to gain extra experience points in WoW is to auto-join any party groups that happen to be detected. In this way, you can get points without really participating. This sort of activity is usually driven by clicking on the user interface (but we know by now about automating that!).

And in Conclusion

In this chapter, we've talked about game weaknesses in both implementation and design. These bugs and flaws are very useful for exploiting online games. Some of the defects we discuss are side effects of massively distributed processing, while others are related to user interface issues and trust models. Still others involve explicitly doing what you're not supposed to do.

Throughout the remainder of the book, we'll show you how to exploit these sorts of problems by specifically perturbing the game client, its state, and its communication with the server.

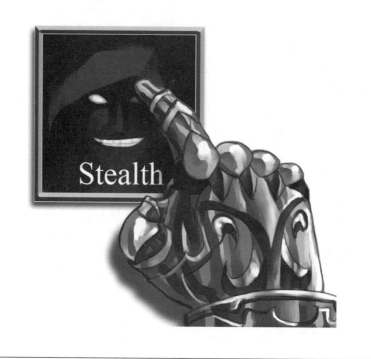

Hacking Game Clients

This chapter is about breaking software—specifically client software found in online games. The methods used to probe, understand, and ultimately control such software are borrowed directly from software testing and assurance. For more on the basics of software exploits, you might want to pick up our book *Exploiting Software* (Addison-Wesley, 2004) as well as David Litchfield's excellent book *The Shellcoder's Handbook* by Jack Koziol et al. (Wiley, 2004).

Malicious Software Testing (Enter the Attacker)

Is software testing malicious? Not always. But often the best testers push the limits of the software they are testing, trying out corner cases and edge conditions. Many times, the best tester in a QA group is not the most well-liked individual among the developers (and sometimes even among management). This is the tester who always finds horrible bugs (leading to headaches for developers); the tester who tells other people that they have made mistakes and has demonstrations to prove it; the tester who naturally thinks about software failure.

The interesting thing is that those software testers who try the hardest to break the code come the closest to probing the edges of security risk. The kind of risk-driven, attack scenario testing described in Chapter 7 of McGraw's *Software Security* (Addison-Wesley, 2006) is driven by the very idea of ferreting out security problems using classic testing techniques.

Though many software developers do not typically think of software QA as a malicious activity, it can be. On one hand, functional testing is designed to make sure that software is reliable and engenders an excellent user experience. But security testing is not just about testing security functionality by asking whether the crypto works. Security testing must probe software like a bad guy, black hat firmly in place. Risk-based security testing, powered by architectural risk analysis and attack patterns, is meant to be malicious. As it turns out, many software bugs bring with them huge amounts of security risk. In this sense, software testing can indeed be malicious.

And it gets worse. Bugs found by the bad guys are only rarely reported to the good guys. That means that testers turned bad are in the game to discover—and then exploit—software problems.

QA Tools and Techniques

Software testers have an impressive arsenal of tools they have developed over the years to help understand and correct software. These include debuggers, coverage tools, fault injection engines, virtual machine simulators, decompilers, and disassemblers—an impressive list. Fledgling bad guys don't need to look far to find effective hacking tools. It turns out that game hackers can use the same kinds of off-the-shelf software testing tools as everyone else. These tools (both open source and commercial) are in common use in QA departments worldwide to find bugs . . . every day.

Software attackers bent on finding and exploiting bugs in online game software make great use of these workaday testing tools. We provide only a basic introduction to the attacker's toolkit in this section. For more, see our previous book *Exploiting Software*.

Decompilers

A decompiler does exactly what a compiler does, only in reverse. The idea with a compiler is to start with source code in a language like C++ and compile it into native executable code for a target platform like Win32. The idea with a decompiler is to start with binary code from some platform and decompile it back into human-readable source code.

The problem with this idea is that it's easier said than done. That is, often it's easier to start with source and render binary than to go back to source from binary. There are many reasons for this that have to do with the arcane inner workings of compilers. As a result, decompilers tend to "shoot from the hip" and don't often yield exact source code. A decompiler is almost guaranteed to mangle comments, variable names, and sometimes even control flow constructs. In the end, decompilers yield an approximate value of what the source code might have looked like.

Decompilers are useful because it is much easier to read and understand source code than it is to read and understand binary code. Some people can read binary directly, but they're in a distinct minority. If you're trying to understand how a piece of code works, it's often easier to do this with source code around.

Game hackers can use a decompiler to help understand what the binary code that makes up a game client is actually doing. Figure 6–1 shows an open source decompiler called Boomerang <http://sourceforge.net/projects/boomerang/>.

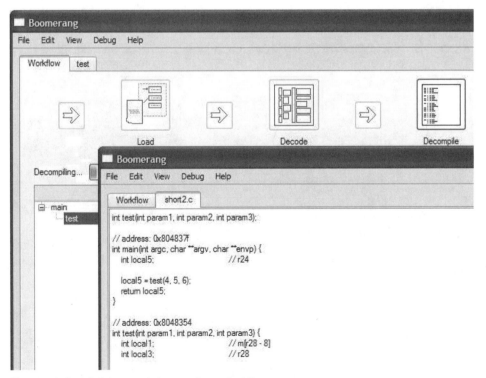

Figure 6–1 A full-featured decompiler called Boomerang.

Disassemblers

Disassemblers are very similar to decompilers. In this case, instead of transforming binary code into source, they tackle the much easier task of converting binary into assembly language (a very low level language, but certainly not as low as a bunch of 1s and 0s). This is a straightforward process as long as you can determine the difference between code and data. Remember, what we're talking about here is a huge set of binary digits. Figuring out whether a given pile of binary is code or not is sometimes a challenge.

Modern disassemblers do a decent job of rendering assembly code. Code analysts interested in figuring out what a piece of executable binary does may start with a decompiler, and if that doesn't work, move on to using a disassembler.

Figure 6–2 illustrates a standard commercial disassembler typically used for reverse engineering. The program is called Inspector by HBGary <http://www.hbgary.com>. Though Inspector has many advanced features, it is in many cases too costly for game hackers. Free disassemblers with

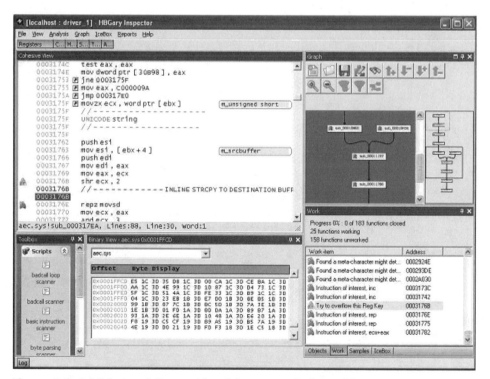

Figure 6–2 A full-featured disassembler of the type typically used for reverse engineering.

fewer features are available for many platforms and can be easily found by searching the Net.

Debuggers

Debuggers are multipurpose tools that allow direct interaction with a program as it runs. Debuggers are considered very low-level tools. They allow a tester to single-step through program instructions, determine program and variable state, insert breakpoints—in general watching very carefully what happens as a program runs.

Debuggers are an essential part of building software. Many debuggers are sophisticated tools—preserving state, displaying stack frames, showing variable bindings, and for the most part allowing huge insight into the code under analysis. A good debugger is thus an essential tool in finding and analyzing bugs in software.

Under the hood, software is a highly choreographed, complex dance of threads, stacks, registers, and memory locations. All of this complexity evolves from the interplay of two things—the program code and the machine it runs on. The machine was designed and manufactured by a hardware designer (think Intel), and the code/program that runs on the machine was created by a compiler (think gcc). To be sure, many rules and regulations are set forth by the operating system (think Microsoft Windows), but overall, software boils down at its core into interactions between specific commands for a given machine and stored data.

A decent debugger allows a person to interact with all of these complex data. Properly driven, a debugger can force a program to do almost anything it is inherently capable of doing, even if the activity was not an *intended* part of the design. This means that although debuggers were originally created to find bugs, people interested in exploiting games can use a debugger as the core component of a bot. In fact, we show you how to write your own basic debugger later for just these reasons.

Figure 6–3 illustrates the very popular (and free) debugger known as OllyDbg <http://www.ollydbg.de/>. This tool is commonly used for reverse engineering and hacking games designed for the Microsoft Windows platform.

Coverage Tools

Coverage tools were created to help testers determine a rough measure of test completeness. Coverage tools do this by keeping close track of which possible paths through a program execute as a program runs. This allows testers to

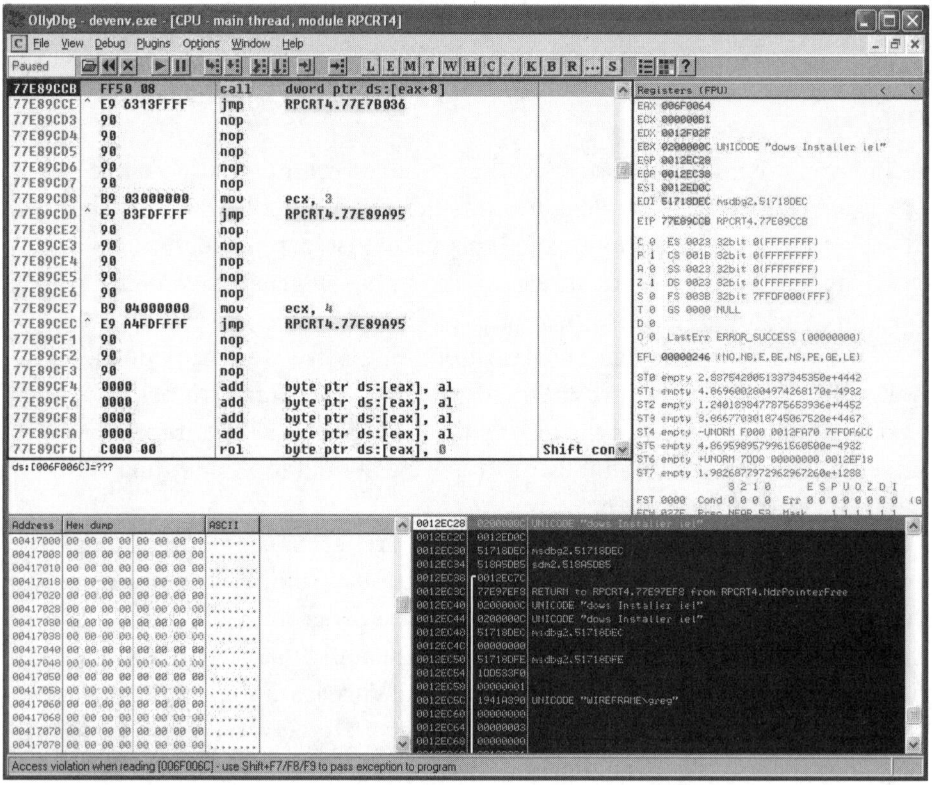

Figure 6–3 OllyDbg is a very popular and free debugger for Microsoft Windows programs (including games, of course).

estimate test effectiveness by determining precisely which parts of a program a test is testing (and which parts it is not). A given test suite may exercise 90% of a program, whereas a different, less effective, suite may exercise only 40% of the code. There are many levels of coverage analysis, ranging from function coverage through multiple condition decision coverage.

Coverage tools work by instrumenting the program under test so that the tool can determine when a given part of the program is exercised (or run). (Note that coverage tools can instrument either program source or binary. Both kinds of tools are common.) Then a set of tests are run dynamically, and as the program runs, coverage data are tracked. For example, a coverage tool might instrument an if then else expression in such a way that the tester can determine whether both the then condition and the else condition are exercised by a given test suite.

Coverage tools are very useful for those interested in exploiting software because in software exploit, getting to the problem is half the battle. An attacker might have discovered an exploitable defect deep inside a program (say, using a code-scanning tool), but somehow the attacker needs to cause the program to arrive at the vulnerable location with just the right state data. Coverage tools are very helpful in getting this done.

Too often, coverage tools are misused to estimate the "goodness" of a program. That is, some misguided testers believe that a 90% coverage result may say something about the program under test. But as we have described, code coverage results are really about test effectiveness. They are not about the program under test itself. Don't be confused by this issue.

Figure 6–4 shows an example coverage graph of a fairly small program. The figure shows which code blocks in the control flow graph have been covered during testing with a given test set (the shaded nodes) and which ones were not exercised during testing (the white nodes). This is only part of a control flow graph; the actual graph is so large that we zoomed in on a subsection of the program and then highlighted a subsubsection of that. We generated this graph by using the open source Graphviz tool from AT&T <http://www.graphviz.org/> combined with a custom debugger that we wrote.

Fault Injection Engines

Fault injection is fairly straightforward conceptually. The idea is to trip up a program as it runs by changing data state, messages, and other basic conditions. In principle, you can do everything that a fault injection engine does with a debugger. But often, having a special-purpose engine for running very large numbers of injections in an automated fashion is extremely useful. The basic idea behind fault injection is to perturb program or data state and then keep an eye out for what happens.

The three basic parts of a fault injection engine are (1) an injection engine (the part that perturbs program or data state), (2) a monitoring system (the part that keeps an eye on things), and (3) a way to run the program. Performing fault injection is a dynamic activity, just like using a debugger or running a coverage tool.

Using a fault injection tool, a tester can supply malformed data to critical parts of a program (including program input) in an attempt to get it to crash or otherwise do something interesting. Variations of fault injection also include forcing error conditions in code (by doing things like returning NULL from a memory allocation) in order to see how the program handles errors. For more on fault injection, see *Software Fault Injection* by Jeffrey Voas and Gary McGraw (Wiley, 1998).

Figure 6–5 shows a fault injection engine being used to crash a server program. The engine is using a genetic algorithm to evolve grammars that

Figure 6–4 This is a large control flow graph of a software program. The shaded nodes were covered during dynamic testing, while the white nodes were not. Coverage analysis is a very useful way to determine testing effectiveness.

Figure 6–5 A genetic-algorithm–based fuzzer at work attempting to crash a server. This fuzzer evolves tests that are more fit by applying the principles of genetic engineering.

are then used to generate input strings to the program. The engine is attached to the target program as a debugger and is measuring code coverage as it runs. Individual genomes that produce better code coverage are allowed to "reproduce" to create the next generation. The inner workings of genetic algorithms are beyond the scope of this book, but interested readers can find a good primer in Melanie Mitchell's book *An Introduction to Genetic Algorithms (Complex Adaptive Systems)* from MIT Press (1998).

Virtual Machine Simulators

Virtual machines (VMs) are a venerable idea from computer science with a long, useful history. The idea is to emulate a machine (or several machines) on top of whatever machine you happen to have in front of you. A modern example of this is the Parallels program that allows a Mac user to run a virtual machine that then runs Windows XP in a window at the same time that it is running Mac OS natively <http://www.parallels.com/>.[1] Interestingly, you can also run XP on top of XP in a VM!

All of this is accomplished by perfectly emulating the underlying machine in software. In the Windows on a Mac example, a software layer sits between the XP operating system and the Mac hardware and translates between the layers. As far as XP is concerned, it is running on native hardware . . . but the VM software knows better.

If you use a VM, you can execute software in an extremely closely monitored fashion. You can do things that are normally difficult to do in hardware, such as rewind state, execute in extreme conditions, and reset quickly if a crash occurs.

When software runs inside a VM, the VM has complete control over it. This is very much like René Descartes' "malicious demon" from his famous "brain in a vat" thought experiment. In the 1600s, Descartes performed a thought experiment, wondering how we might possibly know whether we are not simply a brain in a vat getting just the right kinds of input from a malicious demon as opposed to creatures with free will. It was by performing this experiment that he came up with his famous line, "I think, therefore I am."

Getting back to software, software running on a VM controlled by an experimenter is in the very same state that the brain in a vat is. This yields the experimenter complete control over the software, with nothing left to chance. Turns out this is a great way to defeat anti-debugging tricks.

Countermeasures against Reverse Engineering

Some game developers have gotten wise to the fact that hackers use disassemblers and debuggers to reverse engineer their games and have developed many countermeasures for use against them. These techniques

---

1. In fact, right now I am typing this footnote into Word running on XP running on Parallels on a MacBook Pro.

include obfuscating program code and interlacing runtime checks to see if a debugger is present. Hackers can counter almost all of these tricks, but they must know about them first. This is a classic computer security arms race.

Packing

One very easy countermeasure, and a popular one to boot, is *packing*. A packer changes the way the compiled binary looks on disk. If you try to import a packed binary into a disassembler, the disassembler is not likely to be able to read the file. Instead of getting program code when you disassemble, you simply get an error. In some cases, some of the program may be disassembled, but most of it will remain in data form with no translation back into code.

Packers can be countered by using *unpackers*. There are several universal unpackers available that understand and can undo most popular packing formats. These tools can't cope with custom packers, however. A program that has been packed with a custom packer will need to be read directly from memory instead. This technique requires the ability to read the executable image from memory after the program has launched. In most cases, the memory trawling technique works because packers need to unpack themselves before the program can run. The unpacked version will remain in memory and can be analyzed.

Another approach to the packing problem is to single-step trace the software as it runs and simply capture all the instructions. Assuming the program cannot detect that it's being traced, this approach allows you to recover many of the instructions so that they can be undone.

Anti-Debugging

Programs can also use anti-debugging tricks to defeat reversing. These techniques amount to checking the system to see if a debugger is present—and doing weird things with exceptions if they are—in an attempt to get the debugger to handle an exception rather than forwarding it. The debugger detection flag is an easy trick and can be defeated by clearing the BeingDebugged flag from the process environment block (PEB).

Altering Data in the PEB

The following short snippet of code can be used to get the PEB base address for a program that is being debugged:

```
DWORD GetPEBBase(HANDLE theProcessHandle)
{
       PROCESS_BASIC_INFORMATION pbi;

       DWORD len = sizeof(pbi);
```

This function uses the native API call NtQueryInformationProcess:

```
NtQueryInformationProcess(
              theProcessHandle,
              ProcessBasicInformation,
              &pbi,
              len,
              NULL);

       return (DWORD)(pbi.PebBaseAddress);
}
```

Once the PEB is obtained, the next step is to simply clear the BeingDebugged flag. Remember that if you have attached as a debugger, you need to write the change to remote process memory, not to local memory. To do this, use the ReadProcessMemory and WriteProcessMemory functions:

```
void ClearDebuggerPresentFlag(HANDLE theProcessHandle)
{
       DWORD pebBase = GetPEBBase(theProcessHandle);
       PEB aPeb;
       DWORD lpRead;
```

We make sure to read the PEB from the *remote* process:

```
       ReadProcessMemory(
              theProcessHandle,
              (LPCVOID)pebBase,
              &aPeb,
              sizeof(PEB),
              &lpRead);
```

Once read, we can alter the structure as we want to:

```
       aPeb.BeingDebugged = FALSE;
```

And then write the altered version back to the remote process:

```
WriteProcessMemory(
        theProcessHandle,
        (LPVOID)pebBase,
        &aPeb,
        sizeof(PEB),
        &lpRead)


}
```

This illustrates how to manipulate memory in the remote process. We cover this technique in more detail later.

Forwarding Exceptions

Many anti-debugging tricks rely on the fact that debuggers will not handle or forward exceptions properly. For example, a game program may throw a "divide by zero" exception on purpose to confuse the debugger. This exception would normally be thrown by a bug in the program, but in this case the program throws it on purpose to confuse things.

The game program sets up an exception handler that is supposed to be called when bugs like this occur. When the on-purpose bug is then thrown, the expectation is that the special exception handler will be called. If your debugger is attached, you will see the exception for the on-purpose bug— and if you treat it like a real bug, your debugger may try to handle the situation instead of forwarding the bug to the game program's special exception handler. Ultimately, this means that the game's exception handler doesn't get called, and the game will have subsequently detected your debugger by virtue of this fact.

Exception tricks like these are easy to defeat. All you need to remember is to forward all exceptions to the target program. Debugger events are forwarded to the program using the following call:

```
ContinueDebugEvent(
        thePid,
        dbg_evt.dwThreadId,
        DBG_EXCEPTION_NOT_HANDLED);
```

The key is the DBG_EXCEPTION_NOT_HANDLED flag. This tells the debugger to forward the exception to the target program. The game program is then free to handle its own exceptions, as it should be. We cover the ContinueDebugEvent call in more detail in Chapter 7.

Single-Step Timing

Another form of reversing detection is based on timing. In this case, the game program is set up to read the system time at normal intervals. If the time between samples grows beyond a defined threshold, the program will assume it's being debugged. This works because debuggers can slow a program down. The way to get around this kind of check is to avoid pausing the target game program and to avoid activity that slows the game considerably. Usually the thresholds are not very accurate, and as a result this kind of countermeasure is easy to defeat.

There are many more tricks for anti-debugging than the ones we have described here, but this gives you an idea of the kinds of challenges a budding game analyst may run across. As it turns out, some anti-debugging tricks can get very complex, and subsequently, defeating them also gets quite complex. What results is a constant game of cat and mouse.

The ultimate technique to date involves using virtual machines to perform debugging, but this requires a virtual machine that the game will work with. It also relies on the hope that the game doesn't try to detect that it's running in a VM.

Data, Data, Everywhere

Now that we have some tools strapped on to our belts, let's turn to games. Two kinds of things can be altered in a software program—the code itself and the data that the code interacts with. (Just to complicate matters, the code itself is, of course, a form of stored data.) Ultimately, everything is just data—a sea of perfectly choreographed 1s and 0s. This insight has huge ramifications for the online game hacker.

Any data that are sent to a game client can be accessed or modified. Once data exist in the game client, they are yours for the taking (and yours for manipulating)—even data you're not supposed to see. For example, if the game client knows the location of a hidden secret potion, those data must exist in the game client *somewhere* even if the data are not apparent to you in the user interface. Making this even more fun, many times these game data can be manipulated and changed. For example, if the hidden magic potion is too far away, perhaps you can alter its location coordinates so that it conveniently ends up on the ground right in front of you!

Game clients display information to the game player through the user interface. However, the interface displays only part of the information that the client software possesses—the part that the player is supposed to see.

There is often plenty more information under the hood. Figure 6–6 shows this relationship graphically. Assume that there is a magic potion, and that the potion has properties including strength, power, and duration. Under the hood, a software program is managing the magic potion. In our example, if the strength of the magic potion is greater than 100, you get an extra bonus. Refer to the figure for an example of how this software decision might look. When you click the *Drink* button, the potion's strength will be checked by the software and a bonus may be applied (but only if the condition is met).

As we noted earlier, at the deepest layer of the game client, everything is just data. Even the software itself is stored as data. In Figure 6–6, the software that makes the potion decision is stored in one location, and the data that represent the potion's strength are stored in a different location. This is typically how it is—executable software bytes are stored in a special area away from the rest of the data. To complete our example and see how all of this matters, if you wanted to fool this game into giving you a bonus, you could go into memory and alter the data that control the potion's strength. If you set the potion strength data to a number greater than 100, then when the software executes (after you click the *Drink* button), it will give your character a bonus. You might do this with a fault injection engine or a debugger, or maybe just by poking a value into memory by hand.

This begs the question of how hard it really is to find out where the potion's strength is stored. This may sound a bit like a needle-in-a-haystack

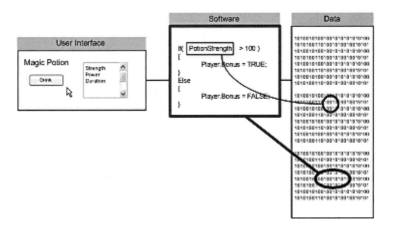

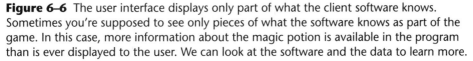

Figure 6–6 The user interface displays only part of what the client software knows. Sometimes you're supposed to see only pieces of what the software knows as part of the game. In this case, more information about the magic potion is available in the program than is ever displayed to the user. We can look at the software and the data to learn more.

problem. There are in many cases millions of bytes of data in a single running program. Simply taking a stroll around in the data without a guide turns out to be not very useful. You need some kind of guide to show you what kind of data you're looking at, and even more specifically, how the data are used. Fortunately, a number of tools and techniques are at your disposal.

First, and most important, data get used. Data are either code or data operated on by code (and in some more complicated cases, both!). If the bits are code, they will be loaded into the CPU at some point and executed. Most disassemblers can find this code and mark it as code, and they'll subsequently show you the instructions that the code translates to in assembly language. Figure 6–7 shows what assembly language looks like once binary has been through a disassembler.

But what about normal data? If you have disassembled the code, the code can provide hints as to the location of data. Figure 6–8 shows the code accessing a data location at 0001F574. Because of the way the code is structured, we now know that memory location 0001F574 stores some kind of data. As it turns out, most code contains volumes of information like this to help us find data of interest.

```
000104D8  ▣ mov edi , edi
000104DA    push ebp
000104DB    mov ebp , esp
000104DD    push ecx
000104DE    mov [ ebp - 4 ] , ecx
000104E1    push 0
000104E3    push dword ptr [ 0001F574 ]
000104E9    push dword ptr [ 0001F578 ]
000104EF    push dword ptr [ ebp - 4 ]
000104F2    push F7
000104F7    call dword ptr [ __imp_ntoskrnl . exe ! KeBugCheckEx ]
000104FD    int 3
000104FE    int 3
000104FF    int 3
00010500    int 3
00010501    int 3
00010502    int 3
00010503  ▣ cmp ecx , [ 0001F578 ]
00010509  ▣ jne 00010514
0001050B  ▣ test ecx , FFFF0000
```

Figure 6–7 A disassembler takes binary code and creates assembly code that looks like this. The numbers in the left column are the memory locations where the machine code is located. The corresponding assembly language is in the right column.

```
000104D8 ▣ mov edi , edi
000104DA   push ebp
000104DB   mov ebp, esp
000104DD   push ecx
000104DE   mov [ ebp - 4 ] , ecx
000104E1   push 0
000104E3   push dword ptr [ 0001F 574 ]
000104E9   push dword ptr [ 0001F578 ]
000104EF   push dword ptr [ ebp - 4 ]
000104F2   push F7
000104F7   call dword ptr [ __imp_ntoskrnl . exe ! KeBugCheckEx ]
000104FD   int 3
000104FE   int 3
000104FF   int 3
00010500   int 3
00010501   int 3
00010502   int 3
00010503 ▣ cmp ecx , [ 0001F578 ]
00010509 ▣ jne 00010514
0001050B ▣ test ecx , FFFF0000
```

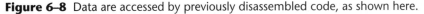

Figure 6–8 Data are accessed by previously disassembled code, as shown here.

Data Exposure and Countermeasures

Obviously you can search for and alter data at will in any target game program. But remember that the game program can also search memory. The game may employ countermeasures that search for modifications made to its own code or data (e.g., through the use of integrity checking), and it can also scan for any injected code or data that you have placed into memory (using active malware scanning). Many of the techniques we show you involve altering code, tweaking data bits, and injecting threads or DLLs into the game process. All of this activity can and will be detected by some game software. The obvious example is Blizzard's Warden, which protects the WoW game (see Chapter 2). There are ways to hide from and defeat many, if not all, forms of scanning, but some of them can get quite complicated.

Data at Rest, Data in Motion

Sometimes data are at rest, say, in the memory of your computer. Sometimes data are in motion, say, as they whiz by on the network connection between two communicating programs. If you focus only on data in memory, you'll be missing out on half the fun. By modifying data in packets that are coming and going, you can deeply affect game play just as readily as you can when you change local instances of data in your computer's memory. In fact, if you know exactly how a given communication protocol works, you can rewrite the game client with a stand-alone client of your own.[2] After all, what you really need is a program that takes in specific input and produces specific output.

Let's make this concrete: Sometimes, by sniffing the right packets, you can determine the location of the secret potion without even using a debugger. Figure 6–9 illustrates an example of such a sniffer. The program, called WoWSniffer, clearly illustrates the ability to sniff chat messages in transit over the network. This is especially interesting because the communications over the network are supposed to be encrypted. Apparently, the author of WoWSniffer has cracked the encryption.

Figure 6–9 The WoWSniffer program is shown here running against World of Warcraft. The messages displayed in the sniffer window have lots of information about the inner workings of the game client. (From <http://www.firepacket.net>; reproduced with permission.)

---

2. This is an example of the attack pattern "Make the client invisible" from our book *Exploiting Software*. Much more on this can be found in Chapter 9.

Looking Elsewhere for Data

In Chapter 2, we introduce the idea of aimbots. Recall that aimbots can provide a player with uncanny, superhuman aim. Aimbots work by detecting the 3D coordinates of your enemy and calculating at exactly what angle to point your weapon to hit him or her with the best possible shot. Automatically pointing your sniper rifle into your opponent's left eye socket requires looking around in the data that store the 3D coordinates of objects being rendered in the game.

What makes aimbots particularly interesting is that they don't just look at data in the game program; instead, they take advantage of how data interact with the video card. The video card itself has a boatload of onboard RAM that stores data structures for rendering 3D objects. (Of course, gamers make a point of having the latest in graphics technology to play their games.) As it turns out, aimbots can take advantage of the 3D data stored in the video card to find the 3D coordinates of objects in the game world. How creative!

Figure 6–10 shows how an aimbot can compute and maintain a carbon copy of all the objects being rendered in the video memory—even those objects not yet directly in the field of view. It does this by intercepting communications between the game and the Direct3D video library provided with Microsoft Windows.

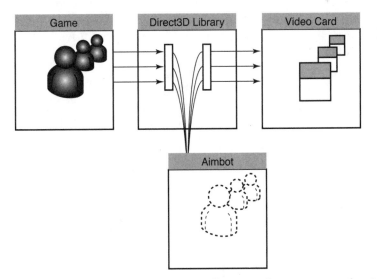

Figure 6–10 How an aimbot intercepts 3D coordinates as they are sent to the video subsystem in order to compute such things as enemy placement.

Getting All Around the Game

By now it should be clear that there are many places we can look around for interesting data in or near the game client. And there are even more places to mess around with these data. You can do this by sending information to the game client through the user interface (we'll call this going *over* the game). You can do this by getting inside the game and looking around in memory (we'll call this getting *in* the game). You can do this by getting between the game and the lower-level services it needs, such as video drivers (we'll call this getting *under* the game). And you can even do this by sitting on the network between the game client and its server (we'll call this standing *way outside* the game).

Here we go.

Going Over the Game: Controlling the User Interface

In Chapter 2, we present a very simple farming game bot that works by interacting with the WoW client interface. This is an extremely common technique and is thus worth another quick look. Refer back to Chapter 2 if you need a more introductory explanation of what's going on here.

The basic idea for getting over the game is to send events to the game client as if the events themselves were coming from the PC. That is, you can send messages to the client that look to it like normal keystrokes, mouse events, or other game-specific messages. This type of utility is sometimes called a *macro*. There are many macro programs available that can post mouse and keyboard events to the screen. Instead of showing you other people's macro programs, we show you how to write your own. What follows are some easy examples to get you started.

Controlling Keystrokes

The first example involves sending keyboard events to the game client just as if we were typing directly on the keyboard. This is important since this can be used to move your game character, click on hotkeys for actions and events, and even type into a chat window.

Here is a snippet of source code that posts a keystroke to the computer. This is handled globally and will post the keystroke regardless of which window is in the foreground or which application is running. This technique is commonly used by macro programs. Many game hacking and macro scripts use basic keyboard and mouse events to interact with the game client. The side effect of using this technique is that you can't use the computer for anything else while you are doing your botting because this technique basically takes over the user interface while it runs.

```
DWORD PostKeystroke(
        BYTE theScanCode,
        DWORD theTime)
{
        keybd_event(
                theScanCode,
                MapVirtualKey(theScanCode, 0), 0, 0);
        Sleep(theTime);
        keybd_event(
                theScanCode,
                MapVirtualKey(theScanCode, 0), 0 |
                        KEYEVENTF_KEYUP, 0);
        return 0;
}
```

This code snippet uses the API call `keybd_event( )`. This call takes the virtual scan code for the key you want to press. This is not the same thing as the ASCII code. The character you want to press needs to be mapped to its respective scan code before you use this API function.

Using Magic Key Sequences

WoW has a character class known as Paladin—quite possibly one of the most difficult classes to play in the game.[3] The key to playing this class is the proper ordering of actions to maximize damage or to preserve mana (an in-game energy rating of sorts). The game offers hotkeys that can be linked to actions for your character. So, one kind of macro might be designed to execute a series of actions to maximize the effectiveness of the Paladin character. Such a sequence might go like this:

F1 key: cast spell Sanctity Aura—increases Holy Damage

F2 key: cast spell Seal of Holy Might

F3 key: cast spell Judgement

F4 key: cast spell Seal of Command

---

3. We know that everyone has their own opinions on matters such as these; this is just our own studied opinion.

F5 key: cast spell Hammer of Justice

F6 key: cast spell Crusader Strike

There are a total of six key bindings set up. Now, using these keys in the correct order and timing could result in the following:

Begin fighting . . .

F1—F2—F3—F4

Wait 15 seconds while fighting

F5—F3—F4

Continue fight for 15 more seconds, if target still alive, then

F5—F3—F4

Repeat above as timers allow

Obviously, that's a lot of keystrokes. At the time of this writing, this sequence would first cast a Sanctity Aura, increasing damage output. Then, the Seal of Holy Might is cast, which is then immediately Judged—effectively placing a curse that makes your opponent take extra damage for a period of time. Next, a Seal of Command is cast, and fighting continues. This spell causes even more damage, and then a Hammer of Justice stuns the target opponent. Next, another Judgement causes a burst of damage that is enhanced by the fact that the opponent is also stunned. The character repeats this sequence as long as the fight is on.

Variations of these kinds of techniques abound, but this gives you an idea of the kind of analysis you can perform up front to engineer your macro for maximum effectiveness. Your mileage may vary.

Controlling Mouse Droppings

We can cause the same effect with the mouse because, just like a keyboard, the mouse generates events as you use it. By sending these events to the game client, we can make it believe that a user is wielding the mouse.

The following source code snippet illustrates use of the mouse_event API call with some inline commentary.

```
DWORD LMouseClick(DWORD x, DWORD y, bool shift)
{
        int ix,iy;
```

This code gets the width and height, in pixels, of the monitor or screen.

```
ix=GetSystemMetrics(SM_CXSCREEN);
iy=GetSystemMetrics(SM_CYSCREEN);
```

This code converts the client coordinates of the foreground window to screen coordinates, letting you move the game client window around—thereby avoiding the annoying problem of having to align the game client screen to the upper left corner of the monitor. Some macro programs require this, but here we show you how to avoid that annoyance.

```
POINT p;
p.x = x;
p.y = y;
ClientToScreen(GetForegroundWindow(), &p);
```

The mouse_event call requires you to specify the coordinates in *mikeys*—the screen is divided into 65,536 (16 bits) mikeys for both x- and y-coordinates—so the upper left is (0,0) and the lower right is (65535, 65535).

```
DWORD mikeysX = p.x * 65535 / ix;
DWORD mikeysY = p.y * 65535 / iy;
```

This sets the mouse position on the screen.

```
mouse_event(
        MOUSEEVENTF_ABSOLUTE | MOUSEEVENTF_MOVE,
        mikeysX,
        mikeysY,
        0, 0);
```

If you want, you can specify that the shift key is pressed before the mouse event. This is useful, for example, when you need to shift-right-click to auto-loot a bag and so on.

```
if(shift)
{
        keybd_event(
                VK_LSHIFT,
                MapVirtualKey(VK_LSHIFT, 0), 0, 0);
```

The sleep here is optional; you may want to experiment with your target game.

```
        //Sleep(20);
    }
```

You can substitute a parameter here to make this a right click instead of a left click. Look up the documentation on mouse_event to see all the available options.

```
    mouse_event(MOUSEEVENTF_LEFTDOWN, 0, 0, 0, 0);
    //Sleep(20);
    mouse_event(MOUSEEVENTF_LEFTUP, 0, 0, 0, 0);
    //Sleep(20);
```

If we used the shift, let's put it back now.

```
    if(shift)
    {
        keybd_event(
            VK_LSHIFT,
            MapVirtualKey(VK_LSHIFT, 0), 0 |
                KEYEVENTF_KEYUP, 0);
        //Sleep(20);
    }
    return 0;
}
```

As you can see, wielding the mouse is just as automatic and easy as wielding the keyboard. This is a classic technique that's as old as the hills.

Sampling Pixels

So you know how to post mouse and keyboard events. How do we also get feedback from the game? For example, what if we want to know the health of a character or of a target opponent? You can learn many things by reading pixel colors from the screen. For example, health bars are typically red and located at a specific place on the screen. If you sample pixel colors from this area, you should be able to tell what value is present on the on-screen health indicator. You can use pixel sampling for a plethora of things, of course; this is just one example.

The following code snippet illustrates how to determine the color of a pixel:

```
COLORREF GetColorOfPixel(DWORD x, DWORD y)
{
        HWND hWnd    = GetForegroundWindow();
        HDC hDC      = GetDC(hWnd);
        COLORREF cr = GetPixel(hDC, x, y);
        ReleaseDC(hWnd, hDC);
        return cr;
}
```

The code first gets the topmost window—which will be the game's client window since it must be topmost (and in focus) in order to interact with your keystroke and mouse messages. This works if the game is in windowed mode as opposed to full-screen mode. Most games support windowed mode. The COLORREF will have values for red, blue, and green, and these can be used to deduce any color.

Figure 6–11 shows an example technique for checking the health, mana, or other information displayed in bars on the WoW interface.

A botting or combat assist program can sample the colors at the locations indicated on the screen. Given a few samples, the botting program can determine whether the character is at full, medium, or low health. See the simple bot in Chapter 2 for an example.

Countermeasures against Macro Bots

Macro-botting programs have one advantage over other types of botting programs—they are easy to understand and build. That's why they are particularly popular. They also have the advantage that they don't manipulate the game's program memory at all, so the game won't be able to detect that it's being hacked. In fact, a macro program such as this is hardly a hack at all—it's merely simulating a real player by pressing keys and clicking the mouse. Game programs that hope to catch players using macro programs

Figure 6–11 By sampling pixel color at the locations on the bar marked with an X, you can keep track of health, mana, and other information displayed as bars on the WoW interface.

like this must resort to scanning the processes and window names on the system. This might seem like a violation of privacy (and we believe it is), but it's the only way games can hope to detect macro programs at this level.

Macro programs like this aren't used just for games like WoW. They are also used for online poker, and in poker games there is often a lot of money at stake. Programs can automatically play cards just as easily as they can drive a Paladin in a fantasy world. In the case of the popular online poker site PartyPoker.com, rumor has it that the game producers resort to taking full screenshots of your computer monitor, including everything visible at the time the shot is taken, and sending those shots home for analysis. Talk about an invasion of privacy!

Hiding from Process Lists

Some games read your PC's process list in hopes of finding a known macro program, such as the AC Tool or something similar. This doesn't work very well because it is trivial to rename your process to something else. Simply rename the .exe file before launching it.

Sometimes scanning a process list is used for more than just determining process names—it is also used to find processes for subsequent memory scans. In this case, renaming the .exe isn't going to work. You need to hide the process entirely. This can be accomplished by using a rootkit.[4] Hiding a program is simple—simply download the easy-to-use and popular FU rootkit from <http://www.rootkit.com>. Running FU will allow you to hide a process.

Changing Window Names

Another method games use to scan for botting software is to read the text of all open windows. If you suspect your target game is doing something like this, you may want to download the tool called the Governor (which we introduce in Chapter 2) from the book's Web site or at <http://www.rootkit .com/vault/hoglund/Governor.zip>. This tool will inform you if the game is attempting to read memory of processes and/or window texts.

To defeat window texts, simply randomize the names of your windows so they can't be trivially fingerprinted.

---

4. *Rootkits: Subverting the Windows Kernel* by Greg Hoglund and James Butler (Addison-Wesley, 2005) is the definitive text on this technology.

Wielding Rootkits for Stealth

The most powerful form of botting stealth can be obtained by using rootkits. Rootkits are programs designed to hide other programs and data on a computer. Rootkits are not intrinsically bad; they are just tools and, like any tool, they can be used by bad guys or good guys. For game hacking, rootkits are particularly useful. More information on how rootkits can be used to hide botting programs is given later.

Generating Windows Messages

Of course, games always have messages specific to the game. If you can generate these messages and get them to the game client, you can in some sense manipulate the game client right through the front door.

Getting In the Game: Manipulating Game Objects

As we've shown, everything in a game eventually boils down to data—even the client code. Many game hacks are based solely on reading data for objects that are normally not visible but are nevertheless present in client memory. (Recall our magic potion example from earlier.) All you need for these hacks is to open your eyes. Other hacks are based on writing select values to process memory, including such things as player position. These hacks merely involve changing things a bit. The hacks we present here don't alter any code, but they do manipulate the data that the client code interprets and uses.

We know by now that game objects, including items, inventory, monsters, and other players, are all stored somewhere in memory. These kinds of things are usually stored as groups or lists of objects. Some games make use of a generic object management system, where the same kinds of list structures are used for everything. Many games are constructed in C++ and make use of object-oriented design, where lists are the basic type (base class), with subclasses for each specific game object type.

Let's make this concrete. In some versions of WoW, the following structure is used to track game objects.[5] The game uses a doubly linked list with a set of object-specific values:

---

5. We say "some versions" because WoW and other online games are in a constant state of evolution.

```
typedef struct
{
        DWORD id;
        DWORD unk1;
        DWORD unk2;
        void *prev;   // previous entry
        void *next;   // next entry
        DWORD unk3;
        DWORD unk4;
        DWORD unk5;
        char *name1;
        char *name2;
        char *name3;
        char *name4;
        DWORD unk6[16];
        DWORD id2;
} gob_list_struct;
```

There are many other ways to store objects in programs that don't rely on doubly linked lists like the one shown here. Sometimes games use standard issue lists, binary trees, or hash tables. In fact, games make use of all of the common data structures you can learn about in computer science classes.

Once you determine how game objects are represented and where they have been squirreled away in memory, you can make adjustments to memory to suit your needs.

The Problem of Moveable Memory

Yet making adjustments to memory by direct manipulation may lead to its own problems. In fact, there is one major obstacle to overcome. Memory locations don't just sit there waiting for you to come along; stuff in memory gets moved around a lot. In many cases, once you find something in memory (such as the magic potion strength field we talked about before), you will want to come back and keep accessing it. That's great if it stays put; but what if it doesn't? You might want to read a coordinate once a second, or write to a variable every time you fire your weapon. If the memory location is not static—that is, if it moves frequently—you may have to go poking around for it each and every time you use it. This is tedious, and in the worst cases it can screw up your plan.

The good news is that sometimes memory locations are static—that is, particular memory locations are hard-coded into the software so they really can't move. The memory location we introduced earlier in Figure 6–7 is such an example. In this case, the memory location is reliable, so you can continue to use it repeatedly. But even in this case there remains a subtle problem—the problem of patching. Games are patched all the time; in fact, most MMOs are patched almost weekly. Patches move things around by altering the actual game client software, thus often moving hard-coded locations for data as a side effect.

Bot developers are plagued by this problem. Figure 6–12 shows an example of source code for a WoW bot. You can see in the code itself how the developer has commented out several previous hard-coded addresses in favor of new ones. Every time a patch is released, the game hacker has been forced to update the bot source code. This can become quite a chore.

There are some nice ways to avoid the problem of updating constantly changing memory locations that are hard coded. The main idea is to use dynamic methods for finding memory locations on the fly so you don't have to update your source code every time a new patch comes out.

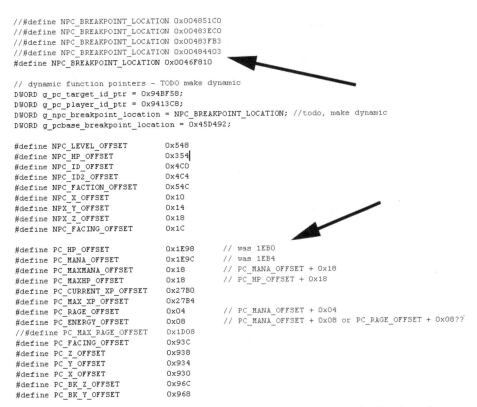

```
//#define NPC_BREAKPOINT_LOCATION 0x004851C0
//#define NPC_BREAKPOINT_LOCATION 0x00483EC0
//#define NPC_BREAKPOINT_LOCATION 0x00483FB3
//#define NPC_BREAKPOINT_LOCATION 0x00484403
#define NPC_BREAKPOINT_LOCATION 0x0046F810

// dynamic function pointers - TODO make dynamic
DWORD g_pc_target_id_ptr = 0x94BF58;
DWORD g_pc_player_id_ptr = 0x9413C8;
DWORD g_npc_breakpoint_location = NPC_BREAKPOINT_LOCATION; //todo, make dynamic
DWORD g_pcbase_breakpoint_location = 0x45D492;

#define NPC_LEVEL_OFFSET          0x548
#define NPC_HP_OFFSET             0x354
#define NPC_ID_OFFSET             0x4C0
#define NPC_ID2_OFFSET            0x4C4
#define NPC_FACTION_OFFSET        0x54C
#define NPC_X_OFFSET              0x10
#define NPX_Y_OFFSET              0x14
#define NPX_Z_OFFSET              0x18
#define NPC_FACING_OFFSET         0x1C

#define PC_HP_OFFSET              0x1E98    // was 1EB0
#define PC_MANA_OFFSET            0x1E9C    // was 1EB4
#define PC_MAXMANA_OFFSET         0x18      // PC_MANA_OFFSET + 0x18
#define PC_MAXHP_OFFSET           0x18      // PC_HP_OFFSET + 0x18
#define PC_CURRENT_XP_OFFSET      0x27B0
#define PC_MAX_XP_OFFSET          0x27B4
#define PC_RAGE_OFFSET            0x04      // PC_MANA_OFFSET + 0x04
#define PC_ENERGY_OFFSET          0x08      // PC_MANA_OFFSET + 0x08 or PC_RAGE_OFFSET + 0x08??
//#define PC_MAX_RAGE_OFFSET      0x1D08
#define PC_FACING_OFFSET          0x93C
#define PC_Z_OFFSET               0x938
#define PC_Y_OFFSET               0x934
#define PC_X_OFFSET               0x930
#define PC_BK_Z_OFFSET            0x96C
#define PC_BK_Y_OFFSET            0x968
```

Figure 6–12 Code for a WoW bot. You can see in the code where the developer has updated the source several times to keep up with patches.

Rounding Up the Usual Suspects

In terms of development technique, several common objects are used in almost all games. These include the following:

- Player object: the structure that represents the player's character
- Other player objects: other, real players in multiuser environments
- Nonplayer characters (NPCs) and mobs (short for "mobiles"): nonplayer entities such as shop merchants and monsters

In the upcoming subsections, we'll take a quick look at examples of each of these objects so you can learn how to find and manipulate these structures for yourself.

Player Data Structures

All MMOs include the concept of an in-game character. The character is your alter ego in the game universe. Somewhere in memory, a data structure exists that describes this character. It contains such things as the 3D coordinates for your character's location, health status, and various ability ratings (e.g., strength, magic power). Clearly these data must be stored on the game server, but sometimes the client program controls the values directly. Whenever this is the case, the character data are at risk. This is a prime example of a software security no-no, where the client is trusted even though it is not trustworthy.

There's often a good reason for this. Storing every bit of state about a game on a central server and keeping all gazillion game clients up to date in real time takes too much bandwidth. Today's Internet can't handle the traffic. To get more specific, consider managing location coordinates in 3D space.

Because it takes too much bandwidth to have the server manage 3D coordinates for every single object in the game as thousands of users manipulate them, the game client controls the position and updates it as you move your character around. Every so often, the client software updates the server with the new location.

Do you see the potential exploit? It's easy! Simply set the 3D coordinates in memory by using a debugger tool. These values are usually stored as three float values corresponding to the three dimensions. In some versions of WoW, the server does not check the validity of any movement. Instead, it blithely accepts new values provided by its client software. That means when you update the 3D values by means beyond the game, you can in some sense instantaneously teleport your character in the WoW universe.

Let's make this clear. The following listing shows a character structure reverse engineered from an early version of the WoW client program. You can plainly observe that the player structures are stored in a doubly linked list (next and prev pointers making up the first two members). Several fields were not reverse engineered, delimited below as unk for "unknown." What is particularly significant are the 48-byte name field, the race_type field, and the class_type field.

```
typedef struct
{
        void *next;
        void *prev_pc;
        DWORD unk1;
        DWORD id;
        DWORD unk2;
        CHAR name[48];
        DWORD id2;
        DWORD unk3;
        DWORD race_type;
        DWORD unk4[2];
        DWORD class_type;
        DWORD id3;
        DWORD unk5[3];
} pc_list_struct;
```

In the structure above, the following integer values for race and class were observed (over the course of checking out several characters). These values were obtained by watching the game program in a debugger and cross-referencing a known character's name with its race and class. Pretty simple!

```
// race:
// 3 = dwarf
// 7 = gnome

// class:
// 1 = warrior
// 2 = paladin
// 3 = hunter
// 4 =
// 5 = priest
// 6 =
// 7 =
// 8 = mage
```

It is easy to determine how characters are represented. Naturally, it is easy to experiment with changing these values as well.

There are many more such data structures present in a game. Part of the task of a game hacker is to identify these structures and use them to some advantage later.

Reading the File from Disk

When dealing with a dynamic environment, patched games, and so on, it can sometimes make sense to read the file from disk and search for symbols or byte sequences. This way, even if the game gets patched, your hacking tools or botting program can still find the location it needs to patch, set a breakpoint on, or otherwise use.

The Windows registry can sometimes help you find the location of the game client on disk. The following code snippet shows how to open and query the Windows registry. This example locates the binary for WoW by checking the keys and values that the game installs in the registry.

```
void WowzerEngine::InitWowLocation()
{
        HKEY hKey;
        char szValue[MAX_PATH];
        DWORD dwSize = MAX_PATH;
        HANDLE hFile, hMap;
```

RegOpenKey takes the root hive you will be reading, in this case, HKEY_LOCAL_MACHINE, and the full path to the key you want to open. If the call is successful, the handle to the key ends up being stored in hKey.

```
        if(RegOpenKeyEx(HKEY_LOCAL_MACHINE,
                "SOFTWARE\\Blizzard Entertainment\\World of
Warcraft",
                0,
                KEY_QUERY_VALUE,
                &hKey) == ERROR_SUCCESS)
        {
```

Once the key is opened, you can query any values stored under the key. Here we query GamePath to learn the path to the WoW client executable.

```
            if(RegQueryValueEx(
                hKey,
                "GamePath",
                NULL,
```

```
                    NULL,
                    (LPBYTE)szValue,
                            &dwSize) == ERROR_SUCCESS)
        {
                    strcpy(wow_location, szValue);
        }
        else
        {
                    MessageBox(
                            NULL,
                            "Warning, could not find WoW.EXE -
cannot init pointer values.",
                            "Cannot continue...",
                            MB_OK);
        }
        RegCloseKey(hKey);
        }
```

Once we find the executable, we open a file handle to it so we can read (and potentially write) to it. In this case, we only read the file and use the data for looking up byte sequences, patterns, and symbols in the file.

```
        hFile = CreateFile(
                wow_location,
                GENERIC_READ,
                FILE_SHARE_READ,
                NULL,
                OPEN_EXISTING,
                FILE_FLAG_SEQUENTIAL_SCAN,
                NULL);
        if(hFile != INVALID_HANDLE_VALUE)
        {
```

This call maps the file into memory so we can scan it more easily.

```
        hMap = CreateFileMapping(
                hFile,
                NULL,
                PAGE_READONLY,
                0,
                0,
                NULL);

        if(hMap)
                pbFile = (PBYTE)MapViewOfFile(
                        hMap,
```

```
                        FILE_MAP_READ,
                        0,
                        0,
                        0);
        }

        if(!pbFile)
        {
                MessageBox(
                        NULL,
                        "Could not map WoW.EXE",
                        "Error",
                        MB_OK);
        }
}
```

Finding game files using the registry is a common and useful technique with Windows-based games.

Parsing the PE Header

The game file itself is a Win32 Portable Executable (PE). Most Windows .exe files are in PE format, which is very well documented.[6] Because of this, we are not going to cover the PE format in detail here. The following code snippets are used to look up various things in the PE header. These examples are based on code adapted from Bubba's WoW Hack (BWH).[7] You can search on the Net if you want to find the original source code to BWH.

Before you can scan the PE file with the techniques shown here, you need to locate the code section. Once you do that, the examples are straightforward.

PE headers can also be used to find other information in the file, including embedded resources such as images, named functions that are imported or exported, and the data section. Some of the scanning techniques shown here rely on parsing the PE header. The basic PE parser support functions used in our examples are shown below.

---

6. An introductory article on the PE file format can be found at <http://www .windowsitlibrary.com/Content/356/11/1.html>.
7. You can find Bubba's WoW Hack hosted at a number of Web sites. Try this one: <http://firepacket.net/WoW>.

```
DWORD OffsetToRva(PBYTE pbImage, DWORD dwOffset)
{
        //ripped from bwh
        DWORD dwSecBorder = -1;
        PIMAGE_NT_HEADERS pNt =
                PIMAGE_NT_HEADERS(
                pbImage + PIMAGE_DOS_HEADER(pbImage)->e_lfanew);
        PIMAGE_SECTION_HEADER pSec =
                PIMAGE_SECTION_HEADER(PBYTE(pNt) +
        sizeof(IMAGE_NT_HEADERS)); for(DWORD x = 0; x < pNt->
        FileHeader.NumberOfSections; x++)
        {
         if( dwOffset >= pSec[x].PointerToRawData &&
             dwOffset < pSec[x].PointerToRawData   +
             pSec[x].SizeOfRawData)
           return (dwOffset -
                   pSec[x].PointerToRawData +
                   pSec[x].VirtualAddress);
         if( pSec[x].PointerToRawData &&
             pSec[x].PointerToRawData < dwSecBorder)
           dwSecBorder = pSec[x].PointerToRawData;
        }
        if(dwOffset < dwSecBorder)
          return dwOffset;
        else
          return NULL;
}
```

The following helper function converts a relative virtual address (RVA) to an actual memory pointer that can be used in a memory read-or-write operation.

```
PBYTE RvaToPointer(PBYTE pbImage, DWORD dwRva)
{
        //ripped from bwh
        DWORD dwSecBorder = -1;
        PIMAGE_NT_HEADERS pNt =
                PIMAGE_NT_HEADERS(
                pbImage +
                PIMAGE_DOS_HEADER(pbImage)->e_lfanew);
        PIMAGE_SECTION_HEADER pSec =
                PIMAGE_SECTION_HEADER(PBYTE(pNt) +
                sizeof(IMAGE_NT_HEADERS));
        for(DWORD x = 0; x < pNt->FileHeader.NumberOfSections; x++)
```

```
{ .
  if( dwRva >= pSec[x].VirtualAddress &&
      dwRva < pSec[x].VirtualAddress   +
      pSec[x].Misc.VirtualSize)
    return( pbImage +
            (dwRva - pSec[x].VirtualAddress +
            pSec[x].PointerToRawData));

  if( pSec[x].PointerToRawData &&
      pSec[x].PointerToRawData < dwSecBorder)
    dwSecBorder = pSec[x].PointerToRawData;
}
if(dwRva < dwSecBorder)
  return pbImage + dwRva;
else
  return NULL;
}
```

PE file basics come in very handy when looking for various game data.

Looking Around for Stuff

As we briefly demonstrate above, many data values are stored globally. When the game code is compiled, hard-coded pointers to these global storage locations are placed inline with the code. We can begin our bot experiment by looking for a hard-coded data pointer.

There are two good ways to find game code you're looking for. The first is to scan code directly from an in-memory image of the loaded code. The second is to map it from the file on disk. Either way works. The in-memory image is often more accurate when it comes to where things end up, but unless the game client specifically reorders itself in memory or employs other sneaky forms of obfuscation, the on-disk version usually works just as well as the in-memory version. With either, you end up dealing with a handle to some memory. If you're loading from disk, you can first map the file into memory and get your memory pointer that way. If you're looking directly at memory, you can just obtain a pointer to the right place.

The following examples are based on code adapted from BWH. Note that many of these techniques are directly detectable now, and use of them will get your character banned. The code uses an open file handle and parses the file's PE header information to locate the code section. Then it subsequently scans through a bunch of opcodes. Finally, it finds a globally stored value and reads it.

The code itself is particularly hard to read because of all the hard-coded values, but it does give a clear indication of the nested data in the game. That is, one pointer points to the next, which points to the next, and so on. Basically, you follow the chain all the way to the particular memory glob you're after.

All of these common data are indispensable for a bot. The data include clues about geometry, hitpoints, positions of objects, and object states. Position information is obviously required for a bot to know where it is in the world and how it exists in relation to other things.

So, once we have the file loaded up, let's look for some interesting items. These examples show you lookups for things specific to the WoW game client.

Player Character Corpse Identification

When your character dies in the WoW game, the corpse is left behind, and your character appears at the graveyard. You need to be able to get back to your corpse in order to resurrect and continue playing. Any good botting program should be able to do this automatically. You can either teleport/telehack to the corpse location or drive the character manually over the terrain to the corpse location. Either way, to proceed, you need to be able to read the coordinates of the corpse location. The following snippet scans for the memory location where the corpse coordinate is stored. Once again, these examples were taken from BWH.

```
DWORD WowzerEngine::GetLoc_PCorpse()
{
        // ripped from bwh
        DWORD x, y;
        PIMAGE_NT_HEADERS pNtHdr = PIMAGE_NT_HEADERS(pbFile +
                PIMAGE_DOS_HEADER(pbFile)->e_lfanew);
        PIMAGE_SECTION_HEADER pSecHdr =
                PIMAGE_SECTION_HEADER(pNtHdr + 1);
        PBYTE pbCode =
                RvaToPointer(
                        pbFile,
                        pSecHdr[0].VirtualAddress );
        DWORD dwCodeSize =
                pSecHdr[0].SizeOfRawData;
```

The code here scans for the following opcodes. The pattern is long enough that it will match only on the intended location—it won't match on any false positives.

```
BYTE bCode[] =
        {0xD9, 0xC0, 0xD8, 0xC9, 0xD9,
         0xC3, 0xD8, 0xCC, 0xDE, 0xC1,
         0xD9, 0xC2, 0xD8, 0xCB, 0xDE,
         0xC1, 0xD8, 0x1D};

for(x = 0; x < dwCodeSize; x++)
{
  if(MemoryCompare(&pbCode[x], bCode, sizeof(bCode)))
    {
```

This rather nasty bit of code dereferences a hard-coded pointer. This is
a pointer to a global value that stores the corpse location. Unfortunately,
the code is very hard to follow and could probably be much cleaner. However, you can see that it scans backwards from the code location that was
matched earlier. If it finds what it's looking for, it returns the hard-coded
pointer.

```
if(*((PWORD)&pbCode[x-6]) == 0x25D8)
  {
     for(y = 0; y < 30; y++)
     {
       if(pbCode[x-6-y] == 0xFF)
          return *((PDWORD)&pbCode[x-4]) - 8;
     }
  }
          }
        }
        return NULL;
}
```

Placing an NPC Breakpoint

Using the same technique that we used to find the corpse for the player
character, this snippet scans for a bit of code that handles the linked list of
NPCs. This code location is then used with a breakpoint on the running
client. The way this works is simple—the breakpoint eventually fires when
an NPC structure is processed. When the breakpoint fires, the pointer to the
NPC structure can be obtained from one of the registers on the CPU. This
first NPC structure points to all of the rest since they are in a linked list.
Thus, using a single breakpoint, you can obtain the entire dynamically
located NPC list.

```
DWORD WowzerEngine::GetLoc_NPC_Breakpoint()
{
        // ripped from bwh
        DWORD x, y;
        PIMAGE_NT_HEADERS pNtHdr =
                PIMAGE_NT_HEADERS(
                pbFile + PIMAGE_DOS_HEADER(pbFile)->e_lfanew);
        PIMAGE_SECTION_HEADER pSecHdr =
                PIMAGE_SECTION_HEADER(pNtHdr + 1);
        PBYTE pbCode = RvaToPointer(pbFile,
                pSecHdr[0].VirtualAddress);
        DWORD dwCodeSize = pSecHdr[0].SizeOfRawData;
```

At this point, the pointer to the code section and its length have been uncovered. What is interesting is that a memory compare with a string of bytes is now used to find the location of interest. Once we find what we're looking for (a match), the address of the location is returned. We'll use this address in a subsequent operation.

```
        BYTE bCode[] =
        {0x8B, 0x41, 0x38, 0x8B,
         0x49, 0x3C, 0x83, 0xEC,
         0x40, 0x8B, 0xD0, 0x0B, 0xD1};


        for(x = 0; x < dwCodeSize; x++)
        {
          if(MemoryCompare(&pbCode[x], bCode, sizeof(bCode)))
            {
            return *((PDWORD)&pbCode[x]);
            }
        }
        return NULL;
}
```

Uncovering the Player Character Camera Angle

This snippet is slightly different than the ones presented earlier, in that it doesn't use an array of opcodes to scan; instead, it just compares values. Otherwise, it does generally the same thing. This snippet returns the location that stores the camera angle.

```
DWORD WowzerEngine::GetLoc_PCameraAngle()
{
        // ripped from bwh
        DWORD x;
        PIMAGE_NT_HEADERS pNtHdr =
                PIMAGE_NT_HEADERS(
                pbFile + PIMAGE_DOS_HEADER(pbFile)->e_lfanew);
        PIMAGE_SECTION_HEADER pSecHdr =
                PIMAGE_SECTION_HEADER(pNtHdr + 1);
        PBYTE   pbCode =
                 RvaToPointer(pbFile, pSecHdr[0].VirtualAddress);
```

The program uses Windows-supplied SDK functions to parse the PE header.
By doing this, it subsequently finds the code section. It now gets the length
of the code section and scans through the entire range looking for the 32-bit
value 0xD8DDD8DD.

```
        DWORD dwCodeSize = pSecHdr[0].SizeOfRawData;
        for(x = 0; x < dwCodeSize; x++)
        {
          if(*((PDWORD)&pbCode[x]) == 0xD8DDD8DD)
            {
```

Now that we have discovered the target value, we need to check several
other values nearby. If everything we're looking for is there, the code
scanner has located the function of interest. This function uses a globally
stored value. The code reads the pointer to this value as x+6 and returns
what is pointed to—in other words, it dereferences the pointer and retrieves
the dynamic value from memory.

```
            if(*((PWORD)&pbCode[x+4]) == 0x05D9)
              {
                if(*((PWORD)&pbCode[x+10]) == 0x05D9)
                  {
                    if(*((PWORD)&pbCode[x+16]) == 0xF3D9)
                      {
                        return *((PDWORD)&pbCode[x+6]);
                      }
                  }
              }
            }
          }
        return NULL;
}
```

Even though this code is ugly and is by no means well documented, the technique is sound. Using this approach, the scanner can locate a given function even if the program is patched (which happens to WoW clients and other game clients with some regularity). This means that even if the function moves about due to a patch, our scanner can still locate it and read the correct global memory address.

Finding the Player Character Block

The next scan locates where the player's character structure is stored. The character structure is very important since it has the character's current location, health, magic points (mana), and so on. Unfortunately, you can't hack WoW simply by overwriting your hitpoints with a new value because the server keeps the hitpoints on its end. But the character block is invaluable for managing your bot.

This snippet shows a rather interesting trick. The WoW client and many other games store debug strings in the binary that are used for error messages or for debugging the game client. You can use some of these strings to locate functions you're interested in. In the case of WoW, some of these strings actually contain the names of the source code files used to build the actual client. Pretty neat. At any rate, the following snippet scans for the character by first finding a known debug string.

```
DWORD WowzerEngine::GetLoc_PCharBlock()
{
        // ripped from bwh
        DWORD x,y;
        PIMAGE_NT_HEADERS pNtHdr =
                PIMAGE_NT_HEADERS(
                pbFile + PIMAGE_DOS_HEADER(pbFile)->e_lfanew);
        PIMAGE_SECTION_HEADER pSecHdr =
                PIMAGE_SECTION_HEADER(pNtHdr + 1);
        PBYTE pbData = RvaToPointer(pbFile,
                pSecHdr[2].VirtualAddress);
        DWORD dwDataSize = pSecHdr[2].SizeOfRawData;
        PBYTE pbCode = RvaToPointer(pbFile,
                pSecHdr[0].VirtualAddress);
        DWORD dwCodeSize = pSecHdr[0].SizeOfRawData;
        PBYTE pbString = NULL;
        BYTE bCode[] = {0xBA, 0, 0, 0, 0};

        // scan for "..\Object/ObjectClient/Player_C.h" in the
        // data section
        for(x = 0; x < dwDataSize - 15; x++)
```

```
      {
        if(MemoryCompare(
              &pbData[x],
              (PBYTE)"..\\Object/ObjectClient/Player_C.h", 33))
          {
            pbString = &pbData[x];
            break;
          }
      }

    // if we didn't find it then return failure
    if(pbString == NULL)
      return NULL;

    // build code search pattern
    *((PDWORD)&bCode[1]) =
          OffsetToRva(
          pbFile,
          (DWORD)(pbString - pbFile)) +
                pNtHdr->OptionalHeader.ImageBase;

    // search for the code
    for(x = 0; x < dwCodeSize - sizeof(bCode); x++)
      {
        if(MemoryCompare(&pbCode[x], bCode, sizeof(bCode)))
          {
            // found the first code, now search for next call
            for(y = x; y < x + 20; y++)
              {
                if(pbCode[y] == 0xE8)
                {
                // found call instruction;
                // decode the instruction for the pointer
                  return OffsetToRva(
                          pbFile,
                          (DWORD)(&pbCode[y] - pbFile)) +
                                pNtHdr->OptionalHeader.ImageBase +
                                5 + *((PDWORD)&pbCode[y+1]);
                }
              }
          }
      }
    return NULL;
}
```

Locating Player Character Data

Again, another snippet of the same flavor, only this time you can locate character data.

```
DWORD WowzerEngine::GetLoc_PCharData()
{
        // ripped from bwh
        DWORD x, y;
        PIMAGE_NT_HEADERS pNtHdr =
                PIMAGE_NT_HEADERS(
                pbFile + PIMAGE_DOS_HEADER(pbFile)->e_lfanew);
        PIMAGE_SECTION_HEADER pSecHdr =
                PIMAGE_SECTION_HEADER(pNtHdr + 1);
        PBYTE pbCode = RvaToPointer(pbFile,
                pSecHdr[0].VirtualAddress);
        DWORD dwCodeSize = pSecHdr[0].SizeOfRawData;

        for(x = 0; x < dwCodeSize; x++)
          {
            // scan for mov ???, [???+D0]
            //          mov ???, [???+D4]
            if(pbCode[x] == 0x8B &&
              *((PDWORD)&pbCode[x+2]) == 0xD0 &&
              pbCode[x+6] == 0x8B &&
              *((PDWORD)&pbCode[x+8]) == 0xD4)
            {
              // found it; now search for the
              // next mov above it to get the pointer
              for(y = x-1; y > x - 20; y-)
                {
                   if(pbCode[y] == 0x8B)
                     return *((PDWORD)&pbCode[y+2]);
                   if(pbCode[y] == 0xA1)
                     return *((PDWORD)&pbCode[y+1]);
                }
            }
          }
        return NULL;
}
```

So, we have seen how to scan the game program to find all kinds of interesting data pointers and code locations. Once we have this basic technique, it would be useful to build a general tool that will scan the game program after every patch in order to update said pointers.

Building a WoW Decompiler

Many game hackers are constantly frustrated by updates and patches game companies release for their online games. Blizzard is no exception. To get around this problem, we built a general tool called the WoW Decompiler. The program is not really a decompiler at all, but rather a very useful pointer finder of sorts.

The strategy is simple: We have a copy of WoW.exe that we have already disassembled in order to find all the code and data pointers. When a new version of WoW.exe is released via a patch, we can leverage what we already know from the previous version and apply it to the new version to find all the same locations. The code to our tool follows.

```
#include "stdafx.h"
```

The program first loads WoW.exe into memory and scans it for structures that we know about. We set up global pointers for this:

```
DWORD g_binBufSize = 0;
char *g_binBuf = NULL;

bool ReadBinaryBuffer(char *filepath);
DWORD FindOffset( char *theName );

int _tmain(int argc, _TCHAR* argv[])
{
```

Our function ReadBinaryBuffer reads the WoW.exe program into memory:

```
        if(true == ReadBinaryBuffer("wow.exe"))
        {
                DWORD offset = 0;
```

Now that the program is loaded, we can scan for various named functions. We use a function called FindOffset that we built for ease of use. Our first call is to find RenderWorld—this function is called constantly during the execution of the game and makes a great hookpoint since it's on the main thread.

```
                offset = FindOffset( "RenderWorld");
                if(offset != -1)
                {
```

If we get the offset, we still must add the base address where WoW.exe is loaded in memory. Remember that we are dealing with a file on disk right now, not the loaded game. That means when the game is actually loaded, everything "starts" at 0x00400000 in memory—we just add this base address to resolve the correct actual address in memory.

```
    // add base of file in memory
    offset += 0x00400000;
    printf(
            "got offset 0x%08X for RenderWorld\n",
            offset );
}
else
{
    printf("could not find RenderWorld\n");
}
```

Next, we look for ProcessMessage, which exists in a C++ class known as NetClient. It allows us to sniff all the network traffic going through the game client:

```
offset = FindOffset( "NetClient::ProcessMessage" );
if(offset != -1)
{
    // add base of file in memory
    offset += 0x00400000;
    printf(
            "got offset 0x%08X for
NetClient::ProcessMessage\n", offset );
}
else
{
    printf("could not find ProcessMessage\n");
}
```

Now we look for ClearTarget, a function in the class known as CGGameUI. This is another great example of botting—calling this function directly from the main thread will cause the current target to be cleared. Using direct function calls like this allows us to make a bot that does not require the keystroke and mouse macros we describe earlier.

```
                 offset = FindOffset( "CGGameUI::ClearTarget" );
                 if(offset != -1)
                 {
                   // add base of file in memory
                   offset += 0x00400000;
                   printf(
                           "got offset 0x%08X for
CGGameUI::ClearTarget\n", offset );
                 }
                 else
                 {
                   printf("could not find ClearTarget\n");
                 }
```

Another big doozy of a function is `CastSpellByID`. When it is called, it allows a bot to make the character cast any spell the character is capable of casting. Again, no keystroke macros required!

```
                 offset = FindOffset( "Spell_C::CastSpellByID" );
                 if(offset != -1)
                 {
                   // add base of file in memory
                   offset += 0x00400000;
                   printf(
                           "got offset 0x%08X for
Spell_C::CastSpellByID\n", offset );
                 }
                 else
                 {
                   printf("could not find Spell_C::CastSpellByID\n");
                 }

                 if(g_binBuf) delete[] g_binBuf, g_binBuf = NULL;
        }
        return 0;
}
```

We could keep loading more functions, but for the sake of a short example, let's now explore how we perform the memory scan to find the offset.

The following code opens a handle to a file and checks it to see if it's in any of the directories in the PATH environment variable.

```
bool ReadBinaryBuffer(char *filepath)
{
      HANDLE hFile;

      hFile = CreateFile(
             filepath,
             GENERIC_READ,
             FILE_SHARE_READ | FILE_SHARE_WRITE,
             NULL,
             OPEN_EXISTING,
             FILE_ATTRIBUTE_NORMAL,
             NULL);

      if(!hFile || hFile == INVALID_HANDLE_VALUE)
        return false;

      g_binBufSize = GetFileSize(hFile, NULL);
      g_binBuf = new char[g_binBufSize];
      DWORD nBytes;
      ReadFile(
             hFile,
             g_binBuf,
             g_binBufSize,
             (LPDWORD)&nBytes,
             NULL);

      CloseHandle(hFile);

      if(nBytes != g_binBufSize)
        return false;

      return true;
}
```

What follows is a special pattern-based memory compare where a * byte is considered a wildcard.

```
bool _f_memcmp(const char *in, const char *pat, int len)
{
      for(int i = 0;i<len; i++)
      {
        if(*pat == '*')
          {
            // skip wildcards
          }
```

```
        else if( *pat != *in )
          {
            // the two don't match
            return false;
          }
        pat++;
        in++;
      }
    return true;
}
```

Next comes the ScanForBytes function that will scan the loaded binary for a given byte pattern.

```
// return -1 if scan fails to find needle, treats * as wildcard
// for now requires at least 4 bytes to search for
DWORD ScanForBytes( const char *haystack,
      DWORD haystack_size, const char *needle,
      DWORD needle_size )
{
      const char *curr = haystack;

      assert(haystack_size >= needle_size);

      while(curr <= (haystack + haystack_size))
      {
        if(*curr == *needle)
          {
            if(true == _f_memcmp(curr, needle, needle_size))
              {
                // haystack is the beginning of the buffer,
                // and curr is where string occurs
                DWORD offset = curr - haystack;
                return( offset );
              }
          }
        curr++;
      }
      return -1;
}
```

Finally, here's the function that defines the byte patterns for each of the functions we want to find:

```
DWORD FindOffset( char *theName )
{
```

Notice how we comment the disassembly for each function we are looking for. Some parts of the disassembly may change between patches (e.g., stack cookies change all the time), so these are converted into wildcards. Also, references to global memory addresses typically change, so these also need to be wildcarded.

```
    if(!strcmp(theName, "RenderWorld"))
    {
      // find RenderWorld
      /*
      .text:00479270          push    ebp
      .text:00479271          mov     ebp, esp
      .text:00479273          sub     esp, 80h
      .text:00479279          push    esi
      .text:0047927A          mov     esi, ecx
      .text:0047927C          lea     ecx, [ebp+var_40]
      .text:0047927F          mov     [ebp+var_40], 3F800000h
      .text:00479286          mov     [ebp+var_3C], 0
      .text:0047928D          mov     [ebp+var_38], 0
      .text:00479294          mov     [ebp+var_34], 0
      .text:0047929B          mov     [ebp+var_30], 0

      55 8B EC 81 EC 80 00 00-00 56 8B F1 8D 4D C0 C7 45 C0 00 00
80 3F
      */
```

We convert the above byte sequence into an array for our scan:

```
            char s[] = {
0x55,0x8B,0xEC,0x81,0xEC,0x80,0x00,0x00,0x00,0x56,0x8B,0xF1,0x8D,
0x4D,0xC0,0xC7,0x45,0xC0,0x00,0x00,0x80,0x3F };
            int offset = ScanForBytes( g_binBuf, g_binBufSize,
s, sizeof(s) );
            if(offset != -1) return offset;
    }
```

Note that we convert the global address of _aCounter to wildcards here since the global address of this variable could change between patches:

```
if(!strcmp(theName, "NetClient::ProcessMessage"))
{
/*
.text:00514630 arg_0              = dword ptr  8
.text:00514630 arg_4              = dword ptr  0Ch
.text:00514630
.text:00514630                     push    ebp
.text:00514631                     mov     ebp, esp
.text:00514633                     mov     edx, _aCounter ****
.text:00514639                     push    ebx
.text:0051463A                     mov     ebx, [ebp+arg_4]
.text:0051463D                     push    esi
.text:0051463E                     push    edi
.text:0051463F                     lea     eax, [ebp+arg_4+2]
.text:00514642                     mov     esi, ecx
.text:00514644                     inc     edx
.text:00514645                     push    eax

55 8B EC 8B 15 * * * * 53 8B 5D 0C 56 57 8D 45 0E 8B F1

*/
        char s[] = { 0x55, 0x8B, 0xEC, 0x8B, 0x15, '*', '*',
'*', '*', 0x53, 0x8B, 0x5D, 0x0C, 0x56, 0x57, 0x8D, 0x45, 0x0E,
0x8B, 0xF1 };
        int offset = ScanForBytes( g_binBuf, g_binBufSize,
s, sizeof(s) );
        if(offset != -1) return offset;
}
```

And again we convert the subroutine call to wildcards here since the subroutine in question might move between patches:

```
if(!strcmp(theName, "CGGameUI::ClearTarget"))
{
/*
.text:004884C0                     push    ebp
.text:004884C1                     mov     ebp, esp
.text:004884C3                     sub     esp, 1Ch
.text:004884C6                     push    ebx
.text:004884C7                     push    esi
.text:004884C8                     push    edi
.text:004884C9                     mov     [ebp+var_4], ecx
.text:004884CC                     call    sub_45DA90
.text:004884D1                     mov     ecx, dword_B13764
.text:004884D7                     mov     edi, eax
```

```
     55 8B EC 83 EC 1C 53 56 57 89 4D FC E8 * * * * 8B 0D * * * *
8B F8
```

```
     */
          char s[] = { 0x55, 0x8B, 0xEC, 0x83, 0xEC, 0x1C,
0x53, 0x56, 0x57, 0x89, 0x4D, 0xFC, 0xE8, '*', '*', '*', '*',
0x8B, 0x0D, '*', '*', '*', '*', 0x8B, 0xF8 };
          int offset = ScanForBytes( g_binBuf, g_binBufSize,
s, sizeof(s) );
          if(offset != -1) return offset;
     }

     if(!strcmp(theName, "Spell_C::CastSpellByID"))
     {
     /*
     .text:006B3270                    push      ebx
     .text:006B3271                    mov       ebx, esp
     .text:006B3273                    sub       esp, 8
     .text:006B3276                    and       esp, 0FFFFFFF8h
     .text:006B3279                    add       esp, 4
     .text:006B327C                    push      ebp
     .text:006B327D                    mov       ebp, [ebx+4]
     .text:006B3280                    mov       [esp+8+var_4], ebp
     .text:006B3284                    mov       ebp, esp
     .text:006B3286                    sub       esp, 28h
     .text:006B3289                    test      ecx, ecx
     .text:006B328B                    push      esi
     .text:006B328C                    push      edi
     .text:006B328D                    mov       [ebp-14h], edx
     .text:006B3290                    mov       [ebp-0Ch], ecx
```

```
     */
```

```
          char s[] = { 0x53, 0x8B, 0xDC, 0x83, 0xEC, 0x08,
0x83, 0xE4, 0xF8, 0x83, 0xC4, 0x04, 0x55, 0x8B, 0x6B, 0x04, 0x89,
0x6C, 0x24, 0x04, 0x8B, 0xEC, 0x83, 0xEC, 0x20, 0x56, 0x8B, 0xF1,
0x85, 0xF6, 0x57, 0x89, 0x55, 0xF4, 0x89, 0x75, 0xE8, 0x0F, 0x8C,
0x97, 0x04, 0x00, 0x00, 0x3B, '*', '*', '*', '*', 0x00, 0x0F,
0x8F, 0x8B, 0x04, 0x00, 0x00, 0xA1, '*', '*', '*', '*', 0x8B,
0x3C, 0xB0, 0x85 };
```

```
                int offset = ScanForBytes( g_binBuf, g_binBufSize,
    s, sizeof(s) );
                if(offset != -1) return offset;
        }

        return -1;
    }
```

What we show here is a basic starting point for building bots that don't require constant rewriting after every patch. The bot can include these scans intrinsically, or you can make this step part of the development/build process for the bot program. These decisions really depend on how you intend to use and/or distribute the bot.

Reading and Writing Process Memory

Reading computer memory is nigh on trivial. Figuring out exactly *where* in memory to look is not. The problem with modern machines is that they have huge amounts of memory. Sometimes finding what you're looking for is akin to searching for a needle in the proverbial haystack.

In many cases, you may have only one dependable known location to begin searching (such as where some basic object is always loaded). From there, you have to calculate the location of what you want to read or write dynamically.

To read and write process memory on Microsoft Windows, the preferred method is to use the following API functions:

```
ReadProcessMemory
WriteProcessMemory
```

Alternatively, some game hackers inject a DLL into the game process itself and use native pointer access to modify memory.

Getting Under the Game: Manipulating Rendering Information

As we have noted, game client software often relies on calling into functionality below it to get things done. One classic approach to game hacking is to get under the game by getting down to graphics.

All objects in the online game world must eventually be rendered. That means that the locations of all 3D-rendered objects are eventually pushed out to the video card for graphics processing.

Even if you have no clue how to obtain object location information outside of the game client, you can be sure that it will eventually end up in the video card in a standard format for rendering. Unlike video games of old, 3D games today all use industry-standard APIs for rendering. Examples of standard packages are OpenGL and Direct3D. But under these programming APIs exists yet another standard—the video hardware standard itself.

As usual, specifics may help clarify things. NVIDIA cards, a popular video card for gamers, all use a documented format for video information. That means that at some layer in the rendering chain, you can access a known format and in this way obtain the exact coordinates of objects in the field of vision.

3D = X Y Z

Anyone who has taken a computer graphics course knows that by using some simple geometry (or better yet, some linear algebra), you can determine where you stand relative to other objects. Automatically calculating how to move toward objects, how to aim at them, and how to flee from them is often valuable information indeed.

Wall Hacking

First-person shooter games were the first computer games in which simple geometric hacks were used. One great example of a hardware-level or API-level hack has come to be known as *wall hacking*. This cheat is used to this day in online FPS games. The idea is simple and elegant: Make walls transparent so that you can tell even from around the corner when someone is sneaking up on you. This allows you to play with a definite unfair advantage. (See Chapter 2.)

The server-side game program itself cannot afford to calculate when it should and should not show you an object in your field of vision. This can get complicated when objects such as walls occlude other objects such as enemies. Instead, the game server sends all of the objects down the rendering pipeline, and the video card itself computes when your vision is blocked by a wall. That means by reading the video buffer, you can tell where everything is. It's not much of a move after that to overlay the information on the screen. Or, even better, you can find the wall object in the video buffer and just change its texture identifier to "transparent"—in which case, the wall simply disappears.

Interestingly, many times the game client can't control this type of information because it has already relinquished rendering control to the video card. Naturally, the video card becomes a target.

DLL Injection

The most common method for introducing new code into an application
(including a game client) is known as DLL injection. With this method, you
force the remote process to load a new DLL of your own design. The DLL
can then take subsequent steps to hook functions or otherwise modify the
target program memory space. DLL injection is by no means the stealthiest
of approaches (in fact, it's fairly easy to spot, and a number of common
countermeasures are set up to do so), but it is very convenient. We cover
more stealthy approaches later in this chapter.

The trick with DLL injection is to make an existing thread in the target
process jump to a code snippet that calls LoadLibrary. This idea has
multiple instantiations. Some people prefer to create a new thread using
CreateRemoteThread. The technique we show you here doesn't create any
new threads—it just hijacks an existing thread for the loading operation.

First, you need to write code to the remote process that can load the
DLL. We define a short code snippet for this purpose:

```
char InjectedCodePage[4096] =
{      0xB8, 00, 00, 00, 00,
       // mov EAX,  0h | Pointer to LoadLibraryA() (DWORD)
       0xBB, 00, 00, 00, 00,
       // mov EBX,  0h | DLLName to inject (DWORD)
       0x53,                          // push EBX
       0xFF, 0xD0,                    // call EAX
       0x5b,                          // pop EBX
       0xcc                           // INT 3h
       // DLL name string will be placed here
};
int length_of_injection_code=15;
```

Our code above has some placeholders that need to be filled in: the address
of LoadLibraryA() and a pointer to the name of the DLL we wish to load.
To get the address of LoadLibrary, we simply assume it will be at the same
address in the remote process as well as our own. We have never seen a
situation where this wasn't the case, so we consider this safe:

```
FARPROC LoadLibProc = GetProcAddress(
        GetModuleHandle("KERNEL32.dll"),
        "LoadLibraryA");
```

For the DLL name, we are going to write the string to the region of memory
that directly follows the above code snippet. That is, we'll write at offset 15.
We calculate all the offsets we are going to use here:

```
char *DLLName;
DWORD *EAX, *EBX;
/////////////////////////////////////////////////////////
// pointers to be used for "stamping" values into the
// injection code (see below)
/////////////////////////////////////////////////////////
DLLName = (char*)((DWORD)InjectedCodePage
        + length_of_injection_code);
EAX = (DWORD*)( InjectedCodePage +  1);
EBX = (DWORD*) ( InjectedCodePage +  6);
```

Now we have pointers to both placeholder addresses, as well as to the spot where we are going to write the DLL name. We can't fill in the values yet because we haven't written the code to remote process memory yet. Remember, we need to use the remote address values, not the local ones!

You might notice the embedded INT3 in the code snippet. Our system is designed to be combined with a debugger. The embedded breakpoint will be used to signal that the injected code snippet has finished executing. Before we get to that, however, let's explore how we find a location to inject code into.

In the following code, we assume that we have connected a debugger and that the initial debugger breakpoint has fired. If this is an attach operation, a new thread will have been created for the initial breakpoint event. This thread will be the one we hijack to run the injected code snippet. We obtain a handle to this thread from within the debug event loop:

```
hThread = fOpenThread(
            THREAD_ALL_ACCESS,
            FALSE,
            dbg_evt.dwThreadId );
```

Don't forget to close this handle when you're done with it!

The DLL name will be a fully qualified path to the DLL we wish to inject. hProcess is the handle to the remote process we are debugging. The hModuleBase can be obtained from the debug event loop, or you can safely assume that it is 0x00400000 (as it almost always is). If you want to obtain it from the debug event loop, use the following snippet:

```
if(dbg_evt.dwDebugEventCode==CREATE_PROCESS_DEBUG_EVENT)
{
        hModuleBase = dbg_evt.u.CreateProcessInfo.lpBaseOfImage;
}
```

The next step in our injection is to locate a valid executable section of memory in the remote process. The process involves a lot of ugly pointer arithmetic to scan the remote process's PE header. First we need to find the DOS header:

```
res = ReadProcessMemory(
        hProcess,
        hModuleBase,
        &DOShdr,
        sizeof(DOShdr),
        &read);
if( (!res) || (read!=sizeof(DOShdr)) )
{
  printf("Could not get DOS header\n");
  return FALSE;
}
```

Now we double-check that the MZ characters are present. This is a magic string used with the DOS header:

```
if( DOShdr.e_magic != IMAGE_DOS_SIGNATURE ) //Check for 'MZ
{
  printf("Could not find MZ for DOS header\n");
  return FALSE;
}
```

We can now parlay the DOS header information to find the NT header information.

```
//Get NT header
res = ReadProcessMemory(
        hProcess,
        (VOID*)((DWORD)hModuleBase +
        (DWORD)DOShdr.e_lfanew),
        &NThdr,
        sizeof(NThdr),
        &read);

if( (!res) || (read!=sizeof(NThdr)) )
{
  printf("Could not get NT header\n");
  return FALSE;
}
```

Again, we check for the magic string—in this case PE:

```
//Check for 'PE\0\0
if( NThdr.Signature != IMAGE_NT_SIGNATURE )
{
  printf("Could not find PE in NT header\n");
  return 0;
}
```

We arrive here if we have a valid .exe header. We now look for a usable writable code page:

```
if( (dwD=NThdr.FileHeader.NumberOfSections) < 1 )
{
  printf("No sections to scan!\n");
  return FALSE;//Section table: (after optional header)
}

// nasty ptr arithmetic (yucky PE)
pSecHdr = (IMAGE_SECTION_HEADER*)
        (
        ((DWORD)hModuleBase + (DWORD)DOShdr.e_lfanew) +
        (DWORD)sizeof(NThdr.FileHeader) +
        (DWORD)NThdr.FileHeader.SizeOfOptionalHeader + 4
        );

res=FALSE;
dwD2 = (DWORD)GetModuleHandle(0);

for( dwD2=0 ; dwD2<dwD ; dwD2++ )
{
```

Next we iterate sections to look for a writable part of memory that is *not* .idata. We don't want to mess with .idata since it's required for the correct operation of the program:

```
    if( !ReadProcessMemory(
            hProcess,
            pSecHdr,
            &SecHdr,
            sizeof(SecHdr),
            &read) )
    {
       printf("ReadProcessMemory failed, error %08X\n",
GetLastError());
       return FALSE;
    }
```

```
      if(read != sizeof(SecHdr))
      {
        printf("section size mismatch!\n");
        return FALSE;
      }

    printf("looking at target section, %s\n", SecHdr.Name);

    //writable section? And
    //not .idata (import data)

    if(
      (SecHdr.Characteristics & IMAGE_SCN_MEM_WRITE)&&
      ( strcmpi((const char*)SecHdr.Name, ".idata")!=NULL ))
    {
      printf("FOUND useable code page: %s\n",
            SecHdr.Name );

      res = TRUE;
      break;//OK!!
    }

    pSecHdr++;
  }

  if(!res)
  {
    printf("couldn't find usable code page!\n");
    return FALSE;
  }
```

We arrive here if we found a writable code section. We are going to write our code snippet to this location after we preserve what is originally found here.

```
      gRemoteSectionPtr = (VOID*)(SecHdr.VirtualAddress +
                          (DWORD)hModuleBase);
      printf("Using section pointer 0x%08X\n", gRemoteSectionPtr);
```

Now that we know the real address in remote memory, we can go ahead and "stamp" the correct values into our placeholder addresses:

```
         strcpy( DLLName, DllName );
         *EAX = (DWORD)LoadLibProc;
         *EBX = length_of_injection_code + (DWORD)gRemoteSectionPtr;
```

Next we save the original code that is in the target memory so we can put it back when we are done:

```
         if(!ReadProcessMemory(
                 hProcess,
                 gRemoteSectionPtr,
                 gOriginalCodePage,
                 gSizeOfRemoteCodePage,
                 &read) )
         {
           printf("ReadProcessMemory failed, error %08X\n",
                  GetLastError());
           return FALSE;
         }

         if(read != gSizeOfRemoteCodePage)
         {
           printf("Could not write the correct number of bytes\n");
           return FALSE;
         }

         printf("writing new code to remote address 0x%08X\n",
                 gRemoteSectionPtr);
```

Next we write our injected code into the remote process memory:

```
         res = WriteProcessMemory(
                 hProcess,
                 gRemoteSectionPtr,
                 InjectedCodePage,
                 gSizeOfRemoteCodePage,
                 &written);

         if( (written!=0) && (written!=gSizeOfRemoteCodePage) )
         {
             printf("Error writing injection code. Remote process MAY
CRASH\n");

             // try to save face and put the old code back...
             WriteProcessMemory(
                     hProcess,
```

```
                  gRemoteSectionPtr,
                  gOriginalCodePage,
                  gSizeOfRemoteCodePage, &written);
          return FALSE;
          }

      if((!res) || (written!=gSizeOfRemoteCodePage))
          {
            printf("Error injecting code\n");
            return FALSE;
          }
```

Now comes the fun part! We have injected code into a remote memory
location, and we now hijack a remote thread (the primary thread in the
remote process) and force its execution instruction pointer (EIP) to point to
the new code location:

```
          printf("setting thread EIP to 0x%08X\n", gRemoteSectionPtr);

          Context = gRemoteThreadOriginalContext;
          Context.Eip = (DWORD)gRemoteSectionPtr;
          res = SetThreadContext(hThread, &Context);
          if(!res)
          {
            printf("Error, could not set remote thread EIP, process
MAY CRASH\n");
            return FALSE;
          }
```

The code snippet will have caused the DLL in question to load. Now what
remains is to put back the original code and restore the original thread
context. Remember that when the snippet is done, it will execute a
breakpoint instruction (INT3). Because we are attached with a debugger, we
can catch this event, put back the original code page, and restore the thread.

```
if(EXCEPTION_BREAKPOINT ==
        dbg_evt.u.Exception.ExceptionRecord.ExceptionCode)
        &&
        g_codepage_breakpoint_has_fired == FALSE )
    {
```

```
/////////////////////////////////////////////
// the breakpoint in our injected code has fired
// this means the "injected" DLL has been loaded
// and it's now time to fix the remote exe
// back to normal and let the DLL do the rest
// of the work.
/////////////////////////////////////////////
CONTEXT ctx;

ctx.ContextFlags = CONTEXT_FULL;
if(!GetThreadContext(hThread, &ctx))
{
  printf("[!] GetThreadContext failed ! \n");
  return 0;
}

printf("Hit codepage breakpoint\n");
printf("EAX: 0x%08X\n", ctx.Eax);
printf("EIP: 0x%08X\n", ctx.Eip);

g_codepage_breakpoint_has_fired = TRUE;
```

The RestoreOriginalCodePage function just puts back our saved version of what we overwrote.

```
RestoreOriginalCodePage( hTargetProc, hThread, 0);

// we are done using the debugging loop
bDoneDebugging = TRUE;
}
```

Note that after the code page is restored, we exit the debugger. If we wanted to, we could keep the debugger running and use the injected DLL in conjunction with it. There are many options at this point, and the way forward depends on what you want to do.

The RestoreOriginalCodePage function is very simple:

```
DWORD RestoreOriginalCodePage(
        HANDLE hProcess,
        HANDLE hThread,
        DWORD *outSize )
{
        BOOL res;
        DWORD written;
        CONTEXT Context;
```

```
        if(outSize) *outSize = gSizeOfRemoteCodePage;

        Context.ContextFlags = CONTEXT_FULL;
        GetThreadContext( hThread, &Context);

        printf("Restoring original code to remote section ptr
0x%08X, len %d\n",
                gRemoteSectionPtr,
                gSizeOfRemoteCodePage);

        res = WriteProcessMemory(
                hProcess,
                gRemoteSectionPtr,
                gOriginalCodePage,
                gSizeOfRemoteCodePage,
                &written );

        if(!res)
        {
          printf("WriteProcessMemory error %08X\n",
              GetLastError());
          return -1;
        }

        if(written!=gSizeOfRemoteCodePage)
        {
          return written+1;
        }

        res=SetThreadContext(
                hThread,
                (CONST CONTEXT*)&gRemoteThreadOriginalContext);
        if(!res)
        {
          printf("SetThreadContext error %08X\n", GetLastError());
          return -1;
        }

        return 0;
}
```

We've just covered a very advanced technique that allows injection and removal from a running program. This technique is still actively used in game hacking.

Pondering Attacker-in-the-Middle DLLs

A much easier way to inject a DLL is simply to replace an existing DLL that the program depends on with your Trojan'ed copy. Your replacement DLL must either forward function calls to the original DLL (the easiest way to mimic functionality) or replicate the functionality of the DLL itself. This can be cumbersome if the DLL supports a lot of functions. This is particularly problematic if the DLL is updated on a regular basis during patching. Overall, the Trojan replacement technique is no longer in wide use. Historically, this technique was used to hook into the rendering chain with OpenGL for wall-hacking cheats in FPS games. One good example is the wall hack associated with Call of Duty 2.

Calling conventions are very important when creating a replacement DLL. You must adhere to the exact function arguments, types, and calling conventions when exporting your attacker-in-the-middle functions. If you don't, the linker will not be able to resolve the call and the DLL will not load. Subsequently, the game program will throw up an error dialog stating it could not find a required DLL.

Some programs may check the version of the DLL before use. A DLL contains housekeeping data in the form of strings, including the name of the manufacturer, the version number, and a human-readable name for the DLL. With the right tool, you can modify all of these strings. A number of PE editing utilities available for free on the Net will do this for you.

Direct3D, DirectX Specifics

Getting back to the graphics story, a common method for intercepting Direct3D or OpenGL rendering data is to replace the original DLL installed by the game with a Trojan version that interposes in an attacker-in-the-middle sense. A Trojan DLL is usually set up to pass through all system calls, keeping an eye on things as they go by and changing things when it's convenient. By interposing between the game client and the video system, a Trojan DLL can hijack, intercept, and alter any rendering function call.

As an example, a wall hack may selectively alter the rendering setting for certain objects, making them show through walls. Or maybe it will alter colors, making enemies appear to be fluorescent orange.

Hiding Injected DLLs

Injected DLLs are very popular, so some games have started scanning for injected DLLs. A DLL can be loaded and removed from the loaded modules list, however, and will escape detection as a loaded DLL. That doesn't mean the DLL's memory is safe, however.

To remove a DLL from the loaded module list, you can adapt a solution based on the NtIllusion rootkit available for download at <http://www.rootkit.com>. What follows is a short description of how NtIllusion removes DLLs from the linked list of loaded modules.

Three different doubly linked lists are referenced from the PEB. We saw earlier how to get the PEB pointer in a remote process. Remember that now we are within an injected DLL, so we don't have the overhead of using remote process calls. Instead, we can just reference the memory directly since it's local (this makes things a bit easier, eh?).

The following call is intended to be called with the list identifier that should be examined for the DLL in question. To be complete, you would want to call this function three times, once for each list: LOAD_ORDER_TYPE, MEM_ORDER_TYPE, and INIT_ORDER_TYPE. All three lists are identical in regards to parsing and removing the DLL entry.

```
#define LOWCASE(a) ((a>='A' && a<='Z')?a-('Z'-'z'):a)
#define LOAD_ORDER_TYPE 0
#define MEM_ORDER_TYPE  1
#define INIT_ORDER_TYPE 2

int WalkModuleList(char ModuleListType, char *szDllToStrip)
{
        PLIST_ENTRY pUserModuleListHead, pUserModuleListPtr;
        PLIST_ENTRY *pHiddenModuleListPtr;

        int i;
        DWORD PebBaseAddr, dwOffset=0;
        DWORD ImageBase, ImageSize;
        PPEB_LDR_DATA pLdrData;
        PUNICODE_STRING pImageName;
        char szImageName[BUFMAXLEN]; // Non-unicode string
```

The following call gets the PEB pointer for local memory; see below for this function.

```
        PebBaseAddr = GetPEB(0);
        if(PebBaseAddr == FUNC_ERROR)
          return 0;
```

```
// PEB.ProcessModuleInfo = PEB + 0x0C
pLdrData = (PPEB_LDR_DATA)(DWORD *)(*(DWORD *)
        (PebBaseAddr + PEB_LDR_DATA_OFFSET));
if(!pLdrData->Initialized)
  return 0;

// Init chained list head and offset
if(ModuleListType == LOAD_ORDER_TYPE)
{
  // LOAD_ORDER_TYPE
  pUserModuleListHead =
  pUserModuleListPtr =
  (PLIST_ENTRY)(&(pLdrData->ModuleListLoadOrder));
  pHiddenModuleListPtr = &pUserModuleListLoadOrder;
  dwOffset = 0x0;
} else if(ModuleListType == MEM_ORDER_TYPE)
{
  // MEM_ORDER_TYPE
  pUserModuleListHead =
  pUserModuleListPtr =
  (PLIST_ENTRY)(&(pLdrData->ModuleListMemoryOrder));
  pHiddenModuleListPtr = &pUserModuleListMemoryOrder;
  dwOffset = 0x08;
} else if(ModuleListType == INIT_ORDER_TYPE)
{
  // INIT_ORDER_TYPE
  pUserModuleListHead =
  pUserModuleListPtr =
  (PLIST_ENTRY)(&(pLdrData->ModuleListInitOrder));
  pHiddenModuleListPtr = &pUserModuleListInitOrder;
  dwOffset = 0x10;
}
else return 0;

do
{
  // Jump to next MODULE_ITEM structure
  pUserModuleListPtr = pUserModuleListPtr->Flink;
  pImageName = (PUNICODE_STRING)(
              ((DWORD)(pUserModuleListPtr)) +
              (LDR_DATA_PATHFILENAME_OFFSET-dwOffset));

  ImageBase = *(DWORD *)(((DWORD)
              (pUserModuleListPtr)) +
              (LDR_DATA_IMAGE_BASE-dwOffset));
```

```
ImageSize = *(DWORD *)(((DWORD)(pUserModuleListPtr)) +
        (LDR_DATA_IMAGE_SIZE-dwOffset));

//Convert string from unicode and to lower case
for(i=0; i < (pImageName->Length)/2 && i<BUFMAXLEN;i++)
  szImageName[i] =
        LOWCASE(*( (pImageName->Buffer)+(i) ));
  szImageName[i] = '\0';

  if( strstr((char*)szImageName, szDllToStrip) != 0 )
  {
```

If there is a filename match, we now hide the DLL. We remove the entry from the doubly linked list.

```
(pUserModuleListPtr->Blink)->Flink =
        (pUserModuleListPtr->Flink);

(pUserModuleListPtr->Flink)->Blink =
        (pUserModuleListPtr->Blink);

  whImageBase = ImageBase;
  whImageSize = ImageSize;

  *pHiddenModuleListPtr = pUserModuleListPtr;
  }
}
while(pUserModuleListPtr->Flink != pUserModuleListHead);

  return 1;
}
```

At this point, if the DLL was found, it will have been stripped from the linked list. This doesn't affect the DLL's ability to work, and it prevents the DLL from showing up in the loaded modules list for the process. Remember, however, that the memory pages allocated for the DLL can still be read and accessed by any countermeasures.

Getting the PEB is straightforward when you're in local memory:

```
DWORD dwPebBase
__asm
{
    push eax
    mov eax, FS:[0x30]
```

```
        mov [dwPebBase], eax
        pop eax
}
```

As we can see, the PEB is referenced at offset 0x30 from the FS register.

Standing Way Outside the Game: Manipulating Network Packets

So far we've discussed ideas that get either above, under, or inside the game client. Another perfectly valid strategy is to focus on the network itself. Obviously, any client-side state must eventually be squirted back over the network if it is going to get to the game server and make any long-term difference. This fact has prompted many game hackers to focus entirely on the network.

There is one major advantage to focusing on the network—network packets are a single point of data interception where all kinds of great data go by. There is no messy process space chock full of data that move around, messing with debuggers by setting breakpoints, disassembling binary into assembly language arcana, and so on.

Encryption on the Wire

Game manufacturers are not idiots, of course. Many of them understand the risk of network-based interception techniques and have begun to combat them with cryptography. That is, they encrypt all traffic to and from the server so that it's all scrambled up when it goes by.

The upshot of this is that intercepting packets, either simply just sniffing them or altering them, requires cracking any encryption scheme being used. There's a problem in crypto land, though—because of the way the communication works, the endpoints need to know about what kind of cryptography is being used as well as secrets like crypto keys. In other words, the game client itself must know how to decrypt said traffic! So reverse engineering the game client should reveal the correct algorithms that an attacker can reproduce in a crypto-savvy sniffer.

Figure 6–13 shows an example of a decryption routine used for WoW packets.

```
BYTE *DecryptPacket(BYTE *Packet, WORD PacketLen, bool type)
{
    int i = 0, cryptedBytes;
    BYTE curKey, tmp, index, lastByte;
    WoWKeyIndex *KeyIndex;

    if(!(IsBadWritePtr(CryptInfo, █████) && CryptInfo->IsCrypted)
    {

        if(type == SENT_PACKET)
        {
            KeyIndex     = &(CryptInfo->SendKey);
            cryptedBytes = █

            //Received packets don't need the key state returned because they haven't been touched by
            for(i = cryptedBytes; i != 0; i--)      //Return our key index to the state it was in when
            {
                KeyIndex->Index--;
                if(KeyIndex->Index == ████        //-1, BYTES are unsigned..
                    KeyIndex->Index = (CryptInfo->KeyLen - 1);
            }

            KeyIndex->LastByte = htons(PacketLen) & ████████  //the length field is stored in network byte
            KeyIndex->LastByte = (KeyIndex->LastByte ^ *(CryptInfo->Key + KeyIndex->Index));
            KeyIndex->LastByte = *Packet - KeyIndex->LastByte;
            lastByte = KeyIndex->LastByte;
            index = KeyIndex->Index;

        }
        else
        {
            cryptedBytes = █
            KeyIndex     = &(CryptInfo->RecvKey);

            index    = KeyIndex->Index;
            lastByte = KeyIndex->LastByte;
        }


        for(i = 0; i < cryptedBytes; i++)
        {
            curKey   = *(CryptInfo->Key + index);
            index++;
            index = index % CryptInfo->KeyLen;

            tmp              = *(Packet + i);
            *(Packet + i)    = (*(Packet + i) - lastByte) ^ curKey;
```

Figure 6–13 This code is cut from a network sniffer hack that uses the packet decryption routine as revealed by the game client. This decryption routine was intended to reveal the contents of WoW packets.

The Ultimate in Stealth: Taking Client Manipulation to the Kernel

Throughout this chapter, we introduce many techniques for manipulating game clients: scanning memory, using breakpoints, hooking, and injecting code. All of these manipulations expose our hacking to potential detection by the game client itself. But there remains one weakness in game countermeasures. Games, for the most part, do not include kernel-level components.

We alluded earlier to the idea that rootkits can be used to hide game hacking programs—but what if we could make the entire bot a kernel-mode entity?

First, since our mythical ultra bot lives in the kernel, it's not exposed as process memory. The game would need to scan the kernel in order to even detect the bot. This is not allowed, however. In fact, the game would need special access privileges to do this. Second, being in the kernel allows the bot to manipulate what the game is allowed to see when it scans for bots. In effect, the bot is also intrinsically a rootkit.

Does this idea sound too good to be true? Well, it does have some major challenges.

1. Kernel-mode software is different.
2. Some games use kernel-mode protection too, including nProtect and PunkBuster.

For the most part, challenge 1 is just a misconception. People who have never written a driver and are unfamiliar with Windows OS internals are naturally reluctant to try botting from the kernel. However, it turns out that the programming in the kernel is not as hard as you might think. It just takes some OS knowledge that many application programmers simply don't have out of the box.

Challenge 2 is a bigger issue. Game protection companies are starting to use rootkit-like techniques themselves to protect their games. If you release your kernel-mode bot to the public, chances are that the kernel-mode protections are going to find it. If you build a private bot, you might still be detected by generic scanning technologies (such as detecting hooks in the IDT or SSDT). But even worse, putting protections in the kernel introduces interoperability problems. For example, putting a bot in the kernel with protection will certainly cause instability and possibly blue-screen the computer.

Of our two major issues, challenge 2 is definitely the bigger problem. However, for games like WoW, kernel-mode protections are not being used. Furthermore, you can always design specific bypasses for any protection technology being used in any game you target. Above all else, having kernel-level options only expands your capabilities.

Memory Cloaking

One kernel-level technique is known as memory cloaking. The OS runs in virtual memory mode, meaning that addresses in one process space are translated separately from addresses in another. The upshot is that two distinct processes can both have memory at address 0x00400000, but the data stored at this address are completely different between the two processes. In other words, the address isn't a real address in physical memory; instead, it's being mapped on a process-by-process basis.

We discuss some nitty-gritty details about this in Chapter 7, but suffice it to say for now that these virtual addresses are translated into actual physical addresses by an operating system component known as the page table. If you manipulate the page tables for a process, you can alter what memory is visible and even remap memory to point somewhere else.

In Figure 6–14, an injected page of code is actually present at the location being viewed. But when the debugger attempts to read this memory, a fake page of data full of the character A is displayed instead. The kernel

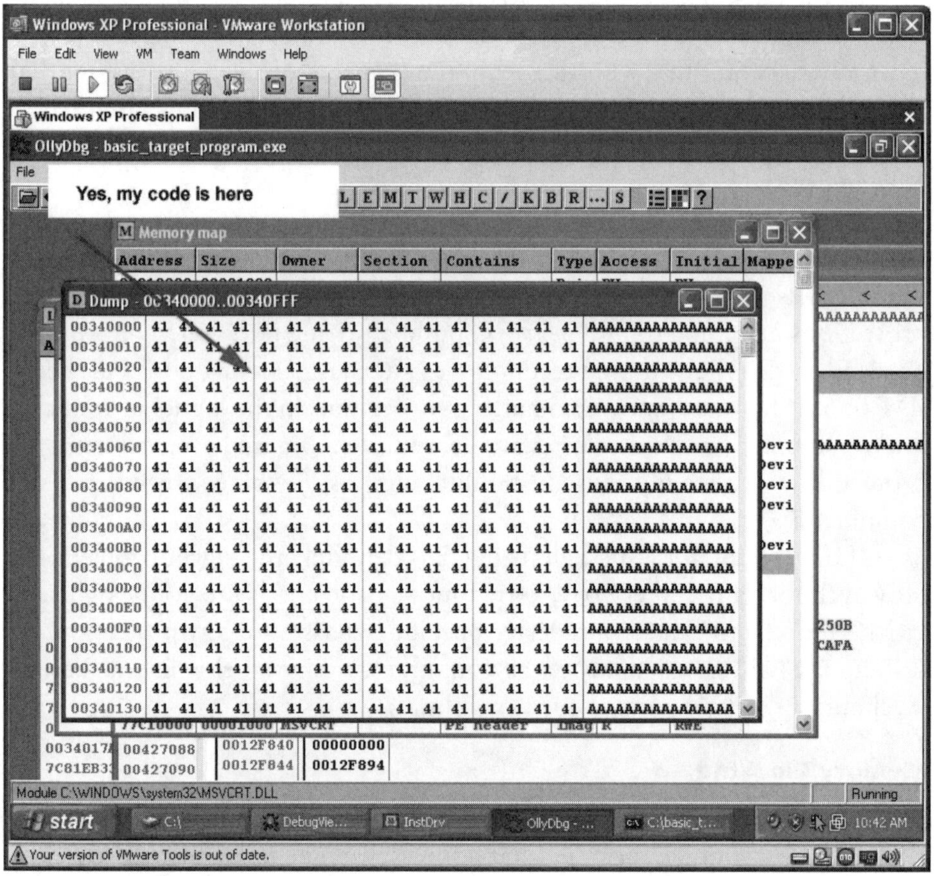

Figure 6–14 Memory cloaking hides the real contents of memory from other processes. Here, memory cloaking is being used to hide the code that is actually in the memory and display a bunch of "A"s instead.

driver is swapping memory translations by manipulating the page tables. This is a very powerful way to hide.

We briefly cover some related kernel-mode techniques, including interrupt hooking, in Chapter 7.

Clients Make Great Targets

This chapter is at its heart a laundry list of techniques that are useful for taking apart and understanding game clients. We show you how to get in, over, under, and way outside clients using common techniques from code analysis. We even hint at kernel-mode techniques.

One of the ultimate tools for client-side game hacking is the bot, and a key component for building a bot is the debugger. Presenting a debugger is a great way to unify our foray into client-side hacking, which we do in the next chapter.

7 Building a Bot

In Chapter 6, we introduce a number of techniques for taking apart and understanding game clients. Each such technique is interesting in its own right, from interposing between the game software and the video rendering system, through injecting new memory values and DLLs, all the way to monitoring and adjusting game-related network traffic. However, a collection of techniques like those described in Chapter 6 is always most powerfully applied in concert. Now that you are armed with a quiver of game manipulation techniques, let's put them all together into a coherent package. To do this, we will build a *bot*.

The bot is one of the ultimate client-side game hacking tools. Bots can use a variety of methods. In fact, ultimately, a bot is simply a layer of intelligence and coherence on top of all the tricks we introduce in Chapter 6. While the ideas of getting in, over, under, and outside a game client are all independent of the particular game being hacked, writing a bot requires much more game-specific information. For example, your character's health status is likely to be stored differently for different games. Likewise, any series of actions you wish your character to take, and the order you take them in, also depends directly on game particularities.

Bots need to know how game logic works, what weapons your character is equipped with, what class your character is, and what skills, spells, and capabilities are available, among other things. For that reason, this chapter may be the most WoW-specific of the book. We don't mean to pick on WoW, but we do want to be as clear as possible about how real game hacks actually work. If you want to build a bot, you must gather these specifics.

Real-world bots come in many flavors, ranging from aimbots for FPS games such as Unreal (e.g., ZelliusBot) to away-from-keyboard (AFK) combat bots for games such as WoW (e.g., WoWGlider, WoWSharp). In almost all cases, bots are explicitly disallowed on game servers. In fact, depending on the game, using one might even get you banned. Blizzard Entertainment, to name just one game company, is notorious for banning people who use bots. You could very well lose all the time you have invested in a game character if you get caught using a bot approach like the one we reveal in this chapter. Use these ideas at your own risk, and don't come whining to us!

This chapter is filled with material to help you understand how bots automatically play a game. In Bot Design Fundamentals, we cover the notion of state and event-driven programming. Using this paradigm, we show how a bot can automatically move a character, locate a mob, cause the character to fight the mob, pick up the loot once a fight is over, and manage agro.[1] In the Bot as Debugger section, we cover the basics of debuggers, describing the basic debugging loop; covering some arcana on process killing and debugger privileges; describing how to set, use, and clear breakpoints; and introducing the idea of sampling and siphoning important data from a running program. We also show in some detail a real example in the form of the Wowzer Botting Engine, a platform for developing multiple bots. Finally, in the Advanced Bot Topics section, we cover three of many active research areas in botting: undetectable kernel-mode bots, pure macro bots, and bot user interfaces.

Bot Design Fundamentals

Let's start with the fundamentals, building on the tools and techniques from Chapter 6 to ease our way into bot design. Be forewarned, however—bot building is a complicated undertaking. There's no avoiding technical issues here, so fasten your seat belt!

---

1. Agro is short for aggression. The basic idea is to monitor character activities closely so that you can avoid having to fight too many monsters at once.

Event-Driven Design

The first key concept in bot design involves a familiar (and basic) design pattern—the event control loop. Take another look at the very simple agro farming bot we introduced in Chapter 2. The basic structure is apparent— the program loops around waiting for something to happen and then reacts accordingly. Every bot program waits for events to occur (possibly in the game client, maybe on the network, perhaps at some specific memory location) and then does something as a reaction. This is called an event-driven design.

State Machines

We talk about the concept of state elsewhere in the book, but it's worth pointing out that a bot program not only keeps an eye on game state to track what's going on but also has plenty of state of its own. The bot's main mission is to keep track of a particular point of view in the game; that is, it needs to track game state according to some character's perception. As we note earlier, it also needs to know some basics about the state of the character—things like health status, position, and so on. Perhaps the bot monitors client health by scraping pixels off the screen like the bot in Chapter 2 did. Or maybe it looks around to make sure it's not being monitored by game minders before doing its dirty work. Whatever it does, the bot requires a state machine model of the world it is interacting with.

Most bots are designed as state machines. The bot controls a character and that character is in some state, such as "running," "sitting," "casting," "healing," and so on. The bot has rules for transitioning between states. For example, a *transition rule* used in the "fighting" state might be "If my health status is less than 25% of normal, enter state 'running away for dear life.'" Each state has its own set of transition rules and can respond to events and status in the game by selecting and executing these rules. Those readers familiar with basic AI will recognize this as a kind of production system. Obviously, for this system to work, the tricks introduced in Chapter 6 should be pressed into service to read things like character health, spell-casting capability (often called mana), target position, target location, and so on. In addition, actions taken while the bot-controlled character is in a given state need to be executed using the tricks from Chapter 6 that allow the character to do things such as move, attack, cast certain spells, and so on.

Figure 7–1 shows a portion of an example bot's state machine. This
state machine controls AFK combat in WoW. As the diagram shows, the bot
begins by reading several structures from the game client's memory. The
initialization of the player character (PC) structure pointer and calculation
of the mob list happens to be performed via sampling breakpoints (see
Chapter 6). Then, character health is calculated as a percentage of total, and
this determines whether a fight should continue. WoW has an odd quirk—
having one hitpoint (a very low health status value indeed) puts the
character into "ethereal spirit form." In this state, a character can travel
back to its body for resurrection (an activity necessary to resume play after
being killed and having your "soul" transported to a central location).

Deeper into our bot's state machine is more logic for finding and killing
mobs. As you can see in Figure 7–2, if a target mob is detected and the

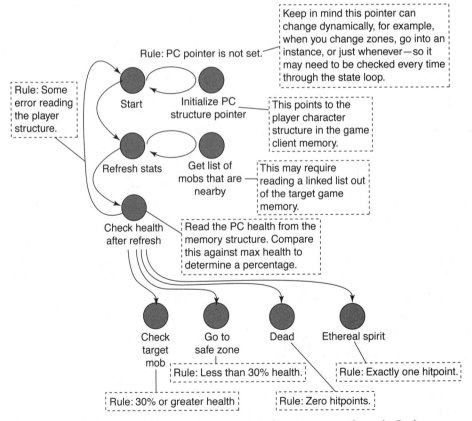

Figure 7–1 A bot state machine can be represented as a connected graph. Each grey
circle is a state, and the arrows show possible state transitions.

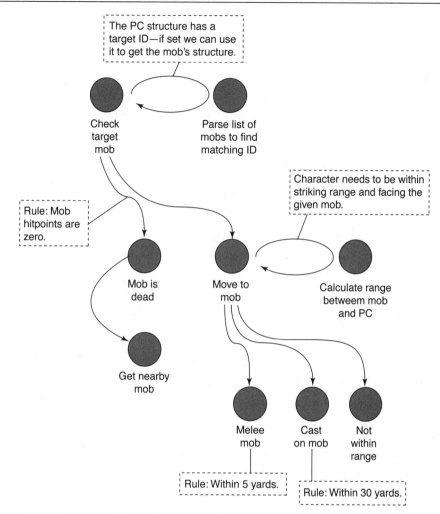

Figure 7–2 A state machine representing closing the range to a target mob.

character has enough health to keep fighting, the bot will attempt to close the distance between the PC and the mob. You could employ several strategies here, such as always maintaining a distance short enough to cast spells but too long for hand-to-hand combat (another example of game specifics). One clever WoW-specific hack known as Z-hacking implements this idea by floating the character far above the heads of mobs so the PC can't be attacked. This hack involves directly changing the z-coordinate corresponding to the PC position.

In Figure 7–2, the bot closes the range between the PC and the mob, then casts spells if within 30 yards and uses melee (hand-to-hand combat) if within 5 yards. If the PC is too far away from the target for either of these, the bot moves the PC toward the mob. In many games, once a target mob has been attacked, it will come to the PC—you don't need to alter position to continue fighting (highly convenient). Of course, if there is no target mob identified, the bot needs to hunt around and find one.

Moving the Player Character

As we said, if the PC is not within range of a mob, it will need to be moved. Movement can be handled in several ways:

- By posting keystrokes that cause movement
- By hijacking the main thread and calling an internal movement function
- By injecting network packets that indicate movement to the server
- By simply setting the PC's coordinates directly in memory (a feat that is sometimes called *telehacking* depending on the distance involved)

The last one is the most straightforward method. If the PC location coordinates set in this manner aren't very far from the current location, this kind of action can even appear to be normal movement.

Telehacking uses the direct PC location setting method, but it usually refers to teleporting over vast regions of the game map, as opposed to small teleports to correct for position within a few virtual yards.

Let's make this concrete. The following code snippet checks range to a mob and presses a key to force movement for a given time period.

First, we refresh the mob structure. This reads a fresh copy of the mob's data from the game client memory.

```
assert(m_target_mob);
m_target_mob->Refresh();
```

We call `SetSelfToFace()` to set the direction of the PC to point directly at the mob. (More detail about this is provided in the Calculating Direction subsection.)

```
SetSelfToFace(m_target_mob->m_x,
              m_target_mob->m_y,
              m_target_mob->m_z);
```

We calculate range between the PC and the target mob. (See the next subsection for a detailed description of this calculation.)

```
float range = CalculateRangeFromSelf(
                 m_target_mob->m_x,
                 m_target_mob->m_y,
                 m_target_mob->m_z);

logprintf("mob range is %f units from self", range);
```

Finally, we press the up arrow key for a calculated time, based on distance. The PostKeystroke() method is defined in Chapter 6 if you need to refresh your memory.

```
// calc time for key press based on distance
// ---------------------------------------------
// try to move the PC only close enough to begin
// ranged attacks

// TODO: make the calculation account for user-supplied
// min range value
DWORD time_to_press = range * 50; //TODO, make configurable

PostKeystroke(VK_UP, time_to_press);
```

Calculating Distance

The range between the PC and the target mob is obviously very important. It not only controls transition rules in our state charts from Figures 7–1 and 7–2 but also allows us to calculate how long to hold down a movement key. We can calculate range by using the x-, y-, and z-coordinates of the two objects involved.

The following function calculates the distance between the player character and a target coordinate:

```
float CalculateRangeFromSelf(float mobX, float mobY, float mobZ)
{
```

The aCharacterMob object represents the PC's data structure. The term *mob* may seem to be overloaded in this case, but technically speaking, the PC is a "mobile" just like all of the other ones!

```
Mob *aCharacterMob = GetSelfMob();
if(!aCharacterMob)
{
    logprintf("warning, could not get self mob");
    return 0;
}
```

The Refresh() call here causes the bot program to read a fresh copy of the PC data structure's values into local memory. This updates the information with accurate xyz positioning data needed for the calculation.

```
aCharacterMob->Refresh();
```

The calculation returns a float as the distance. The sqrt() function calculates square root, and pow() raises the number by the specified power. If you remember your Cartesian geometry from seventh grade, you'll recognize this calculation.

```
//calculate range
float range = sqrt( (float)(
        pow(aCharacterMob->m_x - mobX, 2)
        +
        pow(aCharacterMob->m_y - mobY, 2)
        +
        pow(aCharacterMob->m_z - mobZ, 2)
));

        return range;
}
```

Calculating Direction

In many games, in order to attack something, the PC needs to be facing the target. In WoW, the direction an object is facing is stored within the in-memory data structure. By accessing this value, we can read (and even write) the current direction. Similar to the way the telehacking trick sets x-, y-, and z-coordinates, direction can simply be overwritten in memory and the character's direction will instantly update on screen. (See Chapter 6 for more detail on the necessary techniques.)

The following code calculates the required direction and also overwrites the stored PC direction.

```
void SetSelfToFace( float mobX, float mobY, float mobZ )
{
```

This call gets a pointer to the PC structure.

```
Mob *aMob = GetSelfMob();
if(!aMob)
{
```

```
        logprintf("warning, could not get self mob");
        return;
}
```

The information in the local representation of the PC structure is updated.
This technique reads the data from the WoW.exe memory space and copies it
locally.

```
        aMob->Refresh();
```

We now get the current x/y position of the character and calculate the
direction required to face the point indicated by mobX and mobY. This
function is basically used to turn the character to face a target given by
the coordinates.

```
        float g = 0;
        float RealX = aMob->m_x - mobX;
        float RealY = aMob->m_y - mobY;

        if(RealX < 0)
        {
           RealX = RealX * -1;
        }
        if(RealY < 0)
        {
           RealY = RealY * -1;
        }
```

The next part of the calculation uses the RTOD macro, which converts
radians to degrees and is defined as:

```
#define M_PI 3.14159265358979
#define RTOD(r) ((r) * 180 / M_PI)
```

The value g is in degrees and indicates the direction we want the PC to face.
Trigonometry is handy here.

```
        if((mobX > aMob->m_x) && (mobY > aMob->m_y))
        {
           g = RTOD( atan(RealY/RealX) );
        }
        if((mobX > aMob->m_x) && (mobY < aMob->m_y))
        {
           g = (( RTOD(atan( RealY / RealX )) * -1 ) + 90) + 270;
```

```
     }
     if((mobX < aMob->m_x) && (mobY < aMob->m_y))
     {
       g = RTOD(atan( RealY/RealX )) + 180;
     }
     if((mobX < aMob->m_x) && (mobY > aMob->m_y))
     {
       g = (( RTOD(atan( RealY/RealX )) * -1 ) + 90) + 90;
     }
```

Next, we convert the degrees back to radians and set the PC direction value.

```
     float to_rotate = ((2*3.14159265358979)/360)*g;

     //logprintf("to_rotate: %f\n", to_rotate);

     SetSelfRotation(to_rotate);
}

void SetSelfRotation(float to_face)
{
     Mob *aMob = GetSelfMob();
     if(aMob)
     {
       aMob->SetFacing(to_face);
     }
     else
     {
       logprintf("warning, could not get self mob");
     }
}
```

Finally, here is a small routine that overwrites the in-memory direction value (called to_face in the code). This is a member function in our Mob class:

```
void Mob::SetFacing(float to_face)
{
     SIZE_T bread;
```

Remember here that m_baseaddress is the address of the character structure in the WoW.exe memory space. The PC_FACING_OFFSET is the offset in that structure where the direction is stored. This is a 32-bit value that is treated as a float.

```
//TODO read from config file
if(WriteProcessMemory( m_parent_engine->m_prochandle,
        (void *)(m_baseaddress + PC_FACING_OFFSET),
        &to_face,
        4,
        &bread) == FALSE)
{
  logprintf("error writing to facing");
  return;
}
}
```

This illustrates one of the basic movement operations. It's very important to be able to set the direction of the character and also potentially the camera. Calculations like this can be extended, for example, to teleport the character to a location behind an adversary in player versus player (PvP) combat and subsequently rotate to face the target's back. Since PvP combat is significantly affected by the direction of facing, in theory you can develop a PvP assist macro that puts you behind your target and facing for a swing with one simple key press. Definitely cheating.

Telehacking

While it is possible to calculate a direction to move and manually press the movement keys as we demonstrate earlier, the WoW.exe architecture, and many similar games, simply trust the position values the client reports. They don't evaluate whether a move is physically possible or even plausible. In other words, the server does not attempt to verify whether the PC actually used movement keys to move. Thus, once you set a new position in the PC structure, it will be used.

As we note earlier, this technique is sometimes called telehacking because in effect you teleport the PC directly and instantaneously to a new position. So, when ambling over to the target mob or opponent isn't your style, you can simply teleport directly to the target or, better yet, a short distance away to prepare for battle. There are lots of possibilities. If combat isn't the goal, you can use telehacking to teleport through walls, get into areas you're not supposed to be in, or simply teleport to every treasure location and loot it before you get noticed.

The following code overwrites the xyz position of the character in memory and in this way telehacks the character to the target location.

```
void Mob::SetXYZ(float x, float y, float z)
{
        SetX(x);
        SetY(y);
        SetZ(z);
}
```

Pretty darn easy. And, again, we use the member functions in our Mob class for overwriting remote memory.

```
void  Mob::SetX(float x)
{
        SIZE_T bread;

        // Write new X
        if(WriteProcessMemory( m_parent_engine->m_prochandle,
               (void *)(m_baseaddress + PC_X_OFFSET),
               &x,
               4,
               &bread) == FALSE)
        {
          logprintf("error writing to X");
          return;
        }
```

The following section of code is commented out in the bot we're using as a pattern, but the developers of the bot found that there is a backup location where position is stored. This could be trouble if some kind of verification were being calculated. Ultimately resetting the backup value didn't seem to matter, but the code is here for completeness.

```
#if 0
        // Write new X to backup
        if(WriteProcessMemory( m_parent_engine->m_prochandle,
               (void *)(m_baseaddress + PC_BK_X_OFFSET),
               &x,
               4,
               &bread) == FALSE)
        {
```

```
            logprintf("error writing to backup X");
            return;
        }
#endif

}
```

And, again, we use the member functions in our Mob class for overwriting remote memory.

```
void  Mob::SetY(float y)
{
        SIZE_T bread;

        // Write new Y
        if(WriteProcessMemory( m_parent_engine->m_prochandle,
                (void *)(m_baseaddress + PC_Y_OFFSET),
                &y,
                4,
                &bread) == FALSE)
        {
          logprintf("error writing to Y");
          return;
        }
```

And the backup memory too (just in case).

```
#if 0
        // Write new Y to backup
        if(WriteProcessMemory( m_parent_engine->m_prochandle,
                (void *)(m_baseaddress + PC_BK_Y_OFFSET),
                &y,
                4,
                &bread) == FALSE)
        {
          logprintf("error writing to backup Y");
          return;
        }
#endif
}

void  Mob::SetZ(float z)
{
        SIZE_T bread;
```

```
      // Write new Z
      if(WriteProcessMemory( m_parent_engine->m_prochandle,
            (void *)(m_baseaddress + PC_Z_OFFSET),
            &z,
            4,
            &bread) == FALSE)
      {
        logprintf("error writing to z");
        return;
      }

#if 0
      // Write new Z to backup
      if(WriteProcessMemory( m_parent_engine->m_prochandle,
            (void *)(m_baseaddress + PC_BK_Z_OFFSET),
            &z,
            4,
            &bread) == FALSE)
      {
        logprintf("error writing to backup Z");
        return;
      }
#endif
}
```

Telehacking is a powerful technique you can use in many ways (for one specific example, see the next subsection about ping-ponging). An interesting way to use this concept is to *telestick* onto a target. Telesticking keeps the PC stuck at a precise location with respect to a target mob. This is especially useful in PvP combat situations because you can telestick yourself *behind and facing* your enemy. As is apparent, in WoW, position is critically important during combat. As long as the PC is behind its target, the target can't hit the PC. This works wonders against enemy players who use excessive jumping/strafing as a way to keep your PC from being able to hit them. In WoW, you can render melee classes like warriors almost ineffective when they're using the jumping/strafing combat technique. By using an auto-telestick bot, you can regain the advantage in PvP combat.

Ping-Ponging

For PC types that have a ranged attack (recall that there are different classes of characters, each with its own characteristics), the technique called ping-ponging lets you maintain a consistent distance from a mob while you pound it with attacks. The mob will run to close its distance to the PC, but before it gets there, the PC telehacks to a new location just far enough away to allow another ranged attack before the mob can reach the character again. Ping-ponging relies on telehacking to do most of the heavy lifting.

Making a Player Character Fight

Once the PC is in range of a target, you might use your bot to cause the PC to carry out various actions, such as fighting or using spells. This section of code, cut from a prototype bot, attempts to drive a character through a series of actions for combat.

We first refresh the target's information.

```
assert(m_target_mob);
m_target_mob->Refresh();
bool slapin_extra_range_attack = FALSE;
```

Then we check to see whether we want to melee (close combat) or use ranged attacks (such as magic spells). We use that decision to determine whether telesticking on the target is the desired configuration.

```
if( (FALSE==m_melee_class) && (TRUE==m_telestick) )
{
```

When using a ranged attack, we can ping-pong back and forth between two locations, keeping the mob in constant movement. This prevents the mob from being able to land any blows while the ranged attack does its work.

```
if( m_pingpong_target &&
        (m_pingpong_target == m_target_mob->m_id))
{
  if(m_pingyes)
  {
    //goto pong
    Mob *aSelfMob = GetSelfMob();
    aSelfMob->SetXYZ( m_pong_x, m_pong_y, m_pong_z );
    m_pingyes = FALSE;
    slapin_extra_range_attack = TRUE;
  }
  else
  {
    //goto ping
    Mob *aSelfMob = GetSelfMob();
```

```
            aSelfMob->SetXYZ( m_ping_x, m_ping_y, m_ping_z );
            m_pingyes = TRUE;
            slapin_extra_range_attack = TRUE;
        }
    }
}
```

Once we are in the new location, we need to face the target.

```
SetSelfToFace( m_target_mob->m_x,
               m_target_mob->m_y,
               m_target_mob->m_z);
```

Just setting the position and direction is not enough. We actually have to move a small bit for the location to update to the server properly. The new position information we set isn't used until an actual movement message is posted. We can easily accomplish this with a keystroke.

```
// back up a tap
PostKeystroke(VK_DOWN, 120);

float range = CalculateRangeFromSelf(
               m_target_mob->m_x,
               m_target_mob->m_y,
               m_target_mob->m_z);

logprintf("mob range is %f units from self", range);
```

When we telestick, sometimes we end up too close and the mob ends up behind us. This is bad because now we aren't facing the right direction, and our swings won't take. In this precarious situation, this little bit of code ensures we are back slightly from the mob.

```
// this tick back is needed so we don't move past the target
if( abs(range) < 3.2)
{
        PostKeystroke(VK_DOWN, 120); //TODO, make configurable?
}
```

If ping-ponging, we should fire off a ranged attack, accomplished by sending a hotkey press previously configured in the game's UI.

```
if(slapin_extra_range_attack)
```

```
{
      PostKeystroke(0x32, 120);
      PostPause(m_cast_time);
}
else
{
```

We ensure we're in attack mode here—a state that can be toggled on and off. Sometimes attack mode will already be on; other times it will be off and need to be turned on. The inAttackMode variable tracks state.

```
      // the melee attack is a toggle,
      // so don't apply it unless it's not already on
      if(FALSE == inAttackMode)
      {
        //perform melee attack, slot 1
        PostKeystroke(0x31, 10);
      }

      // tap for a hero strike in slot 3
      PostKeystroke(0x33, 10);
}
```

Instead of reverse engineering the location of the attack mode state, we opted to take a simple approach and sample a pixel location that we know will be colored in a specific way if we are in attack mode. We describe this technique in both Chapter 6 and Chapter 2.

```
// return true if we are in attack mode
// TODO come up with an in-memory way to do this...

BOOL WowzerEngine::GetAttackMode()
{
```

This coordinate is the border of slot 1:

```
      COLORREF cr = GetColorOfPixel(26,731);
      //logprintf(" got %d,%d,%d",
            GetRValue(cr),
            GetGValue(cr),
            GetBValue(cr));
      //DWORD difference = abs(GetGValue(cr) - 138);
      if(GetGValue(cr)>100)
```

```
  {
    // we are in agro mode
    return true;
  }

  return false;
}
```

This section contains lots of central bot actions: how to calculate direction and distance, how to set up and carry out a ping-pong, and how to deliver keystrokes to make the PC fight or cast ranged attacks. This code can be extended to a wide variety of operations, of course.

Looting the Mob

In most games, once you kill a mob, you probably want to loot it (take its items, possibly skin the hide, and so on). In normal play, you can accomplish this with mouse clicks on the screen. But our automated bot version simply right-clicks through an array of locations on the screen that have high probability of causing the loot dialog to pop up. This emulates a shift-click so the loot is taken automatically. We use teleport to make sure the character is positioned properly relative to the mob's dead body.

```
void HunterBot::TeleportAndLootMob(Mob *theMob)
{
        TeleportToTarget(theMob->m_id);
        LootTheDead();
}

void HunterBot::LootTheDead()
{
        logprintf("LOOT THE DEAD");

        RMouseClick(440,390, TRUE, 120);
        RMouseClick(440,443, TRUE, 120);
        RMouseClick(440,500, TRUE, 120);
        RMouseClick(440,550, TRUE, 120);
        RMouseClick(440,600, TRUE, 120);
        RMouseClick(440,680, TRUE, 120);
        RMouseClick(513,390, TRUE, 120);
        RMouseClick(513,443, TRUE, 120);
        RMouseClick(513,500, TRUE, 120);
        RMouseClick(513,550, TRUE, 120);
        RMouseClick(513,600, TRUE, 120);
```

```
    RMouseClick(513,680, TRUE, 120);
    RMouseClick(580,390, TRUE, 120);
    RMouseClick(580,443, TRUE, 120);
    RMouseClick(580,500, TRUE, 120);
    RMouseClick(580,550, TRUE, 120);
    RMouseClick(580,600, TRUE, 120);
    RMouseClick(580,680, TRUE, 120);
}
```

This technique is ugly and relies on brute force, but it works fairly well for
WoW. Other games might require different looting techniques.

Mob Selection and Blacklisting

As the PC fights, it may encounter mobs that it just can't kill, or those that
for some unknown reason have weird data structures. In these cases, you
can blacklist these mobs so you don't attack them anymore.

In the state machine for the bot, we check to see whether we keep
targeting the same mob. We keep a counter for this purpose, and if we
haven't been able to kill this mob for 100 iterations of the state machine, we
blacklist the mob by its ID number. The bot will never try to target it again.

```
if(m_last_target_mob_id == m_target_mob->m_id)
{
      logprintf("grind counter at %d",
            m_number_of_kill_attempts);
      if(++m_number_of_kill_attempts > 100)
      {
        logprintf(" we have been grinding on this mob for a
while...");

        logprintf("blacklisting mob id %d", m_target_mob->m_id);

        AddMobToBlacklist(m_target_mob->m_id);

        m_target_mob = 0;
        m_last_target_mob_id = 0;
        m_number_of_kill_attempts=0;

        // nothing, find one in the database
        SetCurrentState(SH_SELECT_Mob);
        break;
      }
}
```

The blacklist is just a list of mob IDs to ignore. When in the mob selection state, we simply check the targets against this list. The following code selects the mob nearest to the PC and begins the process of closing in for combat.

```
Mob *aSelfMob = GetSelfMob();
if(aSelfMob)
{
  aSelfMob->Refresh();
```

The GetNearestMob() function uses a database of mobs previously siphoned out of the WoW.exe memory.

```
// get the nearest, living mob
Mob *aTargetMob = GetNearestMob(MobTYPE_NPC);
if(aTargetMob)
{
  m_target_mob = aTargetMob;
```

Here we reset the kill counter only if the mob is new. If this is the same mob we just tried to kill, we keep incrementing the kill attempt counter so that we can blacklist it if we find that necessary.

```
if(m_target_mob->m_id != m_last_target_mob_id)
{
  logprintf("detected a new target mob, id %d",
        m_target_mob->m_id);
  m_last_target_mob_id = m_target_mob->m_id;
  m_number_of_kill_attempts=0;
}
else
{
  logprintf("target mob remains the same");
}

// TODO, now attempt to TAB set the
// given mob

SetCurrentState(SH_MOVETO_Mob);
}
else
{
```

```
        m_target_mob = 0;
        SetCurrentState(SH_NO_Mob);
    }
}
```

The mob list itself is a linked list with a global pointer inside the `WoW.exe` process. The following code illustrates how the mob list is siphoned out. Note that this hack is hard coded to a specific patch of WoW and will need to have its addresses updated for any other versions.

```
DWORD WowzerEngine::ReloadMobList()
{
        // empty database (todo: maybe not empty, so we
        // can track ppl who move in and out of area)
        //m_pc_database.clear();
```

The address is a global variable that could change with patch levels of the `.exe`. You can use some of the decompiler tricks we illustrate in Chapter 8 to update this value dynamically for each build of the game.

```
        // contains a ptr to mobTable
        DWORD mobTablePtrAddr = 0x00A41b0C;
        DWORD mobTableFirst = 0;
        DWORD mobTablePtr = 0;
        DWORD bread = 0;

        CHAR name [48];

        if( ReadProcessMemory(
                m_prochandle,
                (void *)mobTablePtrAddr,
                &mobTablePtr,
                4,
                &bread) == FALSE)
        {
          logprintf("failed to read address mobTablePtrAddr");
          return 0;
        }
        logprintf("mobTablePtrAddr: 0x%08X\n", mobTablePtrAddr);

        mobTableFirst = mobTablePtr;
        mob_list_struct mob;
```

This loop parses the entire list of mobs until the list circles back on itself.

```
        do {

                if(ReadProcessMemory(
                        m_prochandle,
                        (LPCVOID)mobTablePtr,
                        &mob,
                        sizeof(mob_list_struct),
                        &bread) == FALSE)
                {
                    logprintf("failed to read address mobTablePtr:
%08.08x", mobTablePtr);
                    break;
                }

                memset (name, 0x00, sizeof(name));

                if(ReadProcessMemory(
                        m_prochandle,
                        (LPCVOID)mob.name1,
                        &name, sizeof(name), &bread) == FALSE)
                {
                    logprintf("failed to read address mob name:
%08.08x", mob.name1);
                }

                logprintf( "%08.08x %08.08x unk1:%08.08x
unk2:%08.08x unk4[0:%d 1:%d 2:%d 3:%d 4:%d 5:%d] %08.08x:%s",
                        mobTablePtr, mob.next,
                        mob.unk1, mob.unk2,
                        mob.unk4[0],mob.unk4[1],mob.unk4[2],
                        mob.unk4[3],mob.unk4[4],mob.unk4[5],
                        mob.id, name);

                mobTablePtr = (DWORD) mob.next;

        } while ((mobTablePtr != 0)
                &&
                (mobTablePtr != 0x00a41b09)
                &&
                (mobTablePtr != mobTableFirst));


        return 0;
}
```

The list of mobs updates on a fairly regular basis, every few seconds or so, and this way the list can be queried for up-to-date mob types and positions. This particular mob list doesn't include player opponents.

Managing Agro

While fighting a target, "adds" or extra monsters may come to attack the PC. For this reason, it's good to keep an eye out for whether the PC is being attacked. Of course, you also need to know when the PC is being attacked even if your bot didn't attack someone first! The following code checks to see whether new adds have been picked up after killing a mob.

```
if(FALSE == amUnderAgro)
{
  if(TRUE == m_loot)
  {
    SetCurrentState(SH_LOOT_Mob);
  }
  else
  {
    SetCurrentState(SH_HEALUP);
  }
}
else
{
  // we are still under agro, try to target the bugger
  PostKeystroke(VK_TAB, 40);
  Sleep(400);
  SetCurrentState(SH_CHECK_TARGET_Mob);
}
```

If the PC is in agro mode (trying to attract attention), immediately begin attacking; otherwise, loot the mob that was just killed.

To determine whether the PC is in agro mode, we perform a very specific pixel sample. This hack is a bit overly specific.

```
// return true if we are being agro'd
// TODO come up with an in-memory way to do this...
BOOL WowzerEngine::AmUnderAgro()
{
        COLORREF cr = GetColorOfPixel(30,65); //the sword's X

        //logprintf(" got %d,%d,%d",
        //      GetRValue(cr),
```

```
//      GetGValue(cr),
//      GetBValue(cr));
DWORD difference = abs(147 - GetRValue(cr));
if(difference<20)
{
  // we are being agro'd
  return true;
}


  return false;
}
```

As we explain in Chapter 2, many kinds of state can be determined using pixel sampling. When developing a bot, it can be very time effective simply to use pixel samples as opposed to investing the energy to reverse engineer the particular locations of state values.

By using pixel samples, however, you introduce requirements that the user interface be visible and in a certain configuration, resolution, and sometimes even position on the screen—all factors that make the setup and use of the bot more complicated for the user.

Let's take a closer look. Using internal state variables may be considered more elite, but remember that you have a limited amount of time for game hacking. If using pixel samples means less development time, it could mean the difference between a working bot and a half-finished project that never runs. There are always tradeoffs in any software development approach. If you intend to release your bot to others, using internal state variables means less setup for users. That is, the bot just works out of the box (or the .rar file, as the case may be).

Bot as Debugger

Savvy readers will have already discerned the relationship between bots and debuggers, especially if you paid close attention in Chapter 6. It turns out that bots can be written as debuggers to great effect. In this section, we show how to attach to a running game client and interject just the right sorts of events in order to create a bot.

Implementing a bot as a program debugger is a convenient way to invasively manipulate the target program. In addition, having a good debugger around is very helpful when you're trying to understand and manipulate any game client. Fortunately, Windows-SDK-compliant debuggers all share a common basic architecture. In this section, we introduce some basic debugging techniques and show how they apply to game hacking using a program called Wowzer.

Please be aware that some game clients can detect whether they are being debugged. Misuse of the techniques presented here may cause you to be banned from the game. Once again, don't come whining to us if you get caught using these ideas and bad things happen!

A Basic Debugging Loop

Here's the main debugging loop for a standard debugger. The code is a console application (i.e., it has no user interface). It prints debug data to stdout as it runs.

```
int _tmain(int argc, _TCHAR* argv[])
{
        HANDLE hProcess;
        DEBUG_EVENT dbg_evt;
        int aPID;

        if(argc != 2)
        {
           printf("wrong number of parameters\nusage %s
<pid>\n",argv[0]);
           return 0;
        }
```

In the code, the program checks its arguments. In this example, the debugger will connect to (or attach to) an already-running process. This is usually the right approach to take when working on a game hack. During start-up, a game may check to see whether it's being launched from a debugger. Obviously that will be disallowed. Attaching to the target program by using these techniques will get you around that common check. (Note that this kind of "Am I being debugged?" check can be run from more than one location, not only at game start-up!) Attaching like this also lets the program get started, for you to log in and so on, before any hacking begins.

```
        // load the ptr to fDebugSetProcessKillOnExit
        fDebugSetProcessKillOnExit = (DEBUGSETPROCESSKILLONEXIT)
           GetProcAddress( GetModuleHandle("kernel32.dll"),
           "DebugSetProcessKillOnExit" );
        if(!fDebugSetProcessKillOnExit)
        {
```

```
        printf("[!] failed to get fDebugSetProcessKillOnExit
function!\n");
    }

    aPID = atoi(argv[1]);
```

The code above loads a pointer to a special utility function that allows us to detach from the running process without killing it. See below for a more detailed description of this feature—it's optional, but highly desired.

```
hProcess = OpenProcess(PROCESS_ALL_ACCESS |
        PROCESS_VM_OPERATION,
        0,
        aPID);
```

Here, we open the target process. In this case, the process must already be running. You can attach to the game once you have already logged into the world and are ready to begin botting or sniffing data.

```
if(hProcess == NULL)
{
  printf("[!] OpenProcess Failed !\n");
  return 0;
}

SetDebugPrivilege(hProcess);

// Alright -- time to start debugging
if(!DebugActiveProcess(aPID))
{
  printf("[!] DebugActiveProcess failed !\n");
  return 0;
}
```

The call above begins the debugging process. If the process doesn't belong to you, you need to enable the debugging privilege. The main loop of the debug event handler is shown below.

```
// don't kill the process on thread exit, XP and above
if(fDebugSetProcessKillOnExit)
        fDebugSetProcessKillOnExit(FALSE);

while(1)
{
```

Next we wait for a debug event. Debug events occur for many reasons, including thread creation and destruction. They also happen when DLLs are loaded. Debug events may also be spawned for debugger-specific reasons, such as when a breakpoint is hit or when a single step occurs. As you can see, there is a timeout option for WaitForDebugEvent. In this case, we specify INFINITE, which means wait forever until an event occurs. This function call blocks until an event occurs.

```
if(WaitForDebugEvent(&dbg_evt, INFINITE))
{
    printf("debug event detected...\n");
```

At this point we're ready to check the debug event code. If the event code is an exception, we check to see whether it's a breakpoint or a single step. A breakpoint is usually in response to an interrupt 3. A single step is in response to an interrupt 1. However, it's important to know that some breakpoint types can result in an interrupt 1 and (even though they are breakpoints) cause the single-step message to be sent. We check for one exception type called an access violation—this is sent whenever invalid memory is read or written.

```
if(EXIT_THREAD_DEBUG_EVENT == dbg_evt.dwDebugEventCode)
{
    printf("[!] Target thread id %d
has finished executing. \n",
            dbg_evt.dwThreadId);
}
    if( dbg_evt.dwDebugEventCode == EXCEPTION_DEBUG_EVENT)
    {
        switch (dbg_evt.u.Exception.ExceptionRecord.
                ExceptionCode)
        {
        case EXCEPTION_ACCESS_VIOLATION:
        break;
        case EXCEPTION_BREAKPOINT:
        printf("breakpoint hit\n");
        break;
        case EXCEPTION_SINGLE_STEP:
        break;
        default:
        break;
        }
    }
```

For fun, we also check for debug strings. This is a special event code used
when debug trace messages are printed. Debug strings are only supposed to
be used in development, but they are often left behind in production builds.
These strings can sometimes contain valuable data about the game—
including function name and purpose.

```
if(dbg_evt.dwDebugEventCode ==
        OUTPUT_DEBUG_STRING_EVENT)
{
  OUTPUT_DEBUG_STRING_INFO *inf =
          &(dbg_evt.u.DebugString);
  LPSTR remote_address =
          inf->lpDebugStringData;
  char _local[4096];
  printf("got debug string len %d\n",
          inf->nDebugStringLength);

  memset(_local, NULL, sizeof(_local));

  if(inf->nDebugStringLength <
          sizeof(_local)-1)
  {
    unsigned long num_read;
    ReadProcessMemory(
            hProcess,
            (LPCVOID)remote_address,
            _local,
            inf->nDebugStringLength, &num_read);

    printf("string: %s\n", _local);
  }
}

printf("continuing...\n");
if(!ContinueDebugEvent(
        aPID,
        dbg_evt.dwThreadId,
        DBG_CONTINUE))
{
  return 0;
}
}
}

return 0;
}
```

What we have now is a basic debugging loop. Use this along with a bot to attach to the target process. This is the basis for breakpoint-based sampling, setting and getting thread contexts, hijacking threads, and so on. Now we turn to some important details you should be aware of.

SetProcessKillOnExit

Before Windows XP joined us in Windows-land, if you connected to a program to debug it, you could not disconnect the debugger without also killing the target program. After Windows XP debuted, Microsoft added a new SDK function to let you disconnect a debugger without also killing the process.

A problem remains, however. The function isn't exported in a way that you can use directly in your programs. Instead, you have to load the function dynamically by using GetProcAddress().

The following code shows how to import an undocumented function dynamically. With this trick, you can get a pointer to any arbitrary function exported from a DLL. You will need to know (or to guess) the types of the arguments passed to the call. (Almost all DLL exports are exported as __stdcall.)

```
typedef
BOOL(__stdcall *DEBUGSETPROCESSKILLONEXIT)
(
   BOOL KillOnExit
);
DEBUGSETPROCESSKILLONEXIT fDebugSetProcessKillOnExit;
```

SetDebugPrivilege

Windows has security features that govern what a logged-on user can do. One of the rights that can be granted or restricted is the right to debug other processes on the system (processes not started by yourself, that is). For a game hack, you probably launched the game client yourself and don't need to invoke this privilege. But, for the sake of completeness, a good debugger should enable the debug privilege so it can be used on system processes and those of other users.

The following code enables the debug privilege in Windows.

```
bool SetDebugPrivilege( HANDLE hProcess )
{
      LUID luid ;
      TOKEN_PRIVILEGES privs ;
```

```
HANDLE hToken = NULL ;
DWORD dwBufLen = 0 ;
char buf[1024] ;

ZeroMemory( &luid,sizeof(luid) ) ;

if(! LookupPrivilegeValue( NULL, SE_DEBUG_NAME, &luid ))
  return false ;

privs.PrivilegeCount = 1 ;
privs.Privileges[0].Attributes = SE_PRIVILEGE_ENABLED ;
memcpy( &privs.Privileges[0].Luid,
        &luid,
        sizeof(privs.Privileges[0].Luid ) ) ;


if( ! OpenProcessToken( hProcess,
        TOKEN_ALL_ACCESS,&hToken))
  return false ;

if( !AdjustTokenPrivileges(
        hToken,
        FALSE,
        &privs,
        sizeof(buf),
        (PTOKEN_PRIVILEGES)buf,
        &dwBufLen ) )
  return false ;

  return true ;
}
```

The debug privilege might not be required for attaching to your game, but the technique is useful if you intend to connect to a service that has already been launched or to a component that starts when the computer boots. Some games may have components like this you might wish to explore.

Breakpoints

Breakpoints are an essential debugging trick. They allow you to cause a program to stop whatever it is doing and pause at a defined location. You can use breakpoints to gain control over the execution of a program, to redirect control flow, to sample data, or to modify select data at a specific time. Breakpoints are like wrenches for the code mechanic—common and extremely useful.

There are two fundamental kinds of breakpoints. *In-memory* breakpoints, the first kind, require a breakpoint instruction to be written over the code. *Memory* breakpoints or *hardware* breakpoints, the second kind, use the debug registers of the Intel chip. Let's take a closer look.

Here we illustrate the placement of an in-memory breakpoint. This requires us to overwrite the code with a breakpoint instruction. This instruction is only 1 byte long (by design, for ease of use). The CC byte, if executed, produces an interrupt 3, which is intercepted by the Windows kernel and filtered down in the form of a breakpoint event. Of course, you could hook interrupt 3 directly, but this requires a kernel driver (see our book *Exploiting Software* for more on that technique).

```
void CreateBreakpoint()
{
        char a_bpx = '\xCC';
```

We define the breakpoint instruction as byte CC. Next, we query the target memory to make sure it's valid. We'll write this CC into the target memory, so we need to make sure the memory actually exists.

```
        MEMORY_BASIC_INFORMATION mbi;
        VirtualQueryEx(
                hProcess,
                (void *)(g_start_breakpoint),
                &mbi,
                sizeof(MEMORY_BASIC_INFORMATION));
        if(VirtualProtectEx(
                hProcess,
                mbi.BaseAddress,
                mbi.RegionSize,
                PAGE_EXECUTE_READWRITE,
                &mbi.Protect ))
        {
```

Our plan to write a CC will overwrite any byte that already exists at that location. Since real code bytes already exist there, we may need to restore the original byte later if we ever wish to remove the breakpoint. To do this, we read the original byte and store it away for later reincarnation.

```
                    // now read the original byte
                    if(!ReadProcessMemory(
                            hProcess,
                            (void *)(g_start_breakpoint),
                            &(g_start_orig_byte),
                            1,
                            NULL))
                    {
                      MessageBox(
                            NULL,
                            "[!] Failed to read process memory ! \n",
                            "oops",
                            MB_OK);
                      return;
                    }
```

Now we write the breakpoint over the memory.

```
                    if(!WriteProcessMemory(
                            hProcess,
                            (void *)(g_start_breakpoint),
                            &a_bpx,
                            1,
                            NULL))
                    {
                       char _c[255];
                       sprintf(_c, "[!] Failed to write process memory, error
%d ! \n", GetLastError());
                       MessageBox(NULL, _c, "oops", MB_OK);

                       return;
                    }
                 }
}
```

At this point, we've set the breakpoint. If this code ever executes, the embedded breakpoint will cause our breakpoint event to fire. Of course, to remove the breakpoint, we simply perform the opposite of what we just did and write the stored original byte back where it goes.

```
void RemoveBreakpoint()
{
        MEMORY_BASIC_INFORMATION mbi;
        VirtualQueryEx(
                hProcess,
```

```
                (void *)(g_start_breakpoint),
                &mbi,
                sizeof(MEMORY_BASIC_INFORMATION));

        if(VirtualProtectEx(
                hProcess,
                mbi.BaseAddress,
                mbi.RegionSize,
                PAGE_EXECUTE_READWRITE,
                &mbi.Protect ))
        {
          if(!WriteProcessMemory(
                hProcess,
                (void *)(g_start_breakpoint),
                &g_start_orig_byte,
                1,
                NULL))
          {
            char _c[255];
            sprintf( _c,
                    "[!] Failed to write process memory, error
%d ! \n",
                    GetLastError());
            MessageBox(NULL, _c, "oops", MB_OK);
            return;
          }
        }
}
```

When the breakpoint is hit, you can do several things. You can alter the control flow to run other code. You can take a memory sample. Or you can overwrite some memory, such as an argument to a function. Regardless of what you do, however, if you intend to allow execution to continue from the current location, you will need to remove the breakpoint. If you don't, it will simply keep firing, and you'll be stuck.

```
if(dbg_evt.dwDebugEventCode == EXCEPTION_DEBUG_EVENT)
{
```

Now perform a switch on the exception code:

```
switch (dbg_evt.u.Exception.ExceptionRecord.ExceptionCode)
{
case EXCEPTION_ACCESS_VIOLATION:
      break;
```

The following exception code is used for CC breakpoints placed into code.

```
case EXCEPTION_BREAKPOINT:
    if(g_initial_break)
    {
      g_initial_break = FALSE;
      printf( "initial breakpoint, debugging started...\n");
      if(g_start_breakpoint) CreateBreakpoint();
    }
    else if(g_start_breakpoint)
    {
```

When we hit a breakpoint, we need to remove the CC byte and replace it with whatever byte was originally present in the code. Furthermore, we need to rewind the instruction pointer by one so that the original instruction can execute now that the CC is out of the way.

```
        printf("user supplied breakpoint hit, removing...\n");
        // breakpoint fired, now remove it
        // roll back the EIP and correct the opcode

        CONTEXT ctx;

        HANDLE hThread =
                fOpenThread(
                THREAD_ALL_ACCESS,
                FALSE,
                dbg_evt.dwThreadId );

        if(hThread == NULL)
        {
          printf("[!] OpenThread failed ! \n");
          return 0; }
```

We use the context of the thread to rewind the EIP (instruction pointer) by one.

```
        // rewind one instruction
        ctx.ContextFlags = CONTEXT_FULL;
        if(!GetThreadContext(hThread, &ctx))
        {
          printf("[!] GetThreadContext failed ! \n");
```

```
                    return 0;
                }

            ctx.Eip--;
            ctx.ContextFlags = CONTEXT_FULL;
            if(!SetThreadContext(hThread, &ctx))
            {
                printf("[!] SetThreadContext failed ! \n");
                return 0;
            }

            RemoveBreakpoint();
            g_start_breakpoint=0;

        }
break;
case EXCEPTION_SINGLE_STEP:
        break;
default:
        break;
}
```

And there you have it, setting a breakpoint in memory and removing it once it has fired.

Snagging Samples from Context

The following example shows how to read the EAX register from the CONTEXT structure that the debugger collects. You can sample any register and then use the sampled value as a pointer, reading further information from memory. You can also sample dynamically allocated structures, grab a pointer to a structure at runtime, or just update a running count or value.

```
void take_sample(CONTEXT ctx)
{
        DWORD reg;
        struct hit *h = new struct hit;
        SYSTEMTIME thetime;
        GetSystemTime( &thetime);
        char addr[32];

        // build report item
        reg = ctx.Eax;
        h->mReport += "EAX: ";
```

```
_snprintf(addr, 30, "v:0x%lx/%d", ctx.Eax, ctx.Eax);
h->mReport += addr;
if(can_read( (void *)reg ))
{
  SIZE_T lpRead;
  char string[32];
  string[31]=NULL;


  // read the target memory
  if(ReadProcessMemory(
       hProcess,
       (void *)reg,
       string,
       30,
       &lpRead))
  {

    h->mReport += " -> ";
    h->mReport += string;
    h->mReport += "\r\n";
  }
  else
    h->mReport += "\r\n";
}
else
  h->mReport += "\r\n";
```

Here we store samples in a list. You can organize and use samples in many ways; this is just one example.

```
gHitList.push_back(h);

char _c[255];
_snprintf(
     _c,
     250,
     "Time: %d:%d:%d:%d",
     (thetime.wHour - 7),
     thetime.wMinute,
     thetime.wSecond,
     thetime.wMilliseconds);
LV_ITEM lvi;
lvi.mask = LVIF_TEXT | LVIF_PARAM;
lvi.iSubItem = 0;
```

```
        lvi.iItem = 0;
        lvi.pszText = _c;
        lvi.lParam = (LPARAM)h;
```

The code here fills a list-view GUI component with the sample information.

```
        ListView_InsertItem(ghWndSplitter, &lvi);
}
```

Next we show how to set the breakpoint and handle the single-step functionality.

```
if(dbg_evt.dwDebugEventCode == EXCEPTION_DEBUG_EVENT)
{
        switch (dbg_evt.u.Exception.ExceptionRecord.ExceptionCode)
        {
          case EXCEPTION_ACCESS_VIOLATION:
          MessageBox(
                  NULL,
                  "[!] Target experienced an ACCESS_VIOLATION ! \n",
                  "hehehe",
                  MB_OK);
          break;
          case EXCEPTION_BREAKPOINT:
          {
            CONTEXT ctx;

            HANDLE hThread =
            fOpenThread(
                    THREAD_ALL_ACCESS,
                    FALSE,
                    dbg_evt.dwThreadId);

            if(hThread == NULL)
            {
              MessageBox(
                      NULL,
                      "[!] OpenThread failed ! \n",
                      "oops",
                      MB_OK);
              return;
            }
```

```
    // rewind one instruction
    ctx.ContextFlags = CONTEXT_FULL;
    if(!GetThreadContext(hThread, &ctx))
    {
      MessageBox(
              NULL,
              "[!] GetThreadContext failed ! \n",
              "oops",
              MB_OK);
      return;
    }

    if(ctx.Eip == g_bp_address+1)
    {
      ctx.Eip--;
      ctx.ContextFlags = CONTEXT_FULL;
      if(!SetThreadContext(hThread, &ctx))
      {
        MessageBox(
                NULL,
                "[!] SetThreadContext failed ! \n",
                "oops",
                MB_OK);
        return;
      }

      RemoveBreakpoint();

      take_sample(ctx);
```

After the breakpoint has fired and we have taken a sample, we probably
want to put back the breakpoint so we can sample again the next time this
location executes. We do this by setting single step and replacing the CC once
the next instruction finishes executing.

```
      // we are going to run the instruction,
      // and then put the breakpoint back.
      SetSingleStep(dbg_evt.dwThreadId);
    }
    CloseHandle(hThread);
  }
  break;
  case EXCEPTION_SINGLE_STEP:
  {
    // put the breakpoint back, single step
```

```
        // is no longer active
        SetBreakpoint();
    }
    break;
    default:
    break;
}// end switch
}
```

Now you know a general way to use a breakpoint to take samples. Using this technique, you could, for example, set a breakpoint on a function in the game where one of the arguments to the function is something you're interested in. A function might process the list of NPCs, for example, and then by using this breakpoint sample method, you could siphon a pointer to the linked list of all NPCs. Let's look at this more closely in the next subsection.

Siphoning with Breakpoint Samples

Breakpoints can also be used to set up memory pointers. Later, you can use these pointers for siphoning information out of the running program. Our example again targets WoW to get the pointer to the all-important PC structure.

```
DWORD g_npc_breakpoint_location = NPC_BREAKPOINT_LOCATION;
DWORD g_pcbase_breakpoint_location = 0x45D492;
```

Setting up the one-shot sample breakpoint can be accomplished as follows:

```
// this is a one-shot sampler that grabs the PC_BASE structure
m_pcbase_sampler = CreateBreakpoint(g_pcbase_breakpoint_location);
AddBreakpoint(m_pcbase_sampler);
```

The associated handler is shown here:

```
DWORD WowzerEngine::OnBreakpoint(Breakpoint *theBreakpoint)
{
        if(theBreakpoint == m_pcbase_sampler)
        {
          // read EAX for the PC-BASE
          DWORD pc_base = theBreakpoint->m_context.Eax - 0x08;
          logprintf("SNAGGED PC BASE!  0x%08X", pc_base);
          m_player_character->m_baseaddress = pc_base;
        }
```

We can see in the handler that when the breakpoint fires, EAX has the pointer to the PC structure we were looking for.

Now you're armed with a set of basic debugger tricks allowing you to attach a bot to a running game client. This is a very common and powerful game hacking technique that's important to master.

The Wowzer Botting Engine

Since you have accumulated plenty of bot basics, the time has come to put together everything we have described so far into an actual bot program. Our approach involves building a general-purpose bot engine that can then be instantiated as a large set of particular bots. We devote this section to describing a particular bot engine for WoW. This engine, called Wowzer, has not been publicly released.

At the highest level, the Wowzer engine is a collection of program classes that implement a state machine botting approach of the sort we introduce earlier. Figure 7–3 shows Wowzer's primary class packages.

The base class for Wowzer implements low-level debugging functions and is agnostic to any particular game. This is a good way to build an abstraction layer you can reuse for many games. From this class, we derive WowzerEngine, a specialization of the generic debugger specifically for WoW. The WowzerEngine subclass is responsible for things like calculating NPC lists and determining and manipulating PC structure. Basically, anything specific to WoW goes in this class. Finally, specific bots are developed as subclasses of the WowzerEngine. In Figure 7–4, we show HunterBot—a reasonably effective AFK combat bot.

In Figure 7–4 you can see a number of other types of bots (mostly under development) that can be subclassed from WowzerEngine. Our design allows us to reuse basic code as efficiently as possible.

Each bot type has a state machine specific to it. For example, the possible states for the AFK combat bot, HunterBot, are illustrated in Figure 7–5.

We can, similarly, create a different state machine for a bot called ZHackBot, as shown in Figure 7–6.

The ZHackBot is particularly interesting. It moves the PC above the ground to a point where mobs can't attack and then casts spells to kill dozens of mobs at once, all while remaining immune to attack (by

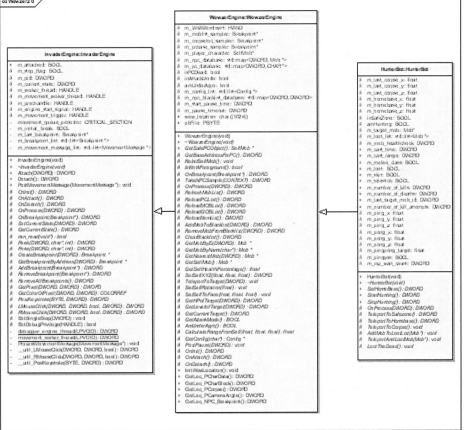

Figure 7–3 The Wowzer bot engine uses a number of classes in three packages.

remaining out of range). Unfortunately for game hackers, the efficiency of this kind of hack was seriously degraded by changes Blizzard made to WoW once the company realized this kind of bot strategy was a problem.

The Wowzer engine project is very large and encompasses many months of development, so describing Wowzer in great detail is far beyond the scope of this book. We do want you to see what a real botting engine looks like, though, so we have been careful to describe Wowzer basics. We also believe that Wowzer can help you generate ideas for your own botting platform.

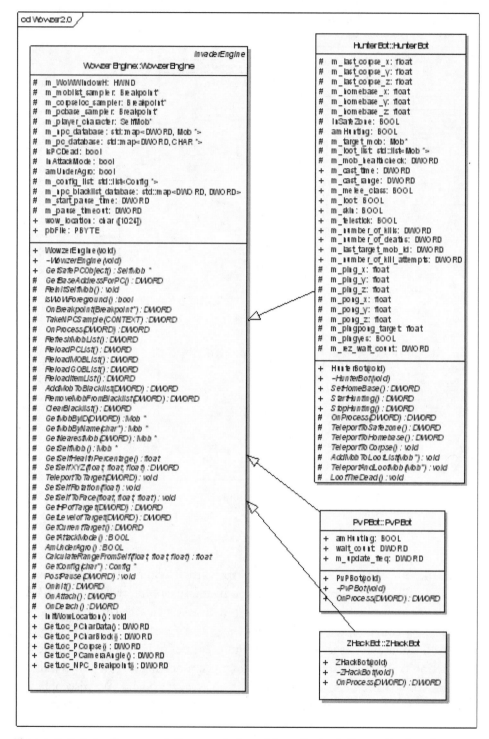

Figure 7–4 Bots of many varieties are subclassed from the basic WowzerEngine class.

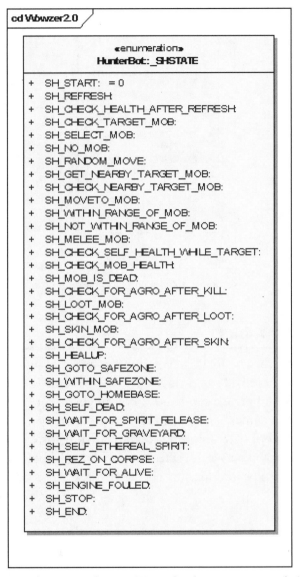

Figure 7–5 State machine states for an AFK combat bot, HunterBot, derived from the Wowzer engine.

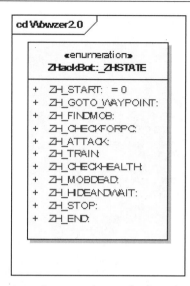

Figure 7–6 State machine states for a ZHackBot, also based on the Wowzer engine.

Advanced Bot Topics

The remainder of the chapter is devoted to a number of new ideas that can be (and are being) applied to botting. First, we examine the use of kernel-mode support for a bot. We can make a bot much harder to detect by borrowing some technical ideas from rootkits. Second, we introduce the idea of building a bot that is simply a collection of helpful macros. Finally, we look at developing a user interface for an advanced bot program. While we're at it, we describe graphics interposition hacks in some detail.

Bots and Kernels

As you might imagine, there is quite an arms race between botters and game companies, involving detection and remediation on the part of the game companies, and evasion and evolution on the part of bot developers. Like checkers or chess, the game involves one move at a time for each side, but unlike these simple games, there is no clear end in sight.

Based on the state of this continual arms race between detection and antidetection, the ultimate step in the evolution of bots emerged—kernel-level stealth of the sort that rootkits use.[2] The fact is, most games don't

---

2. We won't be describing rootkits and rootkit evolution in detail in this book. See *Rootkits* by Greg Hoglund and James Butler (Addison-Wesley, 2005) for more.

include any sort of kernel-mode protection, although that is changing with programs like nProtect GameGuard <http://eng.nprotect.com/nprotect_gameguard.htm> and PunkBuster <http://www.punkbuster.com/index.php>.

We now present a general architecture for a kernel-mode assisted bot.

General Architecture of a Kernel-Assisted Bot

The first design decision we made was to determine that the only component that would execute on the game machine would be the kernel driver. Our reasoning is that without access to the kernel, a game client won't be able to scan for our code. By keeping everything out of user process space, we attain one level of stealth beyond normal bot approaches.

To make this move, we had to move all bot application functionality to another machine and set up a communications channel. The resulting bot architecture consists of several components (Figure 7–7).

The controller machine is the computer that runs the logic and scripts that drive the bot. The slave machine is the computer running the game (in this example, WoW.exe) as well as a kernel-mode driver called supervisor (shown as "Super" in the figure). Message traffic is passed over the TCP/IP network between the two machines. On the slave machine, an implant is placed into the WoW.exe process, but it's a very simple tap that isn't connected to any loaded or injected DLL or thread, making it particularly

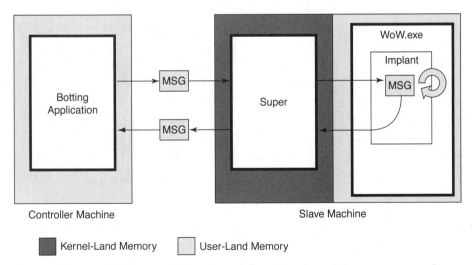

Figure 7–7 The architecture of a kernel-mode bot. Kernel-mode bots are among the most sophisticated hacks in existence today for online games.

difficult to scan for. Furthermore, kernel-level memory cloaking hides the memory from user space, so that even a generic scan of all memory will not reveal the implant.

It turns out that the implant is the key to the whole system. For `WoW.exe` in particular, the implant is responsible for executing a special byte-code language. So, in many ways, the implant is a virtual machine, similar in nature to (although far less robust than) a Java virtual machine. The implant is designed to execute a general-purpose instruction set, just like a virtual CPU.

Developing the supervisor botting system took many months and required the use of some extremely low level tools, many of which had to be developed before the actual botting work began. For example, developing a debugger framework for use in the kernel is made difficult by the fact that you can't debug your own code—that is, you can't really run a debugger against it because you would be debugging a debugger (if that makes any sense!). Hoglund delivered a technical presentation on this technology at the Black Hat conference in 2006.[3]

A New Bot Paradigm: Combat Assist Bots

There are many kinds of bots. Possibly the most popular kind of bot category is the away-from-keyboard combat bot. As we describe in Chapter 2, AFK combat is a great way to build experience points from repetitive kills. You may recall that this is also known as grinding.

AFK botting involves several challenges, not the least of which are moving through the game (called pathing) and exhibiting behavior with some kind of artificial intelligence. In this section, we introduce a new botting paradigm for games such as WoW and other turn-based MMOs.

Before MMOs, FPSs were heavily botted. The primary kind of bot for an FPS is called an aimbot—basically, a bot that assists you in pointing your weapon at someone while fighting. The same concept can be applied to turn-based MMOs, except that instead of aiming, our new bot manages the complex set of actions required to maximize damage while taking as little damage as possible. The bot we describe here applies to WoW, of course, but the concept is highly portable.

---

3. "Hacking World of Warcraft: An Exercise in Advanced Rootkit Design," by Greg Hoglund, 2006 <http://www.rootkit.com/vault/hoglund/GregSlidesWoWHack.rar>.

The Combat Assist bot maintains a list of opponent players, derived using a technique similar to the one used to compute the mob list earlier in this chapter. A script manages actions while the PC fights battles in PvP. The idea can easily extend to player versus environment combat as well (fighting NPC monsters).

The architecture is such that a series of functions in the script are called for specific things:

- One function for each opponent type
- One function for each event type occurring to the PC in two categories:
  - Taking damage
  - Casting spells or effects

A single global data state represents the PC. The script could look something like what we present here, and players can set up various assist profiles for each of their characters.

```
ASSIST( character name )
{
```

What follows is a set of callback functions called for different event types.

```
    OnActivate()
    {
      // called when the assist script
      // is activated or deactivated
    }
```

The basic timer is used for any general-purpose state processing the PC may need, such as maintaining buffs.[4]

```
    OnTimer()
    {
```

The preset variable ME represents the PC.

---

4. A buff is an effect such as a magic spell that adds strength to a character with an associated time period. Maintaining buffs involves keeping track of the time periods in order to keep the spell in effect.

```
        // called once per second, to manage all buffs
        if( ME.Buffs.Has( "Concentration Aura" ) )
        {
        }
        else
        {
```

The `Cast` command is used to cast a named spell or ability.

```
            Cast( "Concentration Aura" );
        }
    }
```

We can use the damage metering function to detect whether the current rate of damage is large and whether a subsequent death will occur if the PC does not cast a protection spell.

```
        OnDamage()
        {
          // called when taking damage
          if(RATE > 50%)
          {
            // RATE is a % of damage, measured against
            // total hitpoints, taken in the last second

            Cast( "Divine Shield" ); // cast a spell
            RETURN;
          }

          if(ME.Health < 20%)
          {
            TargetSelf();
            Cast( "Holy Light" );
            TargetLastTarget();
          }
        }
```

The following function is just an example. The callbacks here occur one after the other for each opponent type. If there are three opponents in range, the callback is called once for each of the opponents (i.e., three times). Ultimately, you need a callback for each opponent type.

```
        ForHunter()
        {
          // called for any opponent who is of the Hunter class
```

While in callback, if the player has targeted the opponent in question, then certain attack steps need to happen.

```
if(ME.Target == HUNTER)
{
  if(RANGE < 30)
  {
```

The following pseudocode illustrates what a Paladin character might need to do to set up for maximum damage.

```
if(ME.Buffs.Has("Seal of Crusader"))
{
  Cast("Judgement");
  Cast("Seal of Command");
}

EnsureMeleeMode();

if(ME.Buffs.Has("Seal of Command"))
{
```

The following check would allow a Judgement spell to be cast if there is enough mana and the Seal of Command has less than 10 seconds left.

```
    if(ME.Mana > 10%)
    {
      if(ME.Buffs.TimeLeft(
           "Seal of Command") < 10)
      {
        Cast("Judgement");
        Cast("Seal of Command");
      }
    }
  }
}
else
{
if(ME.Mana > 60%)
  CastIfNotBuffed( "Seal of Crusader" );
}
}
}
```

Some opponents have pets, so you can use this callback to deal with the pet. In this case, the script would automatically stun the pet and inform the player that the Hunter is the priority target.

```
ForHunterPet()
{
  // called for any Hunter's pet

  // RANGE in meters between character and the pet
  if(RANGE < 10)
  {
    // pet is close
    if( PET.Target == ME OR PET.Owner.Target == ME )
    {
      // this opponent is going for us
      // stun the pet and go for the opponent
      Target(PET);
      Cast( "Hammer of Justice" );

      // set target with priority 5
      PriorityTarget(PET.Owner, 5);
      SelfMessage(" GO FOR THE HUNTER ");
    }
  }
}
```

You can set up similar callbacks for other opponent types. Of course, this is only one potential architecture for the system. The impetus for this design is that each particular opponent type requires a different combat strategy.

```
ForMage()
{
}

ForWarlock()
{
}

//etc...
```

Bot User Interface

The basic guts of the debugger bot design just described include a number of very powerful techniques, but they're not exactly user friendly. If we want our bot to be more useful, we need to add some kind of interface to it. In

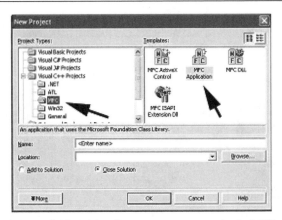

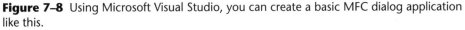

Figure 7–8 Using Microsoft Visual Studio, you can create a basic MFC dialog application like this.

this section, we introduce the concept of a dialog-based application to control and wield a bot.

Our approach is to create a simple Microsoft Foundation Class (MFC) Dialog application. You can create one automatically by using Microsoft's Visual Studio Application Wizard (Figure 7–8).

Once you have instantiated the MFC dialog app, you can add various controls to do such things as display lists of world objects, add buttons to control behavior, and so on. Figure 7–9 shows how this is done. Using this prefab functionality is a very convenient way to interface to the bot and to the game.

Integrating 3D Rendering

Most online games use sophisticated 3D rendering to create a compelling world. If our bot program is going to keep up with the coolness factor of the game, it needs 3D rendering capability, too! This kind of capability is good for doing things like plotting the locations of various in-game objects as you track them. You can even go so far as to create a completely new user interface for the game (for more on this, see the discussion of total conversions in Chapter 9).

The OGRE 3D Rendering Library

Fortunately, there are a number of great graphics libraries that you can use for 3D game rendering (well, actually, for 3D rendering in general). That means you don't have to start from scratch. Among the best is the OGRE (Object-Oriented Graphics Rendering Engine), a C++ set of classes designed

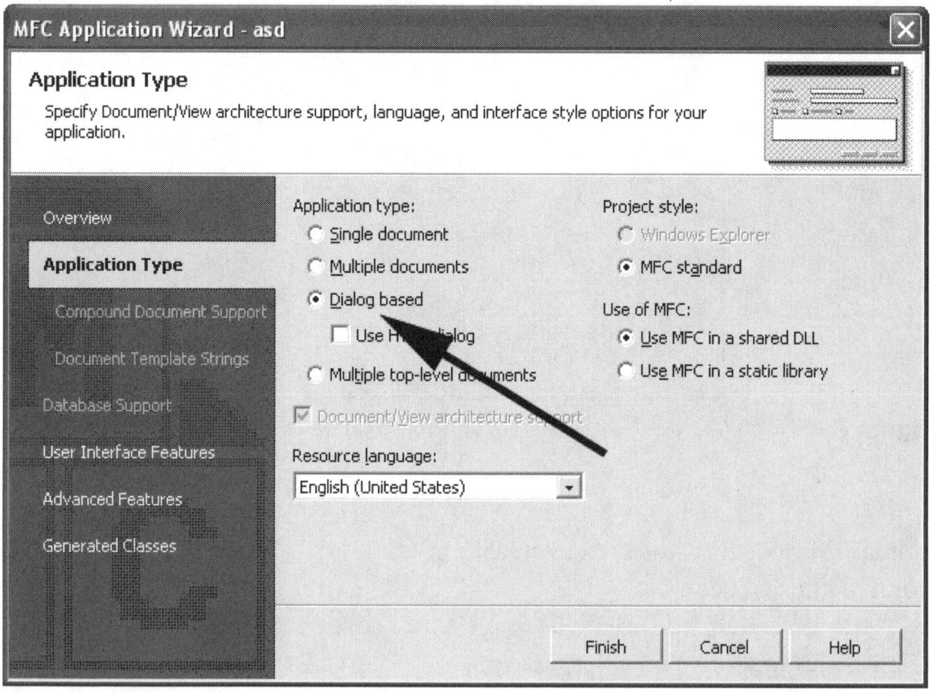

Figure 7–9 Using the Application Wizard, you can add various capabilities to your dialog app. This is an easy way to make a sophisticated display for your bot.

to make 3D graphics easier. For more about OGRE, including a GNU Lesser General Public License (LGPL) download, see <http://www.ogre3d.org/>.

We're happy to report that the OGRE rendering library is very easy to use. Using OGRE, we built a simple client interface that can plot the locations of objects in a 3D world. Figure 7–10 shows what a basic OGRE rendering can look like.

The code below uses the OGRE package to do some basic rendering in a 3D virtual world. We have integrated comments into the code, as usual.

```
#include "Ogre.h"
#include "OgreConfigFile.h"
#include "OgreKeyEvent.h"
#include "OgreEventListeners.h"
#include "OgreStringConverter.h"
#include "OgreException.h"
#include <map>

using namespace Ogre;
```

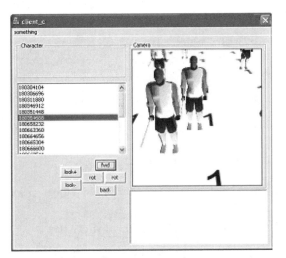

Figure 7–10 Using OGRE, we can create a rudimentary 3D interface for objects in a virtual world.

```cpp
RenderWindow *          m_renderwindow;
Root *                  m_root;
Camera *                m_camera;
RenderSystem *          m_RenderSystem;
SceneManager *          m_sceneMgr;
Viewport *              m_viewport;

Entity *                m_miner;
Entity *                m_bldg;

void Init(HWND hWindow);
void Update();
void Kill();
void UpdateObjectPosition( DWORD id, POINT p);

void MoveCamera( float distance );
void RotateCamera( float degrees );
void PitchCamera( float degrees );
void LookAt( int id );

BOOL selectRenderingPlugin( char *theName );
void loadResources();
void createDebugObjectsInScene();
void createPlane();

std::map<DWORD, SceneNode *> g_points;
```

The code we show below requires that you pass in a parent window handle. If you create an MFC Dialog application as we discuss earlier, you can obtain the handle you need for the dialog box as the m_hWnd member. The code below creates an OGRE rendering window and places it on the parent window. This is how we created Figure 7–10.

```
void Init(HWND hWindow)
{
```

OGRE requires a Root object to be created first.

```
    m_root = new Root("",""); //root without config files
```

We now load the two graphics subsystems and try to use OpenGL.

```
    m_root->loadPlugin("RenderSystem_Direct3D9");
    m_root->loadPlugin("RenderSystem_GL");

    // use the openGL renderer
    if(FALSE == selectRenderingPlugin("OpenGL")) return;
```

After calling initialise (can you tell that the authors of OGRE are European?), we next load the resources. Resources are the meshes and textures used in the scene. You can download many tools from the Net that support translating objects into OGRE mesh files.

```
    m_root->initialise(false);
    loadResources();
```

Next we create the rendering window. Although OGRE manages it, we obtain its actual window handle using getCustomAttribute. After we get the handle, we use SetWindowLong( ) to change its style to WS_CHILD.

```
    m_renderwindow =
            m_root->createRenderWindow(
                    "theCamera",
                    280,  //width
                    290,  //height
                    false,  //fullscreen or not
                    0 );  //optional
    // dirty tricks to make it a child window
    HWND aHandle;
```

```
m_renderwindow->getCustomAttribute(
        "HWND",
        &aHandle);

SetParent(aHandle, hWindow);
SetWindowLong(
        aHandle,
        GWL_STYLE,
        WS_CHILD | WS_BORDER | WS_VISIBLE );
```

Now we get the `SceneManager`. The `SceneManager` is a very important object in OGRE, as it manages all 3D objects directly.

```
m_sceneMgr = m_root->getSceneManager( ST_EXTERIOR_CLOSE );
```

Now we create a camera. The camera can be moved around, changing the perspective and viewpoint. We use the camera metaphor to look at various objects.

```
m_camera = m_sceneMgr->createCamera("MainCam");
m_camera->setNearClipDistance(1.0f);
m_camera->setFarClipDistance(50000.0f);
```

As part of the process, we also need to create a viewport for the camera.

```
m_viewport = m_renderwindow->addViewport(m_camera);
m_camera->setAspectRatio(
        Real( m_viewport->getActualWidth()) /
        Real(m_viewport->getActualHeight()));
```

Finally, we can load some meshes and place some objects in the world.

```
// load the default objects
m_miner = m_sceneMgr->createEntity("miner", "knot.mesh");
m_miner->setMaterialName("MinerMaterial");

m_bldg = m_sceneMgr->createEntity("bldg", "knot.mesh");
createPlane();
createDebugObjectsInScene();
}
```

```
void Kill()
{
        HWND aHandle;
        m_renderwindow->getCustomAttribute("HWND", &aHandle);
        DestroyWindow(aHandle);
}

void Update()
{
        m_renderwindow->reposition( 260, 27 );
        m_renderwindow->resize( 280, 290 );
        m_renderwindow->update();
}

// for testing, create a debug object
void createDebugObjectsInScene()
{
        Entity* myKnot =
                m_sceneMgr->createEntity("knot", "knot.mesh");
        myKnot->setCastShadows(true);


        SceneNode* myNode1 =
                m_sceneMgr->getRootSceneNode()->
                createChildSceneNode( "node_1" );
        myNode1->attachObject(myKnot);


        // set the nodes position
        myNode1->setPosition( Vector3(0, 0, 0) );
        m_camera->setPosition( Vector3(0,300,0) );
        m_camera->lookAt( Vector3(0, 0, 0) );

        // Set ambient light
        m_sceneMgr->setAmbientLight(ColourValue(0.4, 0.4, 0.1));

        // Create a light
        Light* l = m_sceneMgr->createLight("MainLight");
        l->setType(Light::LT_POINT);
        l->setDiffuseColour( 200, 200, 200 );
        l->setPosition(30,30,30);
}
```

```
BOOL selectRenderingPlugin( char *theName )
{
        assert(m_root != NULL);

        // list them
        RenderSystemList *rList = m_root->getAvailableRenderers();
        RenderSystemList::iterator it = rList->begin();

        // example of iterating them
        while( it != rList->end() )
        {
          RenderSystem *rSys = *it;
          it++;
          if(rSys->getName().find(theName))
            {
               m_root->setRenderSystem(rSys);
               m_RenderSystem = rSys;
               break;
            }
        }

        // how to end if we can't find one
        if(m_root->getRenderSystem() == NULL)
        {
          assert(m_RenderSystem == NULL);
          return FALSE;
        }

        return TRUE;
}

void UpdateObjectPosition( DWORD id, POINT p)
{
        if( g_points.find(id) == g_points.end() )
        {
          char node_name[64];
          _snprintf(node_name, 62, "node_%d", id);

          // it was not found, create a new object
          SceneNode* a_node =
                  m_sceneMgr->getRootSceneNode()->
                  createChildSceneNode( node_name );
```

```
          Entity *e =
                m_sceneMgr->createEntity(node_name, "ninja.mesh");
          e->setMaterialName("MinerMaterial");

          a_node->attachObject(e);
          a_node->setPosition( Vector3(p.x, 0, p.y) );
          g_points[id] = a_node;
        }
        else
        {
          // it exists, so update its position
          SceneNode *a_node = (SceneNode *)g_points[id];
          a_node->setPosition( Vector3(p.x, 0, p.y) );
        }
}

void loadResources()
{
        ResourceGroupManager::getSingleton().addResourceLocation(
              "./media/models",
              "FileSystem",
              "General");

        ResourceGroupManager::getSingleton().addResourceLocation(
              "./media/scripts",
              "FileSystem",
              "General");

        ResourceGroupManager::getSingleton().addResourceLocation(
              "./media/textures",
              "FileSystem",
              "General");

        ResourceGroupManager::getSingleton().
              initialiseAllResourceGroups();
}

void MoveCamera( float distance )
{
        m_camera->moveRelative( Vector3( 0, 0, distance) );

        char _t[255];
        Vector3 v = m_camera->getPosition();
```

```
        _snprintf(_t, 252, "camera is %f %f %f", v.x, v.y, v.z );
        OutputDebugString(_t);
}

void RotateCamera( float degrees )
{
        m_camera->yaw( Radian(degrees) );

        char _t[255];
        Vector3 v =m_camera->getDirection();
        _snprintf(
                _t,
                252,
                "camera direction at %f %f %f",
                v.x, v.y, v.z );
        OutputDebugString(_t);
}

void PitchCamera( float degrees )
{
        m_camera->pitch( Radian(degrees) );

        char _t[255];
        Vector3 v =m_camera->getDirection();
        _snprintf(
                _t,
                252,
                "camera direction at %f %f %f",
                v.x, v.y, v.z );
        OutputDebugString(_t);
}

void createPlane()
{
        Plane plane;
        plane.normal = Vector3::UNIT_Y;
        plane.d = 0;
        MeshManager::getSingleton().createPlane(
                "plane_1",
                ResourceGroupManager::DEFAULT_RESOURCE_GROUP_NAME,
                plane,
                50000,
```

```
                    50000,
                    10,
                    10,
                    true,
                    1,
                    50,
                    50,
                    Vector3::UNIT_Z);

        Entity *aPlaneEntity_1 =
                m_sceneMgr->createEntity(
                        "e_plane_1",
                        "plane_1" );
        aPlaneEntity_1->setCastShadows(false);
        SceneNode *aSceneNode_1 =
                m_sceneMgr->getRootSceneNode() ->
                        createChildSceneNode("n_plane_1");
        aSceneNode_1->attachObject(aPlaneEntity_1);
        aPlaneEntity_1->setMaterialName("PlaneMaterial");
        aSceneNode_1->setPosition( 0,-1000,0 );
}

void LookAt( int id )
{
        SceneNode *a_node = (SceneNode *)g_points[id];
        Vector3 v = a_node->getPosition();
        m_camera->setPosition( Vector3( v.x, v.y+500, v.z-200 ) );
        m_camera->lookAt( v );
}
```

Of course, your user interface can get quite complex, almost to the point of recreating a game client. In fact, as we already stated, some bots *are* complete client replacements.

The three advanced topics we introduce, kernel-mode bots, macro-derived bots, and bot user interfaces, demonstrate only three of many areas of active bot research and technology development. Perhaps botting requires a book of its own.

Bots for Everyone

As you can tell from the length of this chapter, botting is a central topic in game hacking. There's nothing quite as compelling as having a program automatically play and win a game for you, especially if it ends up creating monetizeable wealth as a side effect.

We've covered plenty of ground in this chapter. Don't forget that the central ideas here apply to most games. We used WoW as a target so our examples would be concrete, but every idea we covered can be applied to any number of online games.

8

Reversing

Reverse engineering is the art of taking something apart in order to understand how it works. The game hacking community focuses plenty of energy on reverse engineering, with special attention paid to game clients and the communications between a game client and game servers. Getting a handle on the logic of the game client and its data structures is a great way to understand how a game really works. A deep understanding gained through reversing is the bedrock on which game hacks are developed.

The techniques we describe in this chapter are in some sense prerequisite skills you'll need to tackle any new game title. New MMO titles are released all the time, each of which is likely to suffer from the same kinds of security problems we illustrate and describe throughout this book. That is, the techniques and vulnerabilities we describe aren't limited to one game or another.

Some techniques are more equal than others. Reverse engineering, for example, is an absolutely required skill if you want to craft an emulation server for any new game (see Chapter 9). Given a complete picture of the network protocol used between the game client and its associated central servers, it is possible to build a third-party server of your own. Once you've tackled reversing, you can construct sniffers, attacker-in-the-middle packet injectors, bots, client-side state hacks, and more.

The bottom line is that you can use reverse engineering skills to determine the logical structure of a game client, to understand how objects are organized and handled, and to reveal which portions of code do what.

Taking Games Apart

Software has all kinds of structure. Game hackers often focus all of their time and energy probing and poking around in one small area of a game, maybe with a myopic focus on a particular snippet of code, usually because they're trying to get something specific to work. However, stepping back and understanding the whole situation is often a superior approach.

The ability to see the big picture is just one of the things that professional reverse engineers have trained themselves to do. Reverse engineering is sometimes called a black art—but in fact it's becoming a well-documented discipline. The art of reversing is slowly becoming a science.

Knowledge of how computing machines work and how software is constructed is a must to be effective at reverse engineering. For example, most games are written using object-oriented programming concepts. A good reverse engineer will know how to program using an object-oriented language and will further know how compilers convert a high-level programming language such as C++ into native, executable instructions in machine code. Deep knowledge of software and operating system architecture allows a reverse engineer to determine how objects are organized and used within the game. Is the game multithreaded? Does it include message queues between multiple threads? Do objects use inheritance? Are lists of objects abstracted, or do they use templates and iterators? Are single or doubly linked lists in use? Are objects deleted explicitly, or are they garbage collected via reference counts? The answers to these questions significantly impact the game's operation and thus the kinds of hacks likely to work.

The Reverse Engineering Process

When starting a reverse engineering project, you probably already have some idea about how the software operates. However, if you are looking for exploits in the software, it's best to start with a blank slate. Assuming almost nothing about the target software keeps you open to unanticipated and quite possibly novel attack vectors. Yet if you already know about a problem area in the game (e.g., that the game tends to be buggy when you move items around in inventory), you might have some half-baked notion of what kind of exploit you want to write (given this example, an item dupe exploit). In both cases, you want to expose the assumptions made by the developers of the game and leverage those assumptions to your advantage. For example, you might work the assumption that players would never alter their x-, y-, and z-coordinates in memory during combat.

One critical lesson security people often emphasize—and software builders just as often ignore—is the importance of assumptions. People who create software build up a large set of complex interacting assumptions about their systems; in the worst cases, these assumptions lead to security vulnerability. Attackers and security analysts do all they can to expose these assumptions and then undermine them. "Assume nothing" is for this reason an important security mantra for either side.

If we approach a reversing project with an "Assume nothing" attitude, we'll be much more successful than if we wallow in too many details about why this or that attack would never work. For example, it might seem far-fetched that you could discover the IP address of another player on the server to use in an attack. But how would you really know if you don't explore the idea? The server could accidentally copy uninitialized memory into a chat message. Maybe the IP address of the person you're chatting with can be found in the garbage bytes. If you know another player's IP address, you can then use a network hacking tool to boot that player offline, thus disconnecting his or her character from the game.

In any case, you should always start with a rough sketch of the system when getting started with a reversing project. A good way to begin is to load the game and use a tool like Process Explorer NT <http://www.sysinternals.com> to list all the loaded DLLs and open files (Figure 8–1).

Many reverse engineers find it convenient to draw diagrams of the software system. The modeling language known as UML (once short for Unified Modeling Language) is well suited to describe software systems. In UML, a software module, such as a DLL, is known as a package. We use the term *package* to refer to any arbitrary collection of things. Almost all of the packages we're interested in will be closely associated with a grouping of code and data. So, by examining the loaded DLLs as we do in Figure 8–1, we can develop a diagram of packages and determine how they interrelate. Clumping software parts into packages results in an extremely useful initial view of the software under analysis.

To get started grouping things into packages, begin with a list of EXEs and DLLs and assign each one a particular package. The example in Figure

Process Explorer - Sysinternals: www.sysinternals.com [FIRELIGHT\hoglund]

File Options View Process Find DLL Users Help

Process	PID	CPU	Description	Company Name
System Idle Process	0	97.01		
explorer.exe	1184		Windows Explorer	Microsoft Corporation
LaunchPad.exe	3416			

Name	Description	Company Name	Version
clbcatq.dll		Microsoft Corporation	2001.12.4414.0308
comctl32.dll	Common Controls Library	Microsoft Corporation	5.82.2900.2982
comctl32.dll	User Experience Controls Library	Microsoft Corporation	6.00.2900.2982
comres.dll		Microsoft Corporation	2001.12.4414.0258
crypt32.dll	Crypto API32	Microsoft Corporation	5.131.2600.2180
cryptui.dll	Microsoft Trust UI Provider	Microsoft Corporation	5.131.2600.2180
ctype.nls			
dnsapi.dll	DNS Client API DLL	Microsoft Corporation	5.01.2600.2938
gdi32.dll	GDI Client DLL	Microsoft Corporation	5.01.2600.2818
hnetcfg.dll	Home Networking Configuration Manager	Microsoft Corporation	5.01.2600.2180
imagehlp.dll	Windows NT Image Helper	Microsoft Corporation	5.01.2600.2180
imm32.dll	Windows XP IMM32 API Client DLL	Microsoft Corporation	5.01.2600.2180
index.dat			
index.dat			
index.dat			
index.dat			
index.dat			
iphlpapi.dll	IP Helper API	Microsoft Corporation	5.01.2600.2912
kernel32.dll	Windows NT BASE API Client DLL	Microsoft Corporation	5.01.2600.2945
LaunchPad.exe			
locale.nls			
mlang.dll	Multi Language Support DLL	Microsoft Corporation	6.00.2900.2180
msasn1.dll	ASN.1 Runtime APIs	Microsoft Corporation	5.01.2600.2180
msctf.dll	MSCTF Server DLL	Microsoft Corporation	5.01.2600.2180
mshtml.dll	Microsoft (R) HTML Viewer	Microsoft Corporation	6.00.2900.3020
msimtf.dll	Active IMM Server DLL	Microsoft Corporation	5.01.2600.2180
msls31.dll	Microsoft Line Services library file	Microsoft Corporation	3.10.0349.0000
msv1_0.dll	Microsoft Authentication Package v1.0	Microsoft Corporation	5.01.2600.2180
msvcrt.dll	Windows NT CRT DLL	Microsoft Corporation	7.00.2600.2180
mswsock.dll	Microsoft Windows Sockets 2.0 Service Provider	Microsoft Corporation	5.01.2600.2180
netapi32.dll	Net Win32 API DLL	Microsoft Corporation	5.01.2600.2976
ntdll.dll	NT Layer DLL	Microsoft Corporation	5.01.2600.2180
ole32.dll	Microsoft OLE for Windows	Microsoft Corporation	5.01.2600.2726
oleaut32.dll		Microsoft Corporation	5.01.2600.2180
psapi.dll	Process Status Helper	Microsoft Corporation	5.01.2600.2180
rasadhlp.dll	Remote Access AutoDial Helper	Microsoft Corporation	5.01.2600.2938
rasapi32.dll	Remote Access API	Microsoft Corporation	5.01.2600.2180
rasman.dll	Remote Access Connection Manager	Microsoft Corporation	5.01.2600.2180

CPU Usage: 2.99% Commit Charge: 15.27% Processes: 40

Figure 8–1 DLLs loaded by an upcoming (at the time of this writing) MMO called Vanguard. These DLLs are the software components that work together to render and operate the game.

8–1 shows all the DLLs of an MMO called Vanguard. We can see right off the bat that `crypt32.dll` is being used. This is a library of cryptographic functions provided by Microsoft. We also see that many of the DLLs supplied with the game come as part of the operating system. In fact, only a handful of the DLLs used by the game are actually written by the game developers. Most of the code is third-party code and involves such things as rendering libraries, audio codes, and cryptographic functions. From the list of EXEs and DLLs we develop, we can choose packages of interest and start building a diagram of the software.

Figure 8–2 shows a set of packages resulting from the first few steps of a reversing project.

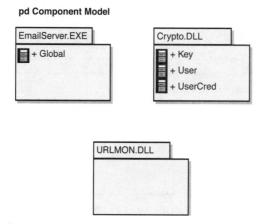

Figure 8–2 A set of packages resulting from the start of a reversing project.

It's very likely that the game programmers assume too much about third-party packages (such as crypt32.dll)—they think they know how they work, what they do, what they would "never do," and so on. For example, the developers might count on the crypto library not to allow secret keys to be swapped out of memory onto disk during paging. By playing with these assumptions, we can gain great insight into the true security posture of the game.

The next step in reversing is to refine our picture a bit into a view of high-level objects that interact as part of the overall system. Note that the resulting interacting objects don't need to be software modules. We might count the network as one of these objects, for example. Figure 8–3 shows the kind of diagram that may result.

Function Imports and Exports

The next step in reversing is to consider each package and think about imports and exports associated with it. Obviously a DLL exists to supply functions for other parts of the program to use. That means that functions are exported from one DLL and imported into another. By using a tool such as Microsoft's Dependency Walker <http://www.dependencywalker.com>, you make it easier to see the various dependency relations between DLLs. This tool will show not only which DLLs are used but also which functions are being used. Figure 8–4 shows a screenshot of Dependency Walker.

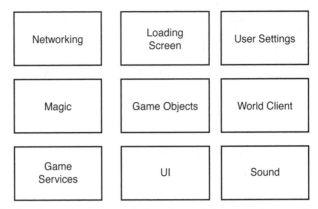

Figure 8–3 We break out the large-scale functions of the game into smaller groups for organizational purposes.

Figure 8–4 Dependency Walker reveals the relationship between the DLLs used by the game Vanguard. In the figure, we can see VANGUARD.EXE uses a DLL called VERSION.DLL, and that DLL in turn uses KERNEL32.DLL, and that DLL in turn uses NTDLL.DLL. These chains layer on one another and can sometimes get very long. In other words, there is a lot of code under the hood to make stuff happen, and the game depends on that code to do the right thing.

Dependency Walker attempts to show us which functions are used in each DLL, but it often misses some functions, and it cannot evaluate or discover code that loads dynamically as the game runs. We also can't know exactly *how* the imported functions are used (or even *if* they are used) by using this tool; nevertheless, we are quickly gaining clues about the software. The level of effort to reach this point of understanding is only about an hour of our time, so the investment is small for a pretty good return.

The next step in our reversing process is to push further into understanding package boundaries and start determining how the packages interact. We show you what we mean with an easy example: Figure 8–5 shows a graph of the imported functions the common Windows program NOTEPAD.EXE uses.

We generated the graph in Figure 8–5 using a graphing package from AT&T Research known as Graphviz <http://www.graphviz.org/> and a simple Perl script that calls the Microsoft command-line utility DUMPBIN <http://support.microsoft.com/kb/177429>. In effect, this is pretty much the same kind of data we found by using the Dependency Walker tool. We include the script here so you can modify it to make other kinds of queries.

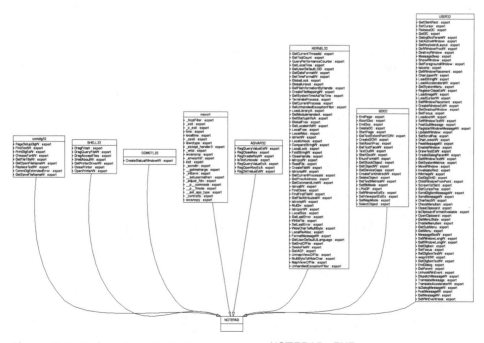

Figure 8–5 Package boundaries from the simple NOTEPAD.EXE program as we understand them early in a reversing analysis

```perl
open(UMLFILE, ">c:\\umlfile.dot");

sub write_header
{
        $header = "digraph G {
                fontname = \"Arial\"
                fontsize = 8
                node [
                        fontname = \"Arial\"
                        fontsize = 8
                        shape = \"record\"
                        ]
                edge [
                        fontname = \"Arial\"
                        fontsize = 8
                        ]\n";

        print UMLFILE $header;
}

sub create_class
{
        my $class_name = shift();
        @function_names = @_;

        # '|' makes a horizontal bar
        # \l makes a new line

        $pkg_string = "
                $class_name [
                        label = \"{ $class_name|";

        foreach $item ( @function_names )
        {
          #print "outputting $item \n";

          $pkg_string .= "+ $item : export\\l";
        }

        $pkg_string .= "}\"";
        $pkg_string .= "]\n";
```

```
            print UMLFILE $pkg_string;
}

sub follow_imports
{
        my $filename = $_[0];
        @dll_names;
        my $dll_name_index = 0;
        my $current_dll_ptr;

        system("dumpbin /imports $filename > c:\\temp.txt");
        open(STUFF, "c:\\temp.txt");
        $current_DLL = 0;

        while($record = <STUFF>)
        {
          print $record;
          if($current_DLL)
          {
            if($record =~ m/[ ]+[0-9A-Fa-f]+[ ]+[A-Fa-f0-9]+
([A-Za-z_0-9]+)$/)
            {
              print "pushing $1 \n";
              # get reference to the anonymous array created below
              $arrayptr = $dll_names[$current_dll_ptr + 1];
              #push import into anonymous array
              push( @$arrayptr, $1);
            }
          }
          if ($record =~ m/[ ]+([0-9A-Za-z]+\.dll)$/i )
          {
            print "got DLL: $1\n";
            $current_dll_ptr = $dll_name_index;
            $dll_names[$current_dll_ptr] = $1;        #name of DLL
            #new anonymous array
            $dll_names[$current_dll_ptr + 1] = [];
            $dll_name_index += 2;

            $current_DLL = $1;
          }
        }

        return( @dll_names );
}
```

```perl
sub write_tail
{
        print UMLFILE "\n}";
}

write_header();

$target_exe = "c:\\windows\\system32\\notepad.exe";
$target_exe_name = "NOTEPAD";

# create base object
print UMLFILE "$target_exe_name [ label = \"{ $target_exe_name| }\"
]\n";

# the return value is a nasty perlism, every other member of the
# array is a reference to another array containing the list of
# functions imported from the given DLL
@import_list = follow_imports($target_exe);

# parse the alien-doubled array
my $count = @import_list;
print "got $count entries\n";
$i = 0;
while($i < $count)
{
        $dll_name = $import_list[$i];
        $arrayptr = $import_list[$i + 1];
        my @myarray = @$arrayptr;

        #foreach $item (@myarray)
        #{
        #  print "dll: $dll_name : got import" . $item . "\n";
        #}

        # get rid of the .dll at the end
        my $safe_name;
        if( $dll_name =~ m/(.+)\./gi )
        {
          print "fixing $1 \n";

          $safe_name = $1;
        }
        else
        {
          $safe_name = $dll_name;
        }
```

```
    # now create a class to represent the imported module
    create_class($safe_name, @myarray);

    #now create a link
    print UMLFILE "edge [ arrowhead = \"empty\" ]\n $safe_name
-> $target_exe_name \n\n";

    $i += 2;
}


write_tail();

close UMLFILE;
close STUFF;

system(".\\graph_bin\\dot -T png -o .\\class.png c:\\umlfile.dot");
```

Strings

Most game programs include a wealth of information in the form of ASCII strings. The program includes error messages, informative text, and sometimes even debug data such as the name of the source code file used to compile a function. This information can help you characterize which functions do what.

Figure 8–6 shows the kinds of useful information you can discover using a simple strings function. Here we can see the names of all the source code files and the directory structure that Blizzard used to build the WoW game client. This is easily obtained by simply dumping the strings from the binary since Blizzard included these strings as part of the game software.

Static Tracing

Now that we have some very basic idea about objects, functions, and package boundaries, we can continue with more static tracing. Static analysis is about understanding what a program will do without actually watching the program run.[1] Using static analysis techniques, we can build a view of our program in terms of control flow (Figure 8–7).

---

1. For more about static analysis and its utility in security analysis, see Chapter 4 of McGraw's book *Software Security: Building Security In* (Addison-Wesley, 2006). Also see how attackers routinely use static analysis in our book *Exploiting Software* (Addison-Wesley, 2004).

Address	Length	T...	▼	String
"--" .data:00...	00000039	C		C:\\build\\buildWoW\\WoW\\Source\\Game\\GameClient\\Minimap.cpp
"--" .data:00...	0000003C	C		C:\\build\\buildWoW\\WoW\\Source\\Game\\GameClient\\PlayerName.cpp
"--" .data:00...	0000003E	C		C:\\build\\buildWoW\\WoW\\Source\\Game\\GameClient\\WardenClient.cpp
"--" .data:00...	00000039	C		C:\\build\\buildWoW\\WoW\\Source\\Glue\\SurveyDownloadGlue.cpp
"--" .data:00...	0000002F	C		C:\\build\\buildWoW\\WoW\\Source\\LoadingScreen.cpp
"--" .data:00...	00000040	C		C:\\build\\buildWoW\\WoW\\Source\\Magic\\MagicClient\\SpellVisuals.cpp
"--" .data:00...	0000003B	C		C:\\build\\buildWoW\\WoW\\Source\\Magic\\MagicClient\\Spell_C.cpp
"--" .data:00...	00000031	C		C:\\build\\buildWoW\\WoW\\Source\\Net\\NetInternal.cpp
"--" .data:00...	0000002F	C		C:\\build\\buildWoW\\WoW\\Source\\Net\\NetInternal.h
"--" .data:00...	0000003C	C		C:\\build\\buildWoW\\WoW\\Source\\Object/ObjectClient/Player_C.h
"--" .data:00...	00000038	C		C:\\build\\buildWoW\\WoW\\Source\\ObjectAlloc\\IObjectAlloc.h
"--" .data:00...	00000039	C		C:\\build\\buildWoW\\WoW\\Source\\ObjectAlloc\\IObjectAlloc.cpp
"--" .data:00...	00000041	C		C:\\build\\buildWoW\\WoW\\Source\\ObjectMgrClient\\ObjectMgrClient.cpp
"--" .data:00...	00000036	C		C:\\build\\buildWoW\\WoW\\Source\\Object\\CreatureStats.cpp
"--" .data:00...	00000038	C		C:\\build\\buildWoW\\WoW\\Source\\Object\\GameObjectStats.cpp
"--" .data:00...	00000031	C		C:\\build\\buildWoW\\WoW\\Source\\Object\\ItemName.cpp
"--" .data:00...	00000032	C		C:\\build\\buildWoW\\WoW\\Source\\Object\\ItemStats.cpp
"--" .data:00...	00000030	C		C:\\build\\buildWoW\\WoW\\Source\\Object\\NPCText.cpp
"--" .data:00...	0000003B	C		C:\\build\\buildWoW\\WoW\\Source\\Object\\ObjectClient\\Bag_C.cpp
"--" .data:00...	0000003E	C		C:\\build\\buildWoW\\WoW\\Source\\Object\\ObjectClient\\Corpse_C.cpp
"--" .data:00...	00000045	C		C:\\build\\buildWoW\\WoW\\Source\\Object\\ObjectClient\\DynamicObject_C.cpp
"--" .data:00...	0000003F	C		C:\\build\\buildWoW\\WoW\\Source\\Object\\ObjectClient\\Effect_C.cpp

Figure 8–6 When we look for strings in a game file, we may find some interesting tidbits. In this screenshot, we can see the names of all of the source code files used to build the WoW client.

Another useful kind of static analysis involves searching for patterns in the code. The pattern can be almost anything, including memory allocations, use of a certain pointer, or use of a certain function.

Figure 8–8 shows the results of a pattern search around the network-related Recv call. The pattern we use searches for any code location that prints a message to the screen. The search criteria is for strings such as %s or %d, which are format specifiers used in string functions. In the figure, the three dark blocks are code locations that print messages to the screen. Pattern searches like these can be used to locate useful information quickly without investing a lot of time. This kind of search might help you think about which areas of a program might be vulnerable. You can then take a look at associated code locations (Figure 8–9).

Searching for parsers and memory allocation procedures is also often fruitful, since parsers that deal with memory are often problematic from a security perspective.[2]

Another way to search through code is to examine the entire binary and disassembly for some pattern of interest. Any location, anywhere, will be

---

2. We describe a number of classic parser-based problems in our book *Exploiting Software*.

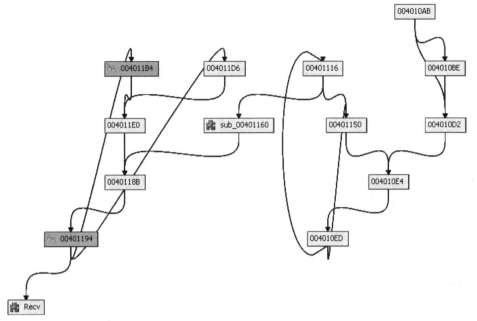

Figure 8–7 A control flow graph shows which code calls which other code. The hexadecimal numbers are the memory addresses where a code block exists. This example shows all the paths that lead to a call to Recv, a function that reads TCP/IP packets from the Internet. You can compute this type of graph by tracing through a target program or package with a disassembler. We generated this screenshot with the reverse engineering tool from HBGary known as Inspector <http://www.hbgary.com/technology.shtml>.

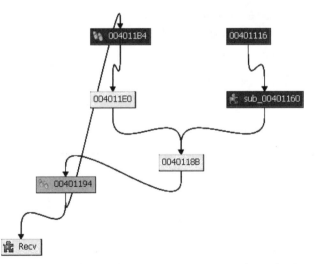

Figure 8–8 A pattern search shows where various interesting things happen near or around our call to the function Recv. In this case, dark blocks represent code regions that print messages to the screen. The code from one of these found locations is listed in Figure 8–9.

```
00401107     mov [ ebp - 000001C0 ] , eax
0040110D     cmp dword ptr [ ebp - 000001C0 ] , FF
00401114  ⊡ je 00401150
00401116  ⊡ mov cx , [ ebp - 000001AE ]
0040111D     push ecx
0040111E  ⊡ call 15
00401123     movzx edx , ax
00401126     push edx
00401127     mov eax , [ ebp - 000001AC ]
0040112D     push eax
0040112E  ⊡ call 12
00401133     push eax
00401134     push 40718C // [ * ] Client accepted from : % s : % d
00401139  ⊡ call sub_0040126E
0040113E     add esp , C
00401141     mov ecx , [ ebp - 000001C0 ]
00401147     push ecx
00401148  ⊡ call sub_00401160
0040114D  ⊡ add esp , 4
00401150  ⊡ jmp 004010E4
00401152  ⊡ xor eax , eax
00401154     mov esp , ebp
00401156     pop ebp
00401157     ret
```

Figure 8–9 One of the code blocks found during our pattern search around Recv. This code obviously prints a string of data.

flagged if it matches the certain pattern. For example, Figure 8–10 shows the results of a scan of a binary for any code that looks like it processes single-byte characters. We performed this search without regard to the proximity of the code to Recv. In fact, we performed the search without regard to the location of the item we happened to find.

A search that covers the whole binary is wide as opposed to deep. The locations we come across may be valid, but whether or not they have any

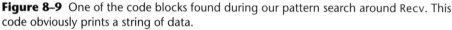

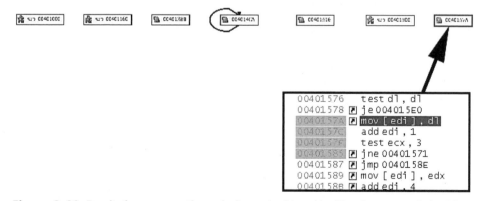

```
00401576     test dl , dl
00401578  ⊡ je 004015E0
0040157A  ⊡ mov [ edi ] , dl
0040157C     add edi , 1
0040157F     test ecx , 3
00401585  ⊡ jne 00401571
00401587  ⊡ jmp 0040158E
00401589  ⊡ mov [ edi ] , edx
0040158B  ⊡ add edi , 4
```

Figure 8–10 Results from a scan through the entire binary looking for any code location that processes single-byte characters. This is a fairly generic search, but it can yield decent results nonetheless.

meaning in the context of our work is an entirely different problem. To extend our example, suppose we want to find any code that parses chat messages for embedded color codes. The generic search illustrated in Figure 8–10 is going to find many more locations in the code than just the color code parser. In fact, such scans can produce hundreds of locations, leaving us to sift through them looking for a needle in a haystack. Granted, the haystack is a lot smaller than it was before we performed our search, but it can still be daunting.

Given a control flow graph (Figure 8–7) and the results of a wide pattern scan (Figure 8–8), we can combine the views to determine which areas we might be able to reach. That is, we trace the regions around our hits to find intersections with areas of code we know we can reach. If we're lucky, we can then connect the dots between known areas and the new location. In the end, we end up with some hypotheses about "how to get to code location 4." Figure 8–11 shows a combined view.

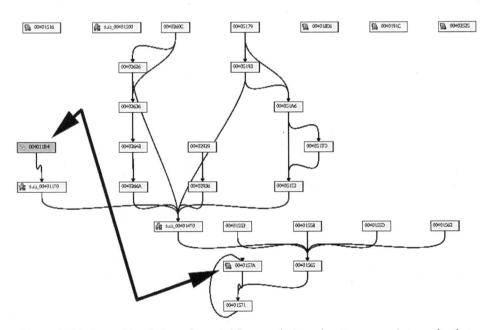

Figure 8–11 A combined view of control flow analysis and pattern scanning results that yields hypotheses about where to focus attention. In this figure, the topmost heavy arrow points to a code location that is reached during normal program operation. A clear path exists between this known location and the suspect location we found with our pattern search. In theory, we should be able to read the code on the path between to determine how to reach the new location.

In our reverse engineering process, we have now reached a point that differentiates formal security analysis from hacking. A security analyst needs to focus attention on the entire program and all of its intricacies; a hacker can go for high-value targets and ignore the rest. Software security is completely lopsided and unfair in this respect, but that's just how things are. As you can see, any game developer is on the losing end of this equation. A game hacker needs to uncover only one way to exploit the game, but the developer must focus on the entire game, identify every conceivable attack, and then remediate them all.

Dynamic Tracing

A large part of our work up to this point involves static analysis—that is, analysis without running the program. The next step is to fire up the program and do some dynamic tracing, making use of static knowledge. The good news is that we can automatically collect dynamic information as a program runs using coverage analysis (see Chapter 6). We can review coverage data and determine whether any interesting spots have been executed in various situations.

Most games are built as a series of interconnected loops. By and large, these loops are event loops, which have other event loops nested inside them. Because of this design, what you see when you look at a dynamic trace is a series of loops within loops that periodically repeat. Using dynamic analysis, you can build a graph of all the code locations visited when you perform certain tests. You can use this graph as a starting point to drill down into other regions of code you have already identified statically. Figure 8–12 hints at the kind of map you can build.

Because software programs are so large (especially games), you would be completely lost without a map to guide you through the process. Instead of looking at the entire software program as a big blob of code, we show you how to target regions of code and work your way around from there.

We can combine static control flow diagrams with dynamic pictures of control flow to yield interesting effects. The result is a hybrid picture (Figure 8–13). We call the resulting view of the program a map—essentially a control flow diagram with coverage information attached to it. In our example, we see a set of subroutines that have not been called during program operation. We might be able to get these locations to execute, but we must reverse engineer the code in order to learn how.

Now that we have developed a map, we can think of the code as a giant city that corresponds to the map. Before you go wandering off into this city,

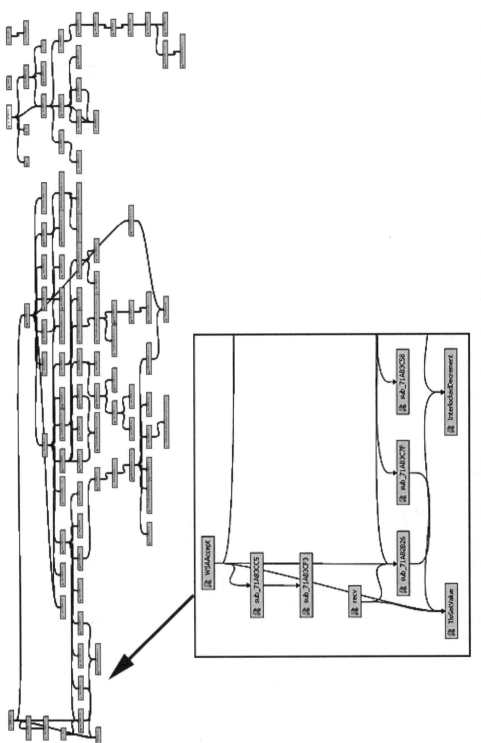

Figure 8–12 A dynamic analysis shows code visited during the game's normal execution—the beginnings of a map of where in the code we have been (i.e., which code has been executed). This information gives us a starting point for drilling deeper into regions we might not have visited.

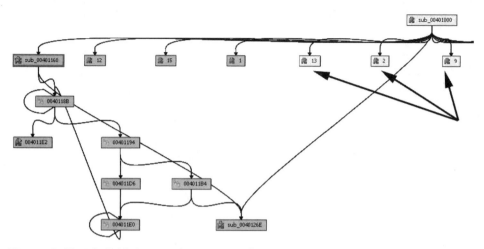

Figure 8–13 A hybrid view combining statically computed control flow information and dynamically computed data about a particular set of runs. We call this view a map.

you can put thumbtacks on the map to indicate all the streets and intersections of interest. That gives your wandering more purpose. This is precisely what we are doing with our reverse engineering process. We build a list of target areas and explore the regions around these locations. We can connect the dots between areas of code and come up with a rough idea of why we should look at a particular region of code.

Unfortunately, though, our reversing work has just begun. The hard part is yet to come—how do you read the code areas once you find them?

Code Patterns in Assembly

Reading code effectively requires an understanding of assembly language; you can find reference manuals all over the Net. There are also several really good books on assembly language, such as *Professional Assembly Language* by Richard Blum (Wrox, 2005), *Hacker Disassembling Uncovered* by Kris Kaspersky (A-List Publishing, 2003), and *Reversing: Secrets of Reverse Engineering* by Eldad Eilam (Wiley, 2005).

Assembly language is not hard to understand; in fact, it's very simple. Each instruction does something very simple and very basic, such as move a byte of data from one place to another. The problem is, ironically, that it's *too simple*. Due to the inane simplicity, it takes tens or even hundreds of assembly instructions to equal a single statement in a higher-level programming language like Python.

An easy-to-understand high-level statement such as:

```
PRINT "You have 30 hitpoints left"
```

may translate to over a thousand individual assembly language instructions! The reason is that high-level languages are designed to mask most of the underlying machine-level detail so that programmers can get more work done in less time. Before there were good high-level languages and compilers, programmers had to hand-code all of their programs using assembly language (or the native equivalent for the computer being used), and before that programmers had to code the binary 1s and 0s directly.

Many people are intimidated by disassembly due to the sheer volume of instructions and perceived lack of high-level structure, but this is because they haven't thought about how to find code patterns. The trick to reverse engineering code is to learn how to identify code patterns visually. Compilers convert high-level statements into predictable sets of assembly language, each of which has an obvious pattern.

This statement:

```
if(somevar == 0)
{
        //do something
}
// after
```

almost always translates to the following assembly language:

```
mov  eax, somevar
test eax, eax
jnz  after
// do something
...

// after
```

Using simple pattern recognition like this, you can perform the translation back to higher-level pseudo-C code simply by finding the pattern and assuming it equates back to the higher-level statement.

In this section, we cover several important patterns that C and C++ compilers typically use. We're going to stick to x86 assembly since the x86 is the most common platform in wide use today. Obviously this approach is C-centric (ignoring myriad other languages that yield the same kinds of assembly constructs), but most games are written in C/C++, so this should give you a good basic start. Be forewarned of things to come, however—the outer-space MMO *EVE Online* uses compiled Python!

In the following material, we take the liberty of assuming that you have some additional assembly language resources available and that you're already familiar with the x86 processor, basic registers, how the stack works, and so on.

Basic Data Movement

Computers do two very basic things: they perform arithmetic on data, and they move data around. Moving data is fairly straightforward with assembly language. The MOV instruction reads data from one location and puts it in another. If a MOV is inside a loop, you can move whole arrays of things. In our notation, the MOV syntax is as follows:

MOV [*to location*], [*from location*]

This is sometimes called *Intel notation*. The first operand is the target of the data move, and the second operand is the source. There are many variations of the MOV instruction.

- MOV EAX, EBX
  This moves stuff from one register into another (from EBX into EAX). The right way to say this is "EAX gets EBX."

- MOV EAX, [EBX] (indirection)
  This moves something from memory to a register. Here, EBX holds a pointer to somewhere in memory, and whatever is out there in memory is put into EAX. EBX is not affected in any way. The right way to say this is "EAX gets indirection EBX."

- MOV EAX, [EBP + 10] (argument)
  In this example, EBP is the pointer, and we add 10 to the pointer address before we grab whatever is out there in memory. EBP remains unaffected; the + 10 is only temporary for this operation. The right way to say this is "EAX gets indirection of EBP plus ten." If we are in a function, anything pointed to as "EBP plus something" is usually an argument to the function.

- MOV EAX, [EBP - 10] (local variable)
  Same as above, except this time EAX gets indirection of EBP minus ten. If we are in a function, EBP minus anything usually means a local variable.

- LEA EAX, [EBP + 10] (taking a pointer)

  This instruction is special, the LEA (pronounced "lee-ah" and short for "load effective address") is used to take the address of some object. Even though the brackets are used, the pointer in EBP is not actually dereferenced. In this case, EAX gets the value that is in EBP plus ten. It's equivalent to:

  ```
  MOV EAX, EBP
  ADD EAX, 10
  ```

  That means EAX ends up pointing to the variable on the stack, a concept used all the time when passing arguments to subroutines. It's equivalent to taking a reference in C/C++:

  ```
  int *pInt;
  int some_int = 0;
  pInt = &some_int;
  ```

  In this case, LEA might be used to initialize pInt.

Global Values

Global values are stored independent of the subroutines, typically in a special data section. These values can be set prior to program execution, or they might vary while the program runs. In either case, it's easy to spot the use of a global value. For example, the following string exists in WoW.exe:

```
.data:0083B7D8 'SPELL_FAILED_ALREADY_AT_FULL_POWER',0
```

The string is referenced at the following code location:

```
.text:006D4D92    mov     eax, 83B7D8h
.text:006D4D97    retn
```

You can see that the global value is referenced through its address. Examining the address clearly shows an ASCII string that says SPELL_FAILED_ALREADY_AT_FULL_POWER.

We cover a bit more about data movement in the Parsing and Strings subsection.

Basic Logic

Basic logic involves the comparison of values and, depending on what the value is, branching this way or that. Combined with arithmetic, this is the basis of all standard computation.

Compare Operations

In a typical compare operation, two values are compared against one another. The values are usually stored in registers, although sometimes one of the values exists in program memory. The result of a compare controls any conditional branches that occur just afterward. Thus, compares are used for higher-level statements such as if and while. Here are some examples of compares:

- CMP eax, ebx
- CMP [eax], ebx
- CMP al, 3Ch
- TEST eax, eax

The function CMP (compare) is interesting because it is the same as SUB (subtract) but does not store the result. It subtracts the two operands, and if the result is zero, the compare is true. We include TEST also because TEST is often used to compare a value against zero. This occurs many times after function calls, when the return value is checked against NULL or zero.

TEST Operations

Like CMP's relationship with SUB, TEST is the same as AND, but it does not store the result. TEST also controls conditional branches that follow it.

TEST is often used to test for a zero result after a function returns, for example:

```
CALL some_function
TEST EAX, EAX
JZ somewhere
```

is equivalent to:

```
result = some_function();
if(result)
{
  // do something
}
```

Function calls on Wintel (Windows on Intel) typically store the return value in the EAX register. This is why you see the CMP and TEST instructions operating on EAX after a call returns.

As we noted, both CMP and TEST control branching operations. They do this by affecting the FLAGS register. The FLAGS register has several bits that record whether an arithmetic operation overflows, results in zero, or has to carry. Conditional branches examine the FLAGS register to determine how to branch.

- TEST affects the following bits in the FLAGS register:
  - Sign flag (SF)
  - Zero flag (ZF)
  - Parity flag (PF)

- CMP affects the following:
  - Zero flag (ZF)
  - Overflow flag (OF)
  - Sign flag (SF)
  - Carry flag (CF)

If the ZF flag is set (ZF = 1), it means the two operands were equal. If ZF is *not* set, the operands were *not* equal. If the operands are not equal, the overflow flag (OF), sign flag (SF), and carry flag (CF) can tell you which of the operands was larger.

True/False Test on a Function Call

Many times a program will check a Boolean variable—a variable that stores TRUE or FALSE. Sometimes a function will return a BOOL result. For example, we can use the function Ellipse to draw an ellipse on the screen in Windows programs.

The function is documented in MSDN <http://msdn2.microsoft.com/en-us/default.aspx> as follows:

> The **Ellipse** function draws an ellipse. The center of the ellipse is the center of the specified bounding rectangle. The ellipse is outlined by using the current pen and is filled by using the current brush.
>
> ```
> BOOL Ellipse(
>   HDC hdc,           // handle to DC
>   int nLeftRect,     // x-coord of upper-left corner of rectangle
>   int nTopRect,      // y-coord of upper-left corner of rectangle
>   int nRightRect,    // x-coord of lower-right corner of rectangle
>   int nBottomRect    // y-coord of lower-right corner of rectangle
> );
> ```

> *Return Values*
>
> If the function succeeds, the return value is nonzero.
> If the function fails, the return value is zero.

As we can see, the return value is BOOL. A programmer might want to check the return value from this function to see whether it succeeded or not.

A check such as this will look like this:

```
if( FALSE == Ellipse( hdc, r1, r2, r3, r4 ))
{
      // error
}
```

In assembly language, the check will go something like this:

```
mov     edx, [ebp-r4]
push    edx
mov     edx, [ebp-r3]
push    edx
mov     edx, [ebp-r2]
push    edx
mov     edx, [ebp-r1]
push    edx
mov     edx, [ebp-hdc]
push    edx
call    Ellipse
add     esp, 4
movzx   eax, al
test    eax, eax
jz      short loc_401128
mov     ecx, [ebp-var_8]
```

There are several interesting things going on in this code block. First, all of the arguments for the function call Ellipse are pushed onto the stack. Notice that they are pushed in reverse order—that is, the first argument to Ellipse (hdc) is pushed last. This leaves hdc as the topmost item on the stack. So, we can see how arguments are passed to functions—on the stack. This is one of the first patterns we learn when starting to think about reversing. When we see push, push, push, followed by a call, we know the pushes are referencing the arguments to the function.

Notice how the values being pushed onto the stack are first moved into a register. This is required for the push to work, but notice how the values are being pulled from locations in memory [ebp +/- this or that]. The operand using EBP is a common pattern. EBP is called the *base pointer* for a reason—it points to the base of a stack frame, a set-aside region of the stack used for the current function. When you see EBP, you know that the variables being used are on the stack, and they are local variables defined in the current function, or sometimes, arguments that were passed into the current function. In our example, we know that the rectangle data and the display context handle are stored in local variables. This would mean the function we're reverse engineering looks something like this:

```
SomeReturnType SomeFunction( SomeNumberOfArguments )
{
        int r1, r2, r3, r4;
        HDC hdc;
        ...
        if( FALSE == Ellipse( hdc, r1, r2, r3, r4 ))
        {
          // error
        }
        ...
}
```

By revealing only a few assembly instructions, we have already learned a great deal about the current function. Next, after the arguments are pushed, there is a call to Ellipse, which after completion stores its return value in EAX. We then see that AL is moved into EAX—this seems odd, and it's another pattern we look for.

This operation:

```
movzx    eax, al
```

is often used when EAX actually contains a BOOL value. Using patterns, we now know that the Ellipse call returns a BOOL. Of course, we already showed you the documentation for Ellipse, so you already knew it was of type BOOL. But assume that you didn't know anything about the Ellipse call—assume that it was an internal call built by the game developers—this pattern would have helped you reverse engineer the return type of the function. That is what this exercise is all about.

Branching Operation: `if`

We already covered comparison operations, so let's explore how higher-level branches translate down into comparisons and jumps. `if` is a common high-level branch statement. It might be used to check the value of some variable:

```
if(somevar == 0)
{
  //do something
}
// after
```

The statement above translates to the following assembly language:

```
mov eax, somevar
test eax, eax
jnz after
// something
...

// after
```

Here we can see that the variable to be compared is first moved into a register. Earlier we saw something similar when we explored the PUSH instruction. Many instructions require that values be present in registers, as opposed to program memory. In this case, `somevar` is first moved into a register, and then it is checked for zero using the TEST instruction. JNZ means "jump if not zero"—so we jump to the `after` block if the variable is nonzero, or we fall through to the `something` block if the variable is zero.

Notice how the `jump` instruction is opposite of the `if` statement? The `if` statement is "if *equal*" but the JNZ is "jump if *not* equal." The `jump` instruction tends to be the opposite of whatever is in the `if` statement, but this makes perfect logical sense if you examine how the branches work. So, for JNZ think `if( something == something2 )` and for JZ think `if( something != something2)`.

Branching Operation: `if else`

Another common statement is to combine `if` with a follow-up `else`. The code would look something like this:

```
if(somevar == 1234)
{
  //do something 1
}
else
{
  //do something 2
}
// after
```

The code above will assemble into something close to this:

```
mov eax, somevar
cmp eax, 1234
jnz something_2
// something_1
...
jmp after
// something_2
...
// after
```

Unlike the code in our first if example, this code has two different blocks that can execute depending on the comparison's result. The key pattern to notice is the unconditional jump in the something_1 block. The JMP after must be there so the execution doesn't fall through into the something_2 block. This keeps the two blocks separated from one another. When you see the unconditional, you are tipped off that an else block is present with the normal if.

Sometimes the else block will also have an additional comparison. The code might look like this:

```
if(somevar == 1234)
{
  //do something 1
}
else if(somevar == 5555)
{
  //do something 2
}
// after
```

In this case, the assembly will go something like this:

```
mov eax, somevar
cmp eax, 1234
jnz something_2
// something_1
...
jmp after
// something_2
cmp eax, 5555
jnz after
...
// after
```

The only difference now is that the something_2 block has an additional CMP and branch so that the something_2 block won't continue executing if the variable is not 5555. The pattern here is the second CMP occurring after the something_2.

Logical Operators

Logical operators (AND, OR, and so on) are used all the time in code to control branching operations. For example, here's a use of the AND operator:

```
if(somevar == 7 && somevar == 42)
{
  //do something 1
}
// after
```

This is similar to the if statement we already explored, except that now we include two variables instead of one. The branching logic is almost the same, having only one additional compare.

```
mov eax, somevar
cmp eax, 7
jnz after
cmp eax, 42
jnz after
// something_1
...
// after (aka "bail out")
```

Note how all of the compares are done up front, with any failing match bailing out to the after block—no hard jumps used. All of the jumps are JNZ.

With an OR operator, the code is only slightly altered:

```
if(somevar == 7 || somevar == 42)
{
  //do something 1
}
// after
```

And the assembly looks something like this:

```
mov eax, somevar
cmp eax, 7
jz something_1
cmp eax, 42
jz something_1
jmp after
// something_1
...
// after (aka "bail out")
```

Just like the AND example, note how all the compares are done up front with a hard jump to the "bail out" at the end. In this case, JZ is used instead of JNZ.

In any set of compares such as the following:

```
if( something && something || something )
{
  // do something
}
// bail out to here
```

there will be a bailout block after the if{ } block. Any jump to the bailout block should be reversed to recover the operation.

- JNZ to bailout block means if(A == B).
- JZ to bailout block means if(A != B).

As we discussed earlier, the jump type is usually the opposite of that of the higher-level statement.

Parsing and Strings

Looping and Incrementing Pointers

Pointers are used for all kinds of things: pointers to structures, functions, or strings of data. Whenever there's an array of objects, a pointer is typically used to iterate through those items. A good example of this is a string, which is actually an array of bytes. If the code were scanning through a string looking for a particular character, you might find disassembly such as:

```
mov     edx, [ebp+var_4]
add     edx, 1
mov     [ebp+var_4], edx
```

Here we see a value stored in a local variable (remember EBP). The value is loaded into a register, incremented by 1, and put back into the register. This value could be anything: a counter, an index into an array, or an actual byte pointer.

If there were a string in memory and it was being copied from one location to another, a loop might be used. Inline string copies are very common. A string may also be scanned for a certain character using a loop. Small loops can always be found in code, and if they contain pointer arithmetic, you can be almost certain they are scanning or copying an array of something. For example:

```
loop:
        mov     al, [ecx]
        mov     [edx], al
        inc     ecx
        inc     edx
        test    al, al
        jnz     short loop
```

This code copies from one buffer to another until a NULL (zero) character is reached. Loops such as this can scan for any kind of character, not just NULL. For example, the following version of the code copies until a ":" character is reached:

```
loop:
        mov     al, [ecx]
        mov     [edx], al
        inc     ecx
```

```
inc     edx
cmp     al, ':'
jnz     short loop
```

You can see in the examples above that ECX and EDX hold pointers to strings in memory and that bytes are being moved from the ECX string to the EDX string. Both pointers are incremented by 1 byte for each pass in the loop.

String Copy

Moving a string from one buffer to another is a very common occurrence. The following code is an inline strcpy. That is, the compiler generates this code directly whenever a strcpy( ) is found.[3] This is done for performance reasons, and this pattern is easy to spot:

```
shr     ecx, 2
mov     [ebx+10h], edi
rep movsd
mov     ecx, eax
and     ecx, 3
rep movsb
```

The length of the string is held in ECX, divided by 4 (shr ecx, 2) and then moved in DWORD-sized chunks (32 bits at a time, the native size of the register). This is much higher performance than the single-byte looping copy we illustrated earlier. The source string is pointed to by the ESI register, and the destination is pointed to by the EDI register.

Because the string is not guaranteed to have a length that is 32-bit aligned, the final few straggler bytes are copied using a single-byte move (the and ecx, 3 is used to determine how many, and the rep movsb is used to copy them). The key thing to look for is the shr arithmetic and the rep mov instructions.

For string moves, remember the following:

- REP MOVS D (moves 32 bits at a time, length in ECX)
- REP MOVS B (moves 8 bits at a time, length in ECX)
- Source: ESI; destination: EDI
- SHR 2 (divides length by 4 in preparation for REP MOVS D)
- ECX (holds length for REP MOVS operations)

---

3. Of course, we all know how dangerous strcpy() can be from a security perspective.

String Comparisons

Many times, a program will compare one string against another. This can be done for a variety of reasons, such as looking for commands or parsing a text-based protocol. The following code makes calls to strncmp to compare a string against some Web address information:

```
push    7                 ; size_t
push    offset aHttp      ; "http://"
mov     eax, [ebp+arg_0]
push    eax               ; char *
call    _strncmp
add     esp, 0Ch
test    eax, eax
jz      short loc_401076
push    8                 ; size_t
push    offset aHttps     ; "https://"
mov     ecx, [ebp+arg_0]
push    ecx               ; char *
call    _strncmp
```

Parsing—Scanning for a Metacharacter

Many strings are formatted with metacharacters, characters that have special meaning in the string, such as ":" or the TAB character. Imagine that a chat message from the server contains special characters to change the font color. These might be encoded with a special character sequence directly in the string. For example, [183 might change the font color to red. The game might parse chat messages looking for the "[" character in order to set the font color appropriately.

The following code scans a string looking for 0x3A (the ":" character) and, if it isn't found, also checks for a NULL:

```
mov     edx, [ebp+var_4]
add     edx, 1
mov     eax, [ebp+var_4]
movsx   ecx, byte ptr [eax]
cmp     ecx, 3Ah
jz      short loc_4010F7
mov     edx, [ebp+var_4]
movsx   eax, byte ptr [edx]
test    eax, eax
jz      short loc_4010F7
jmp     short loc_4010D7
```

You can see there are two checks here, one for 0x3A and the other for NULL (via the TEST instruction). If either check is TRUE, the code branches to location loc_4010F7.

The MOVSX instruction is frequently used when checking for NULL bytes. The following code snippet checks a string for a NULL byte:

```
mov     edx, [ebp+var_4]
movsx   eax, byte ptr [edx]
test    eax, eax
jz      short loc_40109C
```

When looking for string parsers, keep your eye out for the following types of operations:

- MOV AL, BYTE PTR [EBX]
- AL, BL
- CMP AL, 00h
- TEST AL, AL
- CMP AL, 3Ch (different ASCII chars such as ".", "/", "\", ":", "-", and so on)

Of course, you can substitute other registers for AL.

There are many variations of parsing. Sometimes loops are just used to get the length of something or to get a pointer to a certain character in a string. The following loop scans for a NULL, and ESI ends up with a pointer to the end of the string:

```
mov     cl, [esi]
inc     esi
test    cl, cl
jnz     short loc_
```

Code like this might be used when concatenating multiple strings.

Loops can also scan in reverse. The following loop starts from the end of a string (perhaps the pointer being initialized from the previous example) and looks backwards until it finds a space character:

```
cmp     eax, edx
jbe     short loc_
lea     ecx, [eax-1]
cmp     byte ptr [ecx], 20h
jnz     short loc_
```

```
mov     eax, ecx
jmp     short loc_
```

Of course, the code might also use standard functions to get string lengths and such. This depends on how the compiler is set up to build the code. The following code uses the `strlen` function to obtain a pointer to the end of the string:

```
lea     eax, [ebp+var_48]
push    eax                     ; char *
call    _strlen
add     esp, 4
lea     ecx, [ebp+eax+var_48]
mov     [ebp+var_4C], ecx
```

In this example, var_48 is the string, and the result of the `strlen` is added to var_48, such that ECX ends up with a pointer to the end of the string. Notice the use of LEA to calculate the new pointer.

Parsers can look for certain bytes in order to skip over sections of a string. The following parser skips bytes if a delimiter character is found:

```
mov     edx, [ebp+var_4]
add     edx, 1
mov     [ebp+var_4], edx
mov     eax, [ebp+var_4]
movsx   ecx, byte ptr [eax]
cmp     ecx, 3Ah
jz      short loc_4010F7
...
mov     ecx, [ebp+var_4]
add     ecx, 3
mov     [ebp+var_4], ecx
mov     edx, [ebp+var_4]
push    edx
```

If the ":" character is found in the string, the pointer is incremented by 3. This routine assumes that the colon is followed by two other characters, for example, "://" from within "http://". This code snippet was taken from a real program, and the assumption that ":" would always be followed by "//" was actually incorrect! You could supply a string with ":" but without the "//" and cause a serious problem in the program.

Here are some common delimiters:

- 5C = "\"
- 3A = ":"
- 3F = "?"
- 3C = "<"

For a better list, obtain an ASCII chart (easy to find on the Net).

Functions

Functions are collections of instructions. They are the basic containers for code and typically account for how most software is organized. Functions are easy to spot in code because they have a prologue and an epilogue. These structures demarcate the function's start and end, and they always look the same (most of the time, anyway).

Prologue

The prologue of a function sets up the stack, makes room for local variables, and creates the base pointer from the stack pointer:

```
push    ebp
mov     ebp, esp
sub     esp, 176
```

The original EBP is saved on the stack, a new one is created from the current ESP, and then ESP is changed to make room for local variables. Depending on the compiler flags, this prologue might not include the use of EBP. If stack pointer omission is turned on, EBP is not used in this way; instead, it is freed up to be a general-purpose register. Functions that use stack pointer omission are typically much harder to read.

On Windows XP Service Pack 2 systems, you might find that the prologue looks something like this:

```
mov     edi, edi
push    ebp
mov     ebp, esp
sub     esp, 176
```

The addition of "mov edi, edi" is to support patching. What it does is kind of like a NOP used to create space. In this case, the call produces 2

extra bytes that can be overwritten by a fastpatch (a short relative jump),
which subsequently alters the behavior of the call.

Epilogue

The end of a function also has a predictable pattern. Clearly it must RET in
order to return to the caller. The code might look something like this:

```
mov esp, ebp
pop ebp
ret
```

Here we see that the ESP pointer gets put back to its original value, the
saved EBP is restored, and the function uses RET to return to the caller.
Sometimes we will also see the return value from the function placed into
EAX:

```
mov eax, -1
mov esp, ebp
pop ebp
ret
```

In the example, the function is returning –1.
Sometimes the compiler will use the LEAVE instruction:

```
leave
retn    3Ch
```

LEAVE performs the same thing as "mov esp, ebp", and "pop ebp". We
also note an alternative form of RET being used. The RETN instruction
specifies an additional value that is an increment value for ESP. It corrects
ESP by 0x3C in this case.

Calling Conventions

We have already seen an example of pushing arguments on the stack before
a function call is made. This is very common but not always the only course
of action. Instead, arguments can be passed in registers. Also, some functions clean up the stack before they return. Others require the caller to manage the stack (e.g., functions that accept a variable number of arguments).

Fast calling typically passes arguments using registers, as opposed to the stack. For example, the value 5 is being passed to the function here:

```
mov ecx, 5
call ds:some_function
```

Standard calling is used for any function that cleans up its own stack. Note that functions exported from DLLs are typically in this format. They accept their arguments on the stack:

```
push 5
call ds:some_function
```

The *cdecl* calling convention is used for functions that do not clean up their own stack. When using cdecl, the caller cleans up the stack after the function returns. This allows a variable number of arguments to be passed on the stack and is used for functions such as printf that take a variable number of arguments. You can quickly identify cdecl functions because they have a correction to ESP right after they return:

```
push 88
call ds:some_function
add esp, 4
```

Intrinsic Functions

Intrinsic functions are simply functions that are added directly to the binary executable as opposed to being loaded in a DLL. Some functions, such as sprintf, could be loaded in a DLL and used, but for performance and convenience, most compilers will cut and paste the code for a function like sprintf right into the binary so that additional DLLs aren't required.

Here is an example; vsprintf is intrinsic:

```
.text:00630345          push    edx             ; va_list
.text:00630346          push    eax             ; char *
.text:00630347          push    esi             ; size_t
.text:00630348          push    edi             ; char *
.text:00630349          call    ds:_vsnprintf
.text:0063034F          add     esp, 10h
```

Notice that vsnprintf is also cdecl, due to the stack correction. This is because it can take a variable number of arguments.

Inline Functions

For performance reasons, the compiler might inline a function. In addition, a developer might define a function in such a way that it always gets inlined. An inlined function is not called like a normal function. Instead, the entire function is integrated directly into the control flow of the calling function. In effect, the caller and called functions are integrated into one. A good example is the inline `strcpy` we document earlier.

Function Chunking

Modern compilers attempt to optimize the code for better performance. Compilers for Windows might include optimizations known as "function chunking," "working set tuning," or "page optimization." These are all fancy names for breaking a function apart and spreading the little resulting chunks all over the binary. This is terribly annoying for the reverse engineer because the function is not to be found all in one spot. Before such an optimization, all the function blocks would be together in one place. With this new optimization, some pieces might be thousands of bytes away from others, with nothing related in between. You can still reconstruct the function, of course, but that's super inconvenient for people used to using tools such as IDA-Pro (with a linear-file-based interface to the disassembly). Using graphs to explore the function can ease this problem.

The reason such an optimization exists is to keep parts of functions that will be accessed more often in the same memory pages, keeping paging to a minimum. Each time the operating system retrieves a new memory page, it expends critical CPU. Compilers optimize the code to reduce this overhead. This type of optimization is fairly advanced because the compiler has to predict how much each function chunk will be used.

Frame Pointer Omission

Some functions don't use the EBP register to reference variables on the stack. Instead, they make references from the current value of ESP. This makes the function much more difficult to read because ESP is always changing; thus [ESP + 5] and [ESP + 200] could be the same variable depending on when ESP is used.

Variable Reuse

We have seen many examples of variables being used in functions. An odd form of optimization is called variable reuse. If the compiler knows that after a certain point in the code a variable is never used again, it may reuse that same memory location for a second, unrelated variable. This can be very confusing to the reverse engineer if the reverser assumes the memory location is still being used for the original variable! For example:

```
mov [ebp+var_4], edx
push edx
call ds:function
mov [ebp+var_4], eax
cmp eax, 5
```

After the function call completes, var_4 is no longer needed, so the return value from the function is stored in var_4. But you wouldn't know by just glancing at the code that var_4 is being reused. Such nasty little compiler tricks can really catch a reverser by surprise.

C++ Objects

C++ is a very popular language for game development because it allows object-oriented design while maintaining very high performance. Thus, understanding C++ is crucial to reverse engineering games.

ECX *as* this *Pointer*

A C++ class can contain "override-able" functions. These functions are implemented in a table of pointers so that if a new version of the function is available, the pointer can be replaced. Because of this behavior, C++ classes are implemented with a this pointer, which points to the current instantiation of the class object. Many game programs for Windows are compiled with the Microsoft compiler, which commonly uses the ECX register to store the this pointer. You can see how the this pointer is used to get to the function pointer table in the following example:

```
.text:00403D10 sub_403D10      proc near              ; CODE XREF: sub_403AE0+74p
.text:00403D10
.text:00403D10 var_114         = dword ptr -114h
.text:00403D10 var_10          = dword ptr -10h
.text:00403D10 var_4           = dword ptr -4
.text:00403D10 arg_0           = dword ptr  8
.text:00403D10
```

Below we see the typical prologue of the function. The EBP pointer is used as expected to track the locations of variables on the stack. ESP is corrected to make room for local variables.

```
.text:00403D10                    push    ebp
.text:00403D11                    mov     ebp, esp
.text:00403D13                    sub     esp, 114h
.text:00403D19                    push    ebx
.text:00403D1A                    push    esi
.text:00403D1B                    push    edi
```

Notice below that ECX is used. ECX was not initialized first; it already contains the value of the this pointer. So, we can see that this function is a member function of some class, and we know that ECX has a pointer to the virtual function table for this class. Note that ECX is used to load the function table pointer into EAX.

```
.text:00403D1C                    mov     edi, ecx
.text:00403D1E                    mov     eax, [edi]
.text:00403D20                    lea     ecx, [ebp+var_10]
.text:00403D23                    push    ecx
.text:00403D24                    mov     ecx, edi
.text:00403D26                    mov     esi, edx
```

Now we see that the function table pointer is used to make a call. The class must have numerous member functions. The sixth function (which happens to be the fourteenth offset in the table) is being called. We know the class must have at least six member functions.

```
.text:00403D28                    call    dword ptr [eax+14h]
.text:00403D2B                    mov     ebx, [ebp+arg_0]
```

C++ vtables

The virtual function table (or vtable) for a C++ object is found via a pointer. This pointer is the first value in the object instance (Figure 8–14).

Exception Handling

Exception handlers are functions registered to handle errors. In actuality, they don't *have* to be used only for errors, but that is how they're intended to be used by design. Exception handlers are implemented as a linked list of

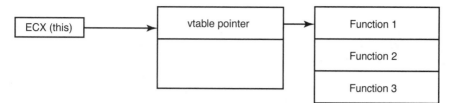

Figure 8–14 This illustration shows how to dereference through the ECX register to find the vtable pointer, and then, finally, the member function pointers.

function pointers. They're called in order until one of the functions in the list handles the exception, at which point the list is no longer traversed.

Frame-Based Exception Handlers

Exception handlers are typically implemented using a series of *exception frames*—which are simply function pointers in a linked list. Each exception frame has a pointer to the next exception frame and an additional pointer to the exception handling function that was registered. The very first exception frame can be found by dereferencing the FS register. The last frame in the linked list will have a NULL pointer to the next exception frame.

In the following code, the exception handler at loc_750A16DB is being registered. Notice how a pointer to the old exception handler, pointed to by FS[0], is stored on the stack along with the loc_750A16DB pointer. This creates the exception frame. A pointer to the new exception frame is then stored in FS[0]:

```
push    offset loc_750A16DB
mov     eax, large fs:0
push    eax
mov     eax, [esp+8+arg_4]
mov     [esp+8+arg_4], ebp
lea     ebp, [esp+8+arg_4]
sub     esp, eax
push    ebx
push    esi
push    edi
mov     eax, [ebp-8]
mov     [ebp-18h], esp
push    eax
```

```
mov     eax, [ebp-4]
mov     dword ptr [ebp-4], 0FFFFFFFFh
mov     [ebp-8], eax
lea     eax, [ebp-10h]
mov     large fs:0, eax
retn
```

In this assembly snippet, we can see the frame-based handler being put on the stack and inserted into the SEH chain.

Switch Statements

Switch statements are a specialized form of branching through which a program can check many values at once and take appropriate action. Switch statements are typically a core part of program logic, so understanding the switch statements in a game program can reveal a great deal of useful information.

Table Switch Statements

When switching multiple values that are in sequence, the compiler will create a table of pointers and use the switched value as an offset into this table. Even if every single value in the sequence is not used, the compiler might still create a table like this for performance reasons (and leave the unchecked values as unused positions in the table).

The kind of code that produces a switch of this nature is as follows:

```
switch(n)
{
  case 1:
  ...
  break;
  case 2:
  ...
  break;
  case 3:
  ...
  break;
  case 4:
  ...
  break;
  case 5:
  ...
```

```
  break;
  default:
  break;
}
```

The example switch table compiles down to code like this:

```
cmp ecx, 5
ja  default_handler
jmp DWORD PTR [dword_40112233 + ecx * 4]
```

In this example, there must be five conditions, numbered 1 through 5. The jump table at address 40112233 is then used to hold the target addresses for each of the value conditions. Note the * 4 on the operation and remember that the address is 32 bits (4 bytes) long for each pointer.

Switch Trees

When cases are not in sequence, the compiler will take a different approach. It will break the conditions into a set of value ranges and compare each range. Then, depending on the range, another subsequent block of code will check even smaller ranges, and the process continues until the exact value has been determined. This is so that every value does not have to be checked, and for this reason it results in higher-performance code.

Code that would produce a switch tree is as follows:

```
switch(n)
{
  case 104:
  ...
  break;
  case 220:
  ...
  break;
  case 3:
  ...
  break;
  case 44:
  ...
  break;
  case 501:
  ...
```

```
  break;
  default:
  break;
}
```

The example code would compile down to this:

```
cmp eax, 104
jge LOC_GROUP_2
cmp eax, 3
jz  LOC_case_3
cmp eax, 44
jz  LOC_case_44
jmp DEFAULT
LOC_GROUP_2:
cmp eax, 104
je  LOC_case_104
cmp eax, 501
je  LOC_case_501
DEFAULT:
```

In this example we can see the switch is broken into groups that further narrow down the value until an exact value is determined and the final branch to the handler for that value can take place.

Self-Modifying Code and Packing

Sometimes game developers will pack a program binary. All this means is that they are adding a secondary step to make the binary difficult to reverse engineer. In many cases, you can undo packing if you figure out the appropriate unpacker utility. If there is no unpacker utility available for the packer in question, you can grab the unpacked binary image from memory by using a debugger.

Sometimes a packer utility will include anti-debugging measures to make grabbing the image from memory difficult. But some unpacker utilities have countermeasures for this. In general, packing is a nuisance, but it doesn't really prevent reverse engineering. Packers, however, do discourage many wanna-be or gonna-be reverse engineering projects and, as such, make a reasonable basic defense against game hackers.

Reversing Concluded

Reversing is an important technique whether or not games are involved. Skill in reversing code is what sets apart wanna-be hackers from the hard core. If you're truly interested in exploiting software—game software or otherwise—it pays to spend some time learning how to reverse engineer code.

9
Advanced Game Hacking Fu

ow that you've come this far in the book, you've learned about client-side state, network-based sniffing, attacker-in-the-middle hacks, and several other standard techniques for hacking online games. In this chapter, we take on what's known as modding—an entertaining way to explore game hacking.

Conversions and Modding

The terms *conversions* and *modding* are hacker slang for custom modifications made to a game. Modding comes in many forms, from creating simple nude patches (changing textures and surfaces to make everyone's character appear to be naked, as shown in Figure 9–1) to completely replacing all the game content (called *total conversion*).

Sometimes the results are a riot. For example, in Figure 9–2 a rather silly game hacker has replaced the fishing lure model in a game with that of a cannon. Wouldn't want to cast that line!

In most cases, modding is applied to visible graphics content (such as models, textures, and levels) and involves substitution. But modding certainly isn't limited to content that you can see and render. In fact, at the other end of the spectrum, the concept can be applied directly to the game software.

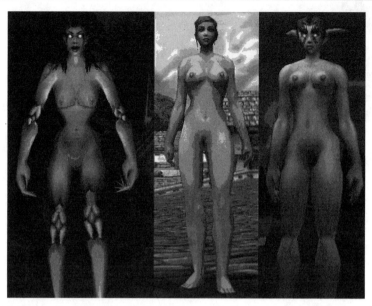

Figure 9–1 Some game hackers replace the textures for character models to make the resulting characters appear to be nude. Apparently they need to get out more. (From <http://www.edgeofnowhere.cc/viewtopic.php?t=314283>; reproduced with permission.)

Modding a game executable allows the game's logic and rules to be altered. At the extreme, a hacker can completely replace the game client with a homegrown stand-in. In such projects, this means completely rewriting the rendering engine and interface logic. Of course, hackers have explored the many possible approaches between simple substitution and complete client replacement. For example, a hacker might refactor some of the graphics, keeping some "as is" while making various changes to the rendering engine or the game client code.

Most modding replaces what are called *media* in the business—pictures and sounds. This modding involves only tweaking the façade of a game. Just under the surface, the game remains essentially the same (that's because the rules that make it work remain the same). With a total conversion, a game hacker can make an existing game look like an entirely new one (e.g., make a medieval game full of knights and dragons instead look like *Star Wars* with droids and Jedi knights).

Some gaming companies frown on the notion of modding, while others encourage it. Game companies obviously want to keep the look and feel of their games intact. A game full of dark, ominous ogres, dragons, and swords can become quite silly when daffodils replace the ogres, giant Teletubbies

Figure 9–2 When games are modded, the results are often amusing. Here, a hacker has replaced the graphics for a fishing lure with the graphics for a cannon. The game client happily renders the result as if nothing were amiss.

replace the dragons, and swords become soap bubble wands. On the other hand, game companies can extend the life of their games if they can foster a healthy modding community, ultimately increasing their revenues.

Modding can be fun because it allows interaction with the game mechanics and story without writing an entire game from scratch. Because of that, modding is an outstanding way to learn how games are built and what their inner workings are really like.

Total Conversions

Total conversions (TCs) are often necessary if modders intend to sell the resulting product. Because a TC replaces all copyrighted content, some people believe that a TC can actually be sold as an add-on to an existing game. Arguably, the most successful TC is Counter-Strike (a TC available for Half-Life from Valve Software). This TC is sold commercially.

Counter-Strike has been cited as not only the most successful TC but also the most widely played FPS game in history.

The logic goes that because commercial game media are copyrighted, redistributing that copyrighted media (including the client engine) is a crime. To avoid that crime, a TC must be installed on a machine that has a legitimate version of the game client already installed. It works by replacing the appropriate media files. You can think of this as piggybacking on an existing game system.

A very popular form of TC is to make *Star Wars* themes for FPS games. Of course, in a TC like this, the game's copyrighted content is being replaced with different, but still copyrighted, content. In such cases it's not legal to redistribute the new content unless you actually own the copyright. On the other hand, sometimes the copyright owners don't mind, nor do they pursue legal action, which has been the case with many *Star Wars* mods.

Rewriting the Client

If you wanted to play a fantasy game based on WoW artwork and models, you could replace the client executable to make a stand-alone game. If you wrote a server program as well, your replacement client-server package could be used to run your own online universe, separate from the commercial one being run by Blizzard Entertainment. Of course, for this approach not to infringe on copyrights, you would need to install the original game first, since redistributing any part of the original game would be illegal.

Consider the following example modding experiment: Build a full-client replacement that would pit the characters of the WoW universe against each other in brutal head-to-head car racing. The modification could be called Orc Speed Racing and could include racetracks in all the popular regions of the WoW universe. This mod makes a good example because it requires a full client replacement with physics engine and additional content in the form of new maps and racecars. Such a modification can be architected as shown in Figure 9–3.

In this process, you discover that rendering the models that come with the standard WoW client is hard work. Fortunately, others have already done much of that work for you. We directly leverage ideas, inspiration, and know-how from the WowMapView and WowModelView projects. These two programs, and others like them, are excellent examples of real-world modding tools. Related projects include scripts for 3D Studio (a popular off-the-shelf program from Autodesk) that convert WoW models to and from .3DS format.

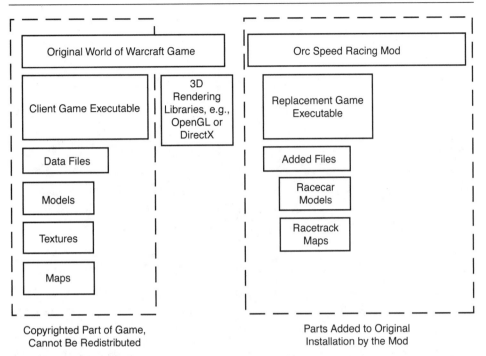

Figure 9–3 The architecture of a fictitious WoW TC called Orc Speed Racing. Notice how parts of the game are replaced while other parts remain the same.

WowMapView was originally created to read WoW terrain files offline (from the disk or a cache) and allow a user to explore the WoW universe without being online with the server. WowModelView does the same thing for rendering—providing the user a way to peruse game models offline. Both programs rely on homegrown 3D rendering built on top of the OpenGL library (which we briefly describe in Chapter 7).

As we mentioned, piggybacking on the game engine and data provided with the WoW client makes it possible to create stand-alone programs that render parts of the WoW universe. Figure 9–4 shows a mod we created that combines two aspects of the WoW universe in a new way: The terrain from the barrens (a location in the WoW universe) has been augmented with orc huts placed in ways not normally found in that region.

Rewriting the Server

If you intend for your mod to work online, there are a number of routes you can explore. The easiest is to leave the game's existing client-server model intact and simply reskin things in individual clients. For example, the

Figure 9–4 This example of a mod uses client-side data and models from WoW in an offline mode. Terrain from the barrens was combined with an orc hut model. (Orc huts are usually not found like this in the barrens.)

infamous nude patch from Figure 9–1 can be applied locally to an individual client program without affecting the online client-server model.

Note that altering game play and logic usually necessitates a change in server mechanics as well. For games like WoW, the server isn't sold with the client, and the game company prefers that you play only on its official servers. Because the game cannot run in server mode, game modders are left with only one option—write their own servers.

You can write servers to make use of the existing client-server protocol that comes with the game, or as an alternative, you can develop an entirely new protocol. If you're not replacing the client executable, the protocol will likely remain intact and your server will need to be compliant with the game's existing protocol. If you do replace the game client logic, you'll need to develop an independent client-server protocol.

Let's return to our fictitious mod. In Orc Speed Racing, we are replacing the entire game client with the new racing game client. Ultimately, we must develop a new game server specifically for this racing game. Note that there

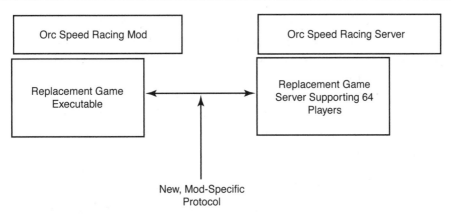

New, Mod-Specific
Protocol

Figure 9–5 The client-server architecture for our fictitious Orc Speed Racing mod.

is no need to use a protocol with any resemblance to the original WoW protocol. Figure 9–5 shows the architecture of the new client-server model for Orc Speed Racing.

Figure 9–6 illustrates a potential model for a game expansion pack. In this scenario, let's say the expansion pack provider has added an entirely new realm to the WoW universe. The provider copyrighted everything in the new world, so the look and feel belongs solely to the provider (new models,

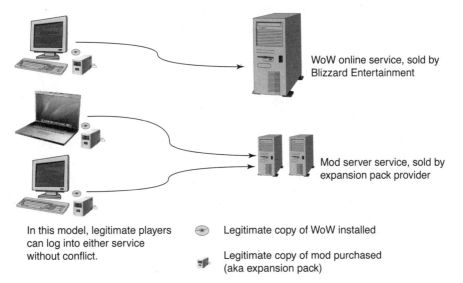

Figure 9–6 A game expansion pack model in which the mod supplier also sells accounts to an online server.

animations, sound, storylines, and so on), and the world server provided for the expansion pack doesn't serve any parts of the universe provided on the original servers. Thus, the new realm is entirely new and distinct (such as a new continent or island).

Players who have the expansion pack can log into this new realm and play on the new continent provided they have an account with the expansion pack provider. In theory, this model would allow the mod company to run a successful business, would not infringe on any copyrights, and would extend the life of the underlying game engine by keeping it fresh with new content. Unfortunately, many game companies don't like this model, which they apparently see either as competition with their own online service or as a system that encourages people to use pirated copies of the game client.[1] In the case of WoW, the third-party service provider may need to pass authentication through to the main WoW servers because part of the game's copyright protection is implemented in the login process.

WoW has a long history of independent server development. Such hacks have traditionally been called *emulation servers*. The problem is that Blizzard Entertainment frowns on the very idea. In fact, Blizzard has threatened to sue pretty much anyone who has ever published an emulation server on the Net. (Recall the fate of the poor BnetD developers we introduce in Chapter 4.) Blizzard's argument has been that emulation servers allow people to play pirated versions of the game (since some security checks require the server). Games have always had ways to check their authenticity, typically with a serial number or key. The WoW game is no different but does have some clever engineering tricks to make the server authentication interdependent with the serial number key check, thus providing a technical platform to support legal action against people who change the server authentication procedure. In short, a brilliant move on the game developer's part.

In some cases, games check their own licenses locally (rendering them susceptible to classic cracking attacks). A problem arises when a game company uses its online service as an additional method of checking authenticity. The game can check a serial number in a traditional client-side manner, but the online service provides an additional layer of security. Because independent servers can't access corporate key servers, they can't

---

1. Remember from Chapter 2 that antipiracy mechanisms usually involve interaction with the original game servers to check game client legitimacy.

check keys online even if they wanted to.[2] Even though the game still requires a serial number to play, companies taking a hard line against server emulation go about shutting down independent servers by using the DMCA law to argue that external servers promote piracy (see Chapter 4).

In reality, such legal efforts haven't worked very well, and many independent game servers operate for WoW clients even as this book goes to press. However, none of these servers are sanctioned by Blizzard, and they could be made instantaneously incompatible with the base game at any point through standard game evolution practices.

Figure 9–7 shows a list of available third-party servers for WoW. The client version required is 1.9.4—the servers don't work with the latest version of WoW. This is because the servers have to be updated whenever

:: Servers :: Click on name for details	Version	Location	Language	XPRate	Click to Connect*	Account	Comments	Rating	% Online	User Online**	Status**
Orange Virus² - 1.12.2	1.9.4	Europe		blizzlike	Connect	Register	12	4.6\5	100.0%	N/A	
WoW GéNéRaTiOn	1.9.4	Europe		blizzlike	Connect	Register	106	2.8\5	96.0%	N/A	
WoWGeR V 3.0 II 1.12.1 / 1.12.2	1.9.4	Europe		blizzlike	Connect	Register	1	5.0\5	100.0%	N/A	
Highlander HighBorne 2005 Romania 1.11...	1.9.4	Europe		blizzlike	Connect	Register	54	4.8\5	100.0%	20	
NordWoW PvP&PvE Server Patch 1.12.2...	1.9.4	Europe		blizzlike	Connect	Register	70	4.3\5	100.0%	N/A	
WoWPortugal	1.9.4	Europe		blizzlike	Connect	Register	6	3.0\5	96.0%	N/A	
New Generation 200MB 24/7 NOW 1.12.1	1.9.4	South-America		blizzlike	Connect	Register	36	3.4\5	98.0%	N/A	
WowApocolypse 1.12.1	1.9.4	Europe		blizzlike	Connect	Register	27	4.0\5	100.0%	0	
Quenya Germany	1.9.4	Europe		blizzlike	Connect	Register	13	5.0\5	96.0%	92	
3server World of Mirro CZ/E...	1.9.4	Europe		high	Connect	Register	5	5.0\5	100.0%	N/A	
DEVASTATOR 1.12.1/1.12.2 officiel	1.9.4	Europe		blizzlike	Connect	Register	6	4.2\5	96.0%	N/A	
Darluok Server FR 1.12.1-1.12.2 DKEmu 0...	1.9.4	Europe		high	Connect	Register	59	4.3\5	100.0%	40	
SGserver	1.9.4	Africa		very high	Connect	Register	9	4.6\5	95.0%	8	
Darluok Server FR 1.12.1-1.12.2 DKEmu p...	1.9.4	Europe		high	Connect	Register	19	4.8\5	100.0%	41	
Némésis	1.9.4	Europe		blizzlike	Connect	Register	1	5.0\5	96.0%	1	
TheBEST!!!CHECK US OUT	1.9.4	North-America		high	Connect	Register	76	4.1\5	100.0%	N/A	
DIABLOS LAIR SERVER (CZ/SK) 1.12.1 pat...	1.9.4	Europe	[?]	low	Connect	Register	3	3.7\5	100.0%	N/A	

Figure 9–7 A list of successful, operational, private WoW servers at the time of this writing. Literally hundreds are available. (From <http://www.wowstatus.net/serverlist.php>.)

---

2. If companies like Blizzard offered a legitimate way for third-party servers to perform a key check, they might be surprised at how willing third-party server developers would be to add this feature. Of course, the main problem is loss of monthly server-subscription revenue. A solution could involve enforcing client "freshness" by using a trusted clock and a cryptographically protected client timestamp that resets only when monthly fees are paid.

a new version of the WoW client becomes available. This makes them always slightly behind the curve.

At the time of this writing, MaNGOS and WoWEmu appeared to be popular choices for setting up a private server.[3] MaNGOS is open source and has an active development staff.[4]

Client Rendering Options

You have many options for rendering a 3D universe, and several open source projects are available for building games. If you need a professional solution for rendering and gaming, consider something like the Torque engine distributed by GarageGames.com. Torque was originally used to create the popular game Tribes. A good open source option is the OGRE 3D platform (described in Chapter 7). In any case, there are several ways to render and reuse models and other client-side media content from an existing game.

In the experiments we describe next, the models, animations, textures, and terrain are all borrowed successfully from WoW media files and reused by the replacement client program. Because media for the WoW universe is usually stored in a set of files located in a directory structure under the game's installation directory, they are particularly easy to find and extract.

Model Construction

Games use a large number of objects to model and then render the game world. 3D models for a game contain many different components. Here is a short WoW-centric list:

- Models
- Animations
- Bone definitions
- Texture animation definitions
- Model vertexes
- Model views
- Model geosets
- Model texture units
- Model render flags
- Model color definitions
- Model transparency definitions
- Model light definitions
- Model camera definitions
- Model particle systems
- Model particle emitter definitions
- Model ribbon emitter definitions

To make this more concrete, consider that a character model in WoW contains many geometry sets for different hairstyles. The player can choose

---

3. Popularity as rated by <http://forum.ragezone.com/world-warcraft/>.
4. For more on the MaNGOS project, see <http://www.mangosproject.org/forum/>.

a hairstyle, and the appropriate hairstyle mesh will be used for rendering. In Figure 9–8, we have imported the 3D model of a character in WoW and separated the various submeshes. You can see a large number of hairstyles, five different cloaks, a sash, a belt, a dress, and various armor pieces. The game chooses which of these to render based on what the character is wearing.

All modern games use similar objects and methods for modeling. Game makers consider these objects important to the look and feel of their games, and they sometimes become perturbed when people talk about and use them. That doesn't stop online game hackers from doing so, however. None of the techniques we describe will come as news to hard-core game hackers.

To help you better understand game objects, we show you a few of the objects contained in the WoW game client. We extracted them from the media files installed with the game by using commonly available tools. We

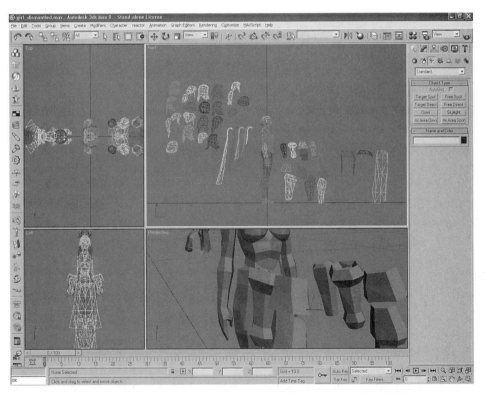

Figure 9–8 Character models are decorated with mesh skin in WoW and most other games. Here we display some of the submeshes stored along with a character model in the WoW client files. (Reproduced with permission from www.wowstatus.net.)

Table 9–1 Tools for Hacking Game Models

Tool	Game
WowMapView	WoW
WowModelView	WoW
MyWarCraftStudio	WoW
Radiant	Call of Duty 2
F.E.A.R. Modification Tools	F.E.A.R.
HL2 SDK	Half-Life
DS2TK	Dungeon Siege II
TES Construction Set	The Elder Scrolls

already introduced one tool, WowModelView, that works against WoW files.

Other games have their share of extraction and manipulation tools as well, as you can see in Table 9–1.

WowModelView has a reasonably sophisticated interface. Figure 9–9 is a screenshot of WowModelView in action. Figure 9–10 shows the same engine rendering a location from WoW.

Some tools were designed specifically for game modding and can be very robust. For example, The Elder Scrolls, a popular fantasy game, has a complete development environment for creating and modifying content. Figure 9–11 shows a TES Construction Set screenshot.

Returning to WoW, the objects in WoW media files can be extracted and used in an alternative environment such as the OGRE environment introduced in Chapter 7. Of course, the objects and media in the files are all copyrighted material, so if you create your own game using Blizzard media, you are not allowed to redistribute it in any way.

Transforming models from one format to another, say, from WoW into 3D Studio Max, can sometimes take some work. Modders quickly collect a whole arsenal of tools that are used together in a pipe (something that anyone who has played with graphics will understand). And when more than one tool is required to get a model or object into a format you need, this process is sometimes called a tool chain. For example, to get a WoW model into 3D Studio, the model is first exported with MyWarCraftStudio (Figure 9–12), then loaded into Milkshape, then exported again, then imported into 3D Studio via a plug-in.

In some cases, tool chains can get quite long, with four or more tools used together to compute a final product. Things get complicated when

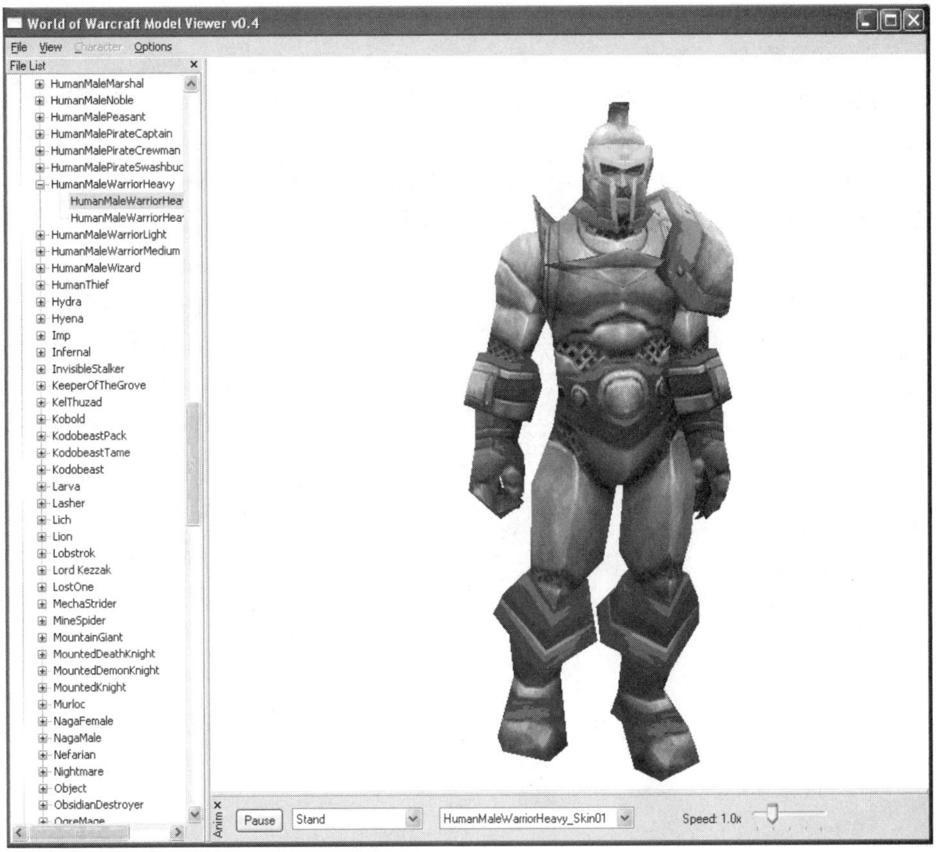

Figure 9–9 This screenshot taken from a session with WowModelView shows the program's reasonably sophisticated interface.

models contain texture data and animations, and each tool in your arsenal may have quirks. Sometimes a tool might not be able to properly convert the animation sequences or bones.

Stand-ins

Hobby game hackers eager to play around with MMO construction can use models and objects belonging to games they own to create their own miniature adventure games and/or MMO projects. Sometimes these objects are called stand-ins because developers may replace the borrowed media later with artwork of their own. Developing a complete set of objects and models from scratch is a huge and expensive undertaking.

Figure 9–10 A picture of a deadmines instance (a location in the WoW universe) as borrowed from WoW and viewed with WowMapView.

Textures

One of the simplest things to mod is game texture. We already show the results of the ever-popular texture modding nude patch at the top of this chapter. One of the reasons texture mods are so easy is that a single graphics file is usually all that needs to be replaced. Image editing programs are fairly easy to use for those with artistic talents.

The coolest thing is that the result of texture work is immediately visible in the game. In other words, you can get quick satisfaction.

Artistic Angles

Some forms of texture modification have taken more of an artistic bent. For example, antiwar activists have created a collection of graffiti art hosted at Velvet-Strike that can be used with the Counter-Strike FPS game, as shown in Figures 9–13 and 9–14.

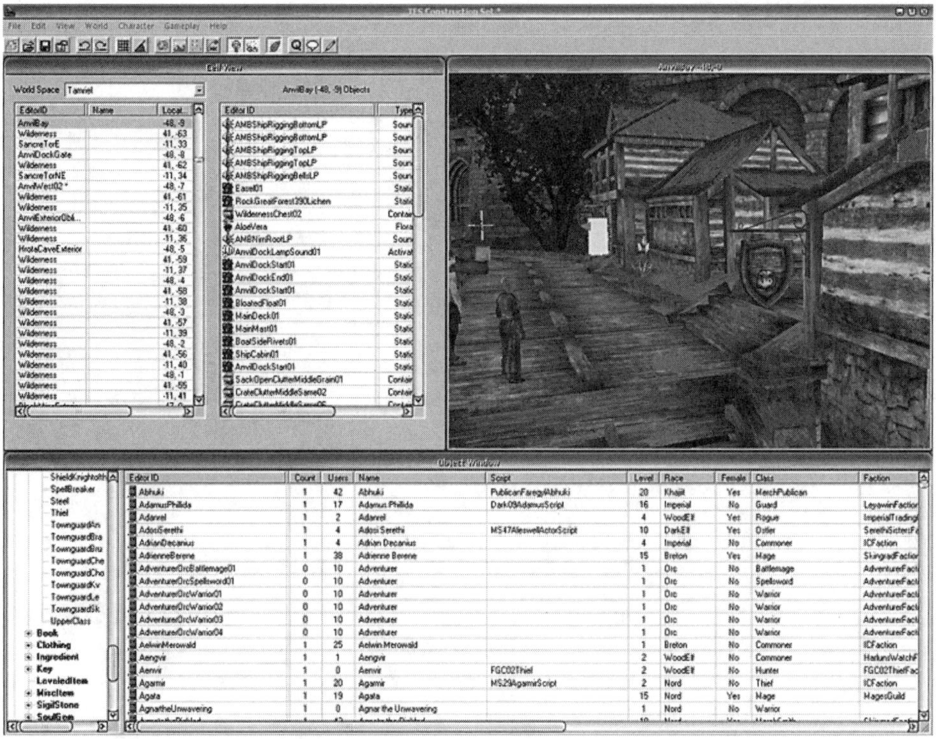

Figure 9–11 A screenshot of the TES Construction Set in action. (From <http://en
.wikipedia.org/wiki/Image:TES4.png>.)

Texture modding is easy and fun. Would-be game hackers who are new
to the sport might try this first. You can see great results with only a few
hours of play.

Terrain

Terrain and levels can be generated automatically (something called *pro-
cedural generation*), or you can construct them ahead of time and store
them as 3D models known as *heightmaps*. Games have their own special file
formats for storing terrain information. In WoW, terrain is stored in the
ADT format (Figure 9–15). In the case of heightmaps, you can use a bitmap
image to define how high the ground should be; the 3D model is generated
on the fly from this information. Figure 9–16 shows an example of a heightmap.

308 *Chapter 9 Advanced Game Hacking Fu*

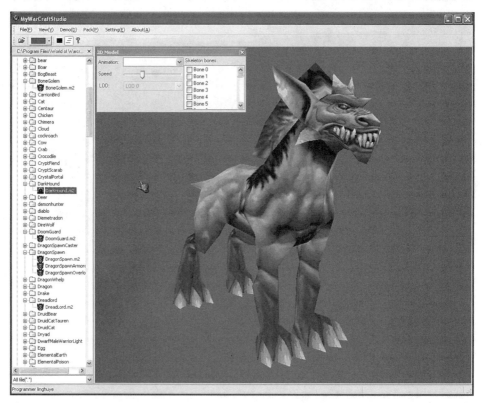

Figure 9–12 The MyWarCraftStudio program allows exporting of WoW models.

Figure 9–13 Antiwar graffiti for Counter-Strike. (From <http://www.opensorcery.net/velvet-strike/sprays.html>. Reproduced with permission from Anne Marie Schleiner.)

Figure 9–14 More antiwar graffiti for Counter-Strike. (From <http://www.opensorcery .net/velvet-strike/sprays.html>. Reproduced with permission from Anne Marie Schleiner.)

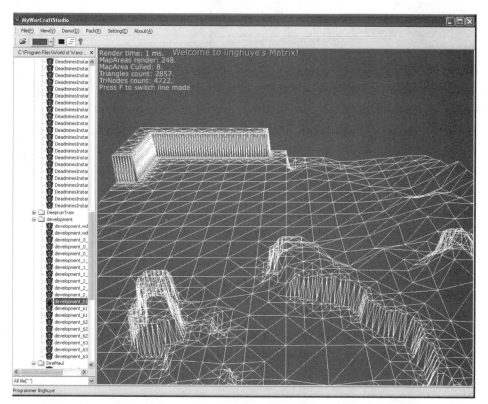

Figure 9–15 Terrain for WoW from an ADT file as viewed in MyWarCraftStudio.

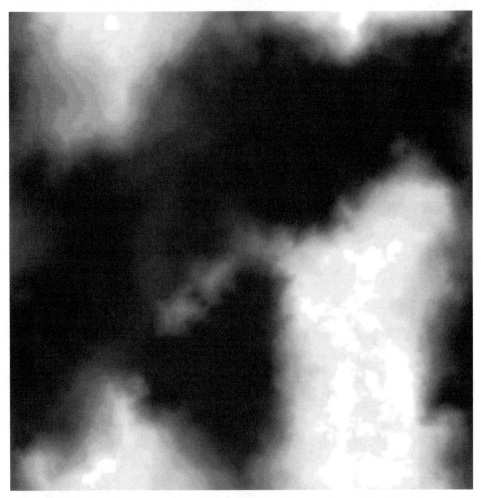

Figure 9–16 A heightmap shows terrain from a "god's eye" view, with different shades used to represent different terrain altitudes.

The rendering engine can use the heightmap from Figure 9–16 to generate terrain, as shown in Figure 9–17.

Wireframe terrain requires textures in order to look like ground, stone, grass, and so on. Depending on the tools used, terrain textures can be painted directly onto the surface, automatically generated, or developed using image editing software such as Adobe Photoshop.

We built a textured terrain using a combination of tools. The result can be seen in Figures 9–18 and 9–19. Figure 9–18 shows a view from above

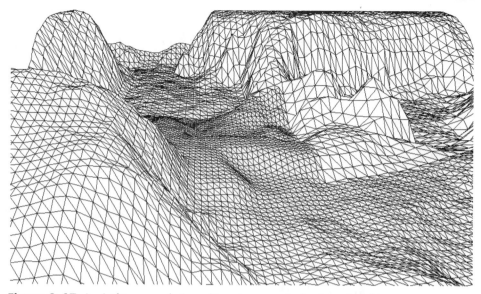

Figure 9-17 A wireframe rendering of terrain generated using a heightmap.

(similar to the heightmap). Figure 9–19 shows a more traditional view from ground level.

Terrain is very important in games. Unfortunately, most hobbyists don't do a very good job with terrain, ending up with silly-looking worlds. This is odd considering how many tools exist for doing decent terrain generation (some with very advanced options). At the time of this writing, a set of upcoming MMOs are leveraging a program called SpeedTree <http://www .speedtree.com> that can procedurally generate lush forests, saving game developers huge amounts of money that would otherwise be spent in terrain development (Figure 9–20).

Another inexpensive program for terrain generation is called Terragen <http://www.planetside.co.uk/terragen/>. Terragen can render photorealistic terrain (Figure 9–21). Terragen can export the terrain in the form of a heightmap, making it particularly easy to import into many existing games.

When it comes to game mods, you can generate entirely new terrains and level maps using more tools than we could possibly cover in a chapter. In fact, entire books already exist that are devoted exclusively to modding

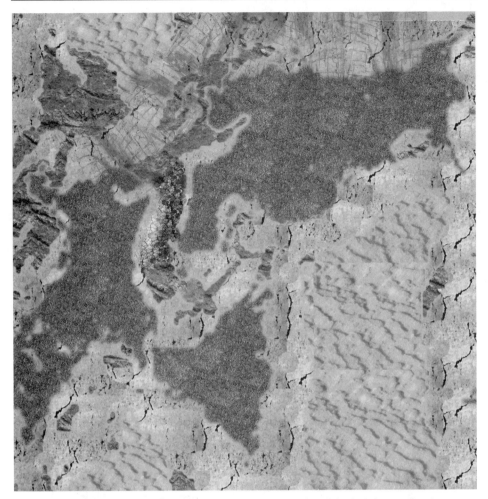

Figure 9–18 With texture added, the "god's eye" view from the heightmap begins to look more like a picture from space.

games. One good example has grown up around the Unreal Engine by Epic Games <http://www.epicgames.com>. Unreal is a particularly popular game engine with a modding community that the game company actively supports. A great book on developing new worlds with the Unreal Engine is *Mastering Unreal Technology: The Art of Level Design* by Jason Busby, Zak Parrish, and Joel Van Eenwyk (Sams, 2004).

Figure 9–19 The same textured terrain rendered from ground level.

Figure 9–20 A SpeedTree-generated view. This image is taken from the game Fatal Inertia, as displayed on the SpeedTree site. (From <http://www.speedtree.com/gallery/index.php?Page=70&Sort=0#>. Reproduced with permission from www.speedtree.com.)

Figure 9–21 A Terragen-rendered landscape, with photorealistic qualities. (From <http://www.planetside.co.uk/gallery/v/tg09gallery/GalleryImage457296.jpg.html>. Reproduced with permission from www.planetside.co.uk.)

Media File Formats

Building a mod like the ones shown throughout this chapter requires a basic understanding of the media file format that the game client uses. In the case of games built by Blizzard Entertainment (including WoW and Diablo), media files are distributed in a proprietary file format called MPQ. The MPQ name is derived from its creator Mike O'Brien and is short for MoPaQ, which is derived from Mike O'Brien PaCK.[5] All games have their selected media formats, whether they are public or homegrown.

To really get into WoW modding, understanding the MPQ file format is essential. Several coders have already built tools to decode the MPQ file format. The open source program libmpq is a code library that simplifies

---

5. The mpq-tools homepage, <https://babelize.org/mpq-tools.php>, describes the origin of the MPQ name.

reading and decoding MPQ files. The code was released under the GNU license and was written by Maik Broemme. You can find the library in the project called mpq-tools available from many sites, including <https://babelize.org/mpq-tools.php>.

A large number of MPQ editors, extractors, and repackers are floating around on the Net. These tools allow you to extract content and replace content inside MPQ files.

Emulation Servers (Private Servers)

Earlier in the book, we introduced the idea of rolling your own game server. At the time, we indicated that when it comes to WoW, a lot of work has already been done in this area. We also made it clear that this kind of activity is frowned upon by Blizzard Entertainment, the makers of WoW. Just so you know, not all game developers take the same hard-nosed stance as Blizzard, and many games have active communities of modders with support by the game developers. Writing a game server is a fascinating programming exercise. In effect, you get to be a microcosmic god over your own little universe, and who doesn't like that?

We need to add an important disclaimer here—even though we cover emulation servers written for WoW in this section, please remember that if you write your own or attempt to redistribute a modded version of the servers we present here, you might find yourself on the sharp end of a lawsuit. Consider yourself forewarned. There is an excellent history of various WoW emulation projects that someone has compiled at <http://www.gotwow.ic.cz/>.

To tell you the truth, we debated whether or not to put this material in the book. In the end, our honest assessment of the material we're sharing is that it doesn't directly violate any copyrights or disable any copyright mechanisms in the stand-alone game. What it does do is enable you to play the game without having an active online account with Blizzard.

We believe that because of fair use protections, if you buy a legitimate copy of a game at the store, you can use the material any way you want, including but not limited to running the game with a private server on your remote tropical island that has no Internet access. Others believe differently.

OK, enough of that.

Protocol Emulation

To emulate a server, you must first be able to communicate directly with the client program. This requires reverse engineering the network protocol, messages, and any encryption or obfuscation the protocol uses.

Here is a partial table of message types for WoW that we obtained from a popular emulation server's source code. This type of data is very expensive to reverse engineer, but others have done all the heavy lifting.

```
public enum OP
        {
        MSG_NULL_ACTION,                        // = 0x0
        CMSG_BOOTME,                            // = 0x1
        CMSG_DBLOOKUP,                          // = 0x2
        SMSG_DBLOOKUP,                          // = 0x3
        CMSG_QUERY_OBJECT_POSITION,             // = 0x4
        SMSG_QUERY_OBJECT_POSITION,             // = 0x5
        CMSG_QUERY_OBJECT_ROTATION,             // = 0x6
        SMSG_QUERY_OBJECT_ROTATION,             // = 0x7
```

We snipped a large number of messages to save room. . . .

```
        SMSG_SET_FORCED_REACTIONS,              // = 0x029D
        SMSG_SPELL_FAILED_OTHER,                // = 0x029E
        SMSG_GAMEOBJECT_RESET_STATE,            // = 0x029F
        CMSG_REPAIR_ITEM,                       // = 0x02A0
        SMSG_CHAT_PLAYER_NOT_FOUND,             // = 0x02A1
        MSG_TALENT_WIPE_CONFIRM,                // = 0x02A2
        SMSG_SUMMON_REQUEST,                    // = 0x02A3
        CMSG_SUMMON_RESPONSE,                   // = 0x02A4
        MSG_MOVE_TOGGLE_GRAVITY_CHEAT,          // = 0x02A5
        SMSG_MONSTER_MOVE_TRANSPORT,            // = 0x02A6
        SMSG_PET_BROKEN,                        // = 0x02A7
        MSG_MOVE_FEATHER_FALL,                  // = 0x02A8
        MSG_MOVE_WATER_WALK,                    // = 0x02A9
        CMSG_SERVER_BROADCAST,                  // = 0x02AA
        CMSG_SELF_RES,                          // = 0x02AB
        SMSG_FEIGN_DEATH_RESISTED,              // = 0x02AC
        CMSG_RUN_SCRIPT,                        // = 0x02AD
        SMSG_SCRIPT_MESSAGE,                    // = 0x02AE
        NUM_MSG_TYPES                           // = 0x02AF
};
```

Of course, the structure doesn't contain all possible messages, and in fact additional tables of response codes, items, object IDs, and so on exist.

In other words, there's literally a ton of data to reverse engineer if you want to build a complete emulation server. That's why emulation servers are so expensive to build.

Exercise: Hooking the Packet Engine

A single function in the WoW.exe client binary handles all packets. The prototype for this function is shown below.

```
NetClient__ProcessMessage(
        int NetClient,
        int dummy,
        unsigned long l,
        DWORD *CDataStore)
```

You can use the techniques shown in Chapter 6 to locate this function dynamically. You can place a detour hook or breakpoint hook on this function using either an injected DLL or an external debugger (as also described in Chapter 6). Once your hook is in place, you can sniff packet traffic to begin reverse engineering what you will need to emulate in your private server. Of course, this is academic for WoW since game hackers have already done this and you can just reuse what they have done. But when you begin reverse engineering a new game, you can implement this same strategy.

Decrypting Warcraft Packets

Note: *A section of this chapter was removed before publication. Readers interested in this subject can learn everything they need to know about decrypting WoW packets by downloading the MaNGOS project and reading the source code.*

The game you reverse engineer will likely have an encryption system for the network communication. Encryption might be too strong a word here; maybe it would better be called an obfuscation system. Because the game client program must decrypt the packets, you will have everything you need to decrypt them yourself. You simply have to reverse engineer what the client program is doing and reimplement that yourself.

Reverse engineering whatever encryption a game uses can certainly take some time, and we don't mean to trivialize it. This kind of activity is a required step in the process of building an emulation server.

To start writing or customizing an emulation server, try downloading MaNGOS or WoWEmu source code and compiling it. We describe how to download MaNGOS in the related text box. As of this writing, MaNGOS reports to be compatible with a fairly recent version of WoW. This exercise can prepare you to craft your own emulation servers for new games that are being released.

Downloading MaNGOS

To download MaNGOS, you need to obtain the source code control program known as Subversion. We suggest you use the program TortoiseSVN, which supports Subversion <http://tortoisesvn.tigris.org>. As of this writing, all you need to do to get the latest version of MaNGOS is to configure Tortoise to perform a CVS Checkout from the URL <https://mangos.svn.sourceforge.net/svnroot/mangos/trunk>. MaNGOS comes with a Microsoft Visual Studio solution file and can be compiled with the Visual Studio compiler.

   MaNGOS must be compiled and configured. It requires MySQL 5.0 to be installed. It also requires a database to be initialized that will represent the game universe. This database is delivered in a separate file. We have tried Azzum'sRepack, which weighs in at about 200MB of compressed data. Several other tools were also required, including Navicat, XAMPP, MaNGOS DB Handler, and nnCron. This sounds like a large pile, and it is. However, the general consensus among game hackers is that it's worth it. A detailed setup and installation guide is available at <http://forum.ragezone.com/world-warcraft>.

Steps Required to Get into the World

A number of steps are required to get an emulation world up and get your character into it. The first step is to build the server, of course.

   Once the emulation server is built, the second step in getting it to work is to have it authenticate a user login. The client program will require a valid login before it will even attempt to render the game world. The client program might establish a session key and then provide a username and password pair to be authenticated. You can simply respond with a success message, or you can write some form of database or flat file of usernames and passwords and actually check.

   After authentication, present the user with a list of servers to log into (at least for WoW). Because many games can't actually create a single world for millions of players, the game is split over many servers. In the case of WoW, each server is distinct and separate, and players must have unique characters for each server. This list of realms must be delivered to the client, and the user will select one.

Next, build a character list. The user may have specific characters on each realm. At this point, the emulation server will likely need to give the user a way to create and/or delete characters as well. The client program will handle most of the details of character creation, but the server might be called upon to make dice rolls, deliver stats, and so on. For example, when the user tries to select a character name, the server will need to check that there isn't a name conflict with an existing character.

Finally, given a working active character, the user should be able to log into the world. The character will have a coordinate position associated with it, which will be used to tell the client where to begin rendering the world. The client program handles all the rendering, so the server just needs to keep track of where all the objects are located.

There are certainly plenty of hoops to jump through before you get to the fun part of actually interacting with the game world. But these steps are necessary in order to get the plumbing working for the game. Once you tackle these steps, you shouldn't need to come back and rework them unless the game company changes something fairly significant in the architecture of its game.

Legal Tangles

The legality of techniques like the ones we describe in this chapter is currently a matter of debate. Some game companies embrace modding and server emulation as a way to build strong user loyalty and ensure perpetual freshness. Others frown on the idea of anyone mucking with their games in any capacity. We're not lawyers, so we can't give you any legal advice. What we can say is that you should be aware of the kinds of legal tangles that can arise when modding a game.

That said, all of the techniques that we show in this chapter are well known by game hackers. Powerful tools for modding and their newfound ease of use make the job much easier than it was in the old days. These are two of the reasons that more people may be looking into modding as a way to understand how games really function.

10 Software Security Über Alles

What exactly are we trying to accomplish with this book anyway? Our primary goal is to understand the security implications of massively distributed software systems that have millions of users. We think MMORPGs—one small sliver of massively distributed systems—are a harbinger of things to come in the rest of the software world. In other words, online games are the systems of the future, today. They are widely used by so many people simultaneously that state is pushed around like sand on a beach. As many security engineers know, securing a distributed system is hard . . . and building a secure distributed system is even harder. In many ways, MMORPGs push the limits of security engineering. By understanding what works and what doesn't in MMORPG security, we can learn important lessons for the future.

Online game companies have to be surprised (in a good way) by their own success. Who would have guessed that more than 8 million people would subscribe to WoW?! But with this success comes a rather large burden—securing a system that millions of people, some of whom aren't trustworthy, use.

Just as with users of other software, most users of WoW and other MMORPGs remain blithely unaware of the security issues exploding around them. Most gamers probably know nothing of how game developers monitor their PCs in the name of security. Few gamers are aware of cheating (in all its many guises), rendering the game unfair for people who play by the rules.

Why have so many turned a blind eye to security issues? It's simple—most people are optimists, believing (for no apparent reason) that the games they use are secure. No false or misleading claims are made about security on the part of game companies trying to appear to be secure (in fact, they cleverly remain mum on the issue if possible); that's just what people naturally believe. Things go very badly for software producers when people suddenly realize the true state of security in the software they count on. Just ask Microsoft, which has spent tens of millions of dollars turning around its poor security reputation (by doing the right kinds of things, we should add)!

As we describe throughout the book, the biggest security risk in online gaming comes when state is pushed to the client. Whenever client-side state is manipulated or otherwise made available in client software, it leaves much room for monkey business. Often, monkey business can turn into real business with the help of middleman companies, including those we describe in Chapter 3.

This chapter is about fixing the problem. First, we make some suggestions to game developers about how to build more secure games. Then we wrap things up with a discussion of what gamers should find out about the games they play.

Building Security In for Game Developers

The biggest problem in computer security today is that most systems aren't constructed with security in mind. Reactive network technologies such as firewalls can help alleviate obvious script kiddie attacks on servers, but they do nothing to address the real security problem—bad software. If we want to solve the computer security problem, we need to do more to build secure software.

Software security is the practice of building software to be secure and to function properly under malicious attack. Online game software is clearly in need of software security.

The trinity of trouble—connectivity, complexity, and extensibility—largely influences the growth and evolution of the software security problem. Clearly these three issues have had a direct influence on computer games. At first, connectivity through the Internet seemed to be a boon for security because a central server could check for legitimate licenses. But now that online games have become large and highly distributed, connectivity adds to security risk, linking people of all stripes, from the trustworthy to the criminal. Complexity and its growth has always been an issue in software, and game software is no exception. Online games are so massively distributed and share so much state with so many users that they're among the most complex distributed software systems in existence. That makes securing them difficult. Finally, because online games are made of software, extensibility is only natural. Sometimes extensibility is explicitly built in as part of the game (as in Second Life), but sometimes a game's true extensibility is brought to light by hackers and hobbyists as in TCs (see Chapter 9).

On the road to implementing a fundamental change in the way we build game software, we must first agree that software security is not security software. This is a subtle point often lost on development people, who tend to focus on functionality. Obviously, there are security functions in the world, and most modern game software includes security features; but adding features such as SSL to your game to cryptographically protect communications doesn't present a complete solution (especially when the client key is so easy to find; see Chapter 6). Software security is a system-wide issue that takes into account both security mechanisms (such as access control) and design for security (such as robust design that makes software attacks difficult). Sometimes these overlap, but often they don't.

Put another way, security is an emergent property of any software system, including online game software. A security problem is more likely to arise because of a problem in a system's standard-issue part (say, the interface to one of the many database modules or the handoff between world servers) than in some given security feature. This is an important reason why software security must be part of a full lifecycle approach. Just as you can't test quality into a piece of software, you can't spray paint security features onto a game and expect it to become secure. There's no such thing as magic crypto fairy dust—we need to focus on software security from the ground up. We need to build security into our online games.

As practitioners become aware of software security's importance, they are increasingly adopting and evolving a set of best practices to address the problem. Microsoft has carried out a noteworthy effort under its Trustworthy Computing Initiative. Many Cigital customers are in the midst of enterprise-scale software security initiatives. Most approaches in practice today encompass training for developers, testers, and architects; analysis and auditing of software artifacts; and security engineering. In the fight for better software, treating the disease itself (poorly designed and implemented software) is better than taking an aspirin to stop the symptoms. There's no substitute for working software security as deeply into the development process as possible and taking advantage of the engineering lessons software practitioners have learned over the years.

Software Security Touchpoints

In the book *Software Security: Building Security In* (Addison-Wesley, 2006), one of us (McGraw) introduces a set of seven best practices called *touchpoints*. Whether or not you're a game developer, putting software security into practice requires making some changes to the way your organization builds software. The good news is that these changes don't need to be fundamental, earth shattering, or cost prohibitive. In fact, adopting a straightforward set of engineering best practices, designed in such a way that security can be interleaved into existing development processes, is often all it takes.

Integrating software security best practices into the software development lifecycle is one of the three pillars of software security. The software security best practices briefly introduced here have their basis in good software engineering and involve explicitly pondering the security situation throughout the software lifecycle. This means knowing and understanding common risks (including the ones described in this book), designing for security, and subjecting all software artifacts to thorough, objective risk analyses and testing.

Figure 10–1 specifies the software security touchpoints and shows how software practitioners can apply them to the various software artifacts produced during software development. This means understanding how to work security engineering into requirements (we now understand that our very customers have darn good economic reasons to break our stuff), architecture (massively distributed systems are particularly tricky), design, coding (remember those timing bugs), testing, validation, measurement, and maintenance.

Although the artifacts in Figure 10–1 resemble a traditional waterfall model, most organizations now follow an iterative approach, which means that they'll cycle through the touchpoints more than once as the software

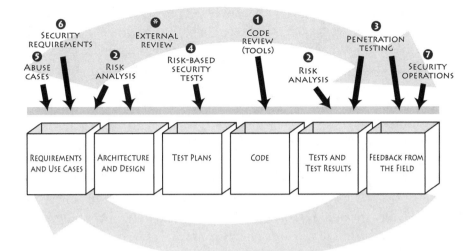

Figure 10–1 The software security touchpoints as introduced and fleshed out in McGraw's book *Software Security: Building Security In.*

evolves. In any event, by focusing on the artifacts, we can avoid broader process issues (including the ever-present warfare surrounding which software process is the one true way and the light).

The software security touchpoints are designed to be process agnostic. That is, you can apply the touchpoints no matter which software process you use to build your software. As long as you're producing some minimal set of software artifacts (and every project should at least be producing code!), you can apply the touchpoints.

Some touchpoints are by their very nature more powerful than others, and you should adopt the most powerful ones first. Here are the touchpoints, in order of effectiveness:

1. Code review with a static analysis tool
2. Architectural risk analysis
3. Penetration testing
4. Risk-based security tests
5. Abuse cases
6. Security requirements
7. Security operations

For much more about the touchpoints, see *Software Security*, where you will find a chapter devoted to each.

The suggested ordering won't be a perfect fit for every organization. In fact, the ordering reflects a bias developed over many years of applying these practices in code-o-centric organizations. For that reason, code review comes before architectural risk analysis. However, the fact is that both of the top two touchpoints are critical. If you do code review and skip architectural risk analysis, you will not properly address the software security problem.

As we've seen throughout this book, the kinds of software defects that attackers go after come in two varieties: bugs and flaws. Code review aims to find the bugs. Architectural risk analysis aims to find the flaws. If you skip one or the other, you're most likely to solve only half the problem. (Bugs and flaws are split 50/50.) Either way, the top two touchpoints can be swapped around without any loss of generality.

As for the rest of the touchpoints, the ranking presented here is based on years of experience applying the touchpoints at many different kinds of organizations, ranging from large independent software vendors to huge investment banks. The ordering is not absolute. However, any attempt to change the order, say, by doing penetration testing before you do code review, is likely to be not as successful as the one we endorse here.

Black Hats and White Hats

Two kinds of activities—black hat and white hat—intertwine to make up software security. This idea serves as inspiration for the yin/yang logo demarking this series of books. The yin/yang design is the classic Eastern symbol related to the inextricable mixing of standard Western polemics. Eastern philosophies are for this reason called holistic. A holistic approach, mixing yin and yang—that is, mixing the black hat and white hat approaches—is just what the doctor ordered.

Destructive activities are about attacks, exploits, and breaking software. This book shows firsthand just what destructive activities are like for online games. Without directly and clearly discussing attacks in a realistic manner (such as we do throughout this book), defenses can't be properly devised and put into place. These kinds of things are represented by the black hat. That is, they are generally considered "bad guy" activities. *Constructive activities* are about design, defense, and functionality. These are represented by the white hat.

Perhaps a less judgmental way to think about the dichotomy is in terms of defense and offense. Neither defense nor offense is intrinsically bad or good, and both are necessary to play almost any sport well.

If you're a game developer who's serious about countering the security problems explained in this book, you should convince your shop to adopt the software security touchpoints.

Security for Everyday Gamers

As a gamer, it's important that you know what the state of security is in your online game. You can start by asking some simple questions sparked by the discussion throughout this book.

- What has your game provider done to secure the game?
- Are people known to cheat in this game?
- What kind of middle market exists for virtual items in the game?
- Are sweatshops and bots common?
- Do security mechanisms invade personal privacy?

Learning about the security mechanisms in the game that you use is also important because they will have a direct impact both on your gaming experience and your personal privacy.

We developed the checklist presented in the Gamer's Security Checklist box to help you learn more about the security posture of the online game you use. Fill out the checklist. Once you have the results, think about whether the answers are acceptable to you as a gamer.

Exploiting Online Games

We cover plenty of ground in this book, from technical issues surrounding bots, cheats, reverse engineering, and total conversions to legal issues and economics. We were often forced to describe technical issues with reference to one particular game or another (mostly because we felt compelled to show you some code), so we must emphasize that the lessons in this book go beyond any one particular game; in short, the techniques and vulnerabilities we describe apply equally to all online games.

Don't forget that many of the technical lessons in this book apply well beyond the field of online games. Other kinds of modern software are evolving toward the very architectures that make online gaming such an interesting security case study. What we learn today about online game security will help us build better software in many other completely unrelated domains.

Gamer's Security Checklist

If your game works online and connects to a central server via the Internet, it carries much more security risk than a game that runs on your PC in a stand-alone fashion. Use this checklist to think about the security of your online game.

☐ Check for security issues with the game on common security mailing lists including these:
  ☐ SecurityTracker <http://www.securitytracker.com>
  ☐ BugTraq <http://www.securityfocus.com/archive/1>
  ☐ The RISKS forum and comp.risks <http://catless.ncl.ac.uk/risks>

☐ Make sure that the game uses SSL or some other cryptographic communications protocol when it connects to the server. You can query the game manufacturer (and believe what it tells you), or you can do some verification yourself by using a packet sniffer like Ethereal <http://www.ethereal.com>, paying special attention to port 443.

☐ Use Hamachi <http://www.hamachi.cc> or some other virtual private network to protect your network traffic, especially if you want to have a virtual LAN party.

☐ Make sure that the game protects private information both at rest (on your PC and on the server) and in transit between machines. You might consider using boron tagging and Ethereal for validation.[1]

☐ Make sure you're comfortable with any spyware the game installed to monitor your PC during gaming sessions.

☐ Read and understand the game's privacy policy (if it has one).

☐ Read the EULA and TOU that came with the game, and know your legal obligations. Reading EULAs is tedious, but if we can get a few people to understand the insane nature of many of these agreements, we will be pleased.

☐ Search for cheats and hacks for the game on the Internet using some of the game hacking terms introduced in this book. If cheating sites are common, you should be aware that fellow players may be cheating.

☐ Determine whether a middle market exists for virtual items in the game. If it's possible to buy items for the game, game hacking is likely taking place.

☐ Don't count on playing an online game for a living, even if the game is set up explicitly to support a virtual economy. Property law is not at all settled in this area, and all of your hard work could disappear overnight.

☐ Run antivirus and antispyware software on your gaming machine. Update it regularly.

☐ Do not run the game as administrator or root. This one is so important that we'll say it again. . . .

☐ Do not run the game as administrator or root.[2]

☐ Read *Exploiting Online Games.*

1. See our book *Exploiting Software* (Addison-Wesley, 2004) for details on this technique.
2. Note that some games require being installed with root or admin privilege.

Our sincere hope is that the material in this book will result in better game security for all. If game companies take security more seriously, they can protect their livelihoods and revenue streams well into the future. If game designers understand the kinds of attacks leveled against their games, they can do a better job of building security in from the start. If gamers understand the implications of security problems to their gaming experience, they will demand better security in the games they love—and as a result, the invisible hand of the market will work its magic.

When we first became interested in online game security, we found the field incredibly fascinating. We have tried hard to explain things as clearly as possible, and we're happy with the result. We hope you are as well.

Index

informIT

Register
Your Book
at www.awprofessional.com/register

You may be eligible to receive:

- Advance notice of forthcoming editions of the book
- Related book recommendations
- Chapter excerpts and supplements of forthcoming titles
- Information about special contests and promotions throughout the year
- Notices and reminders about author appearances, tradeshows, and online chats with special guests

Contact us

If you are interested in writing a book or reviewing manuscripts prior to publication, please write to us at:

Editorial Department
Addison-Wesley Professional
75 Arlington Street, Suite 300
Boston, MA 02116 USA
Email: AWPro@aw.com

Visit us on the Web: http://www.awprofessional.com